MORAL ORDER
AND
SOCIAL DISORDER

SOCIOLOGICAL IMAGINATION
AND STRUCTURAL CHANGE
An Aldine de Gruyter Series of Texts and Monographs

SERIES EDITOR

Bernard Phillips, *Boston University*

Leo d'Anjou
Social Movements and Cultural Change
The First Abolition Campaign Revisited

Frank Hearn
Moral Order and Social Disorder
The American Search for Civil Society

MORAL ORDER
AND
SOCIAL DISORDER

The American Search for Civil Society

FRANK HEARN

ALDINE DE GRUYTER
New York

About the Author

Frank Hearn is Professor of Sociology at the State University of New York College at Cortland. He is the author and editor of three earlier books, including *Reason and Freedom in Sociological Thought*.

ALDINE DE GRUYTER
A division of Walter de Gruyter, Inc.
200 Saw Mill River Road
Hawthorne, New York 10532
This publication is printed on acid free paper ∞

HN
90
. M6
H38
1997

Library of Congress Cataloging-in-Publication Data
Hearn, Frank.
    Moral order and social disorder : the American search for civil society / Frank Hearn.
       p.   cm. — (Sociological imagination and structural change)
    Includes bibliographical references and index.
    ISBN 0-202-30603-8 (cloth : alk. paper). — ISBN 0-202-30604-6 (paper : alk. paper)
    1. United States—Moral conditions. 2. United States—Social conditions—1980– 3. Social problems—United States. 4. Social values—United States. 5. Civil society—United States. I. Title. II. Series.
    HN90.M6H38 1997
    306′.0973—dc21
                              97-18771
Manufactured in the United States of America   CIP

10 9 8 7 6 5 4 3 2 1

Hope implies a deep-seated trust in life that appears absurd to those who lack it.

Christopher Lasch

It is only for the sake of those without hope that hope is given to us.

Walter Benjamin

For Jill, Michael, Caitlin, Jim, and Jack—alone and together you are the hope given to me.

Contents

Acknowledgments   ix

Introduction   xi

1 BAD PARENTS   1

  Two Solutions   3
  Commodification and Juridification   8
  A Sociological View:
    The Importance of Social Institutions   12

2 BAD NEIGHBORS   21

  Bad Neighbors and the Underclass   23
  Two Analyses   27
  A Sociological View:
    The Importance of Social Control
    and Communitarian Interdependencies   33
  Conclusion   45

3 IN THE ABSENCE OF SOCIETY:
  LIBERAL INDIVIDUALISM AND ANOMIE   47

  Portraits of Life in the Absence of Society   48
  Liberal Modernity   55
  Anomie and the Sociological Critique
    of Liberal Modernity   66
  Conclusion   71

4   MORAL INDIVIDUALS:
    IN THE PRESENCE OF SOCIETY   73

    Liberal Views of Morality   73
    Durkheim's Sociology of Morality   77
    Institutions, Communitarian Interdependencies,
        and Morality   84
    Moral Individuals and Liberal Individuals   89

5   SOCIAL CAPITAL:
    GIFTS AND SACREDNESS IN SOCIETY   97

    A Wonderful Life   105
    Gifts   110
    Sacredness   120
    The Loss of Social Capital as the Loss of Soul   128
    Privatization as Individualization Versus Privatization
        as Sacralization   132
    Conclusion   134

6   THE POLITICS OF SOCIAL BREAKDOWN:
    REVITALIZING CIVIL SOCIETY   137

    The Inability to Attend   137
    Inattentive Parents and the Political Right   144
    Civil Society   149
    Conclusion   172

    REFERENCES   187

    AUTHOR INDEX   197

    SUBJECT INDEX   201

Acknowledgments

This book has its roots in two courses I regularly teach at the State University of New York's Cortland College, Sociological Theory and Social Breakdown in the United States. Explicitly in the former course and implicitly in the latter, I try to apply the insights of classical sociological theory to contemporary American society. My efforts in this regard have been enriched invaluably by the undergraduates in these courses. Their interest, inquisitiveness, patience, and demand for clarity and coherence helped bring me to a better understanding of the issues that reside at the center of this book. While elected and appointed officials formally responsible for the well-being of the State University of New York gleefully enact destructive budget cuts and in other ways express their contempt for SUNY and its students, Cortland's undergraduates, most of whom are members of the first generation of their families to attend college, sustain their desire to learn. I am indebted to them.

Helpful comments on early drafts of the manuscript were given by Sheila Myers and Del Palm, each of whom read several chapters, and by Jill Hearn and Gavin Kitching, both of whom gave the entire manuscript a very careful reading. I thank them for their suggestions, criticisms, and kind words of encouragement.

The text itself reveals my debt to those whose work over recent years has cleared and cultivated the ground on which my argument stands. I have been greatly influenced by the writings of Robert Bellah, James Coleman, Christopher Lasch, Michael Sandel, Michael Walzer, and Alan Wolfe, most especially his important and inspiring *Whose Keeper?*.

Gilda Haines, with the assistance of Michelle Pless and Krista Carlton, put the manuscript in shape for publication. A superb administrator and as decent a person as you could ever hope to find, Gilda regularly took time from her extraordinarily busy schedule to assure that my work was done promptly and well. I am grateful to her for this and for all else she does to make life pleasant for faculty and students in the Department of Sociology-Anthropology.

At Aldine de Gruyter, Richard Koffler, executive editor, moved the manuscript through the review process with humor, and attentive care.

Managing editor Arlene Perazzini, brought a sharp eye to her close reading of the manuscript, ridding it of silly mistakes and clumsy formulations. The awkward renderings that remain should be taken as a sign of my stubbornness and Richard's and Arlene's admirable willingness to give the author the "benefit of the doubt."

Introduction

Addressing the moral crisis he found plaguing modern society at the start of the twentieth century, Émile Durkheim ([1912] 1965:475) observed that "the old gods are growing old or already dead, and others are not yet born. . . . Thus we find ourselves in . . . a period of moral cold which explains the diverse manifestations of which we are, at every instant, the uneasy and sorrowful witnesses." Today, at the century's end, all the old gods are dead, but their bodies and souls are marketed to the uneasy and the sorrowful, used to sell candidates for public office to the politically perplexed and indifferent, megachurches to that unchurched multitude— "seekers," as they are called in the business—committed to salvation by entertainment, and a false sense of security to those made anxiously bewildered by their inability to give order to the course of their lives. Family values, community, and personal responsibility are pushed as the institutions of family, marriage and parenthood, and ongoing communal interdependencies decay. Virtue, character, and soul sell well as the social contexts from which they arise deteriorate. Compassion, altruism, morality, and volunteerism are heralded as the social sentiments that fuel them lie uncultivated. In commodified form, designed to stimulate and thereby command the attention of the easily distracted, the dead gods testify to the social breakdown their resurrection is intended to disguise.

This book is about social breakdown in the contemporary United States. Society is made up of social institutions and communitarian interdependencies. The former consist of ideals, statuses, and obligations that define people as social beings and order their relations to one other in ways that both assure the reliable satisfaction of important human and social needs and sustain solidarity. Interdependencies are communitarian when the people they link share a community of concern characterized by mutuality and trust. In John Braithwaite's (1989) words, they combine a thick network of individual reciprocal attachments "with strong cultural commitments to mutuality of obligation" (p. 85). A society breaks down when social institutions lose their legitimacy and ability to motivate and shape the identity of their participants, and when the communities of concern supported by communitarian interdependencies lose the capacity for social control that enables them to regulate their members' behavior in accordance with common expectations. Social breakdown displays itself robustly in both forms, in deinstitutionalization and in the deregulation of social life that results from the diminution of social control, in the United States today.

The visible weakening of social institutions like the family, and the deep erosion of the communitarian interdependencies that feed neighborhood, community, and associational life represent the culmination of a long-standing conflict between liberal modernity and society. First established in the West in the eighteenth and nineteenth centuries, liberal modernity takes as its unassailable end the creation of arrangements that secure the individual his freedom to chose how to live. From this view, society—the virtuous constraints imposed by social institutions and the collective expectations sanctioned by communities of concern—is the enemy of the individual and his freedom. Championing the individual are the two most powerful carriers of liberal modernity, the liberal or capitalist market economy and the liberal state that grows to become a welfare state. Over the years each expanded in the name of furthering individual freedom.

That the expansion of liberal modernity's defining and driving forces has come at the expense of the social institutions and communitarian interdependencies within which people acquire the dispositions and sensibilities and learn the practices that anchor individual freedom, comes as no surprise to those familiar with the classical sociological tradition. From the diverse and often contending critiques of liberal modernity fashioned by Émile Durkheim, Karl Marx, Max Weber, and George Herbert Mead came a common warning: left unabated, the rationalizing, commodifying, proletarianizing, desecrating, and demoralizing dynamics propelled by the structures of liberal modernity surely will poison the ground of sociability and solidarity. Forgotten for a long time, even within sociology, this warning recently has been renewed in the important work of Jurgen Habermas and Alan Wolfe. Habermas's analysis of the colonization of the lifeworld (the realm of active sociability) by the system (the rationally depersonalizing logics of the capitalist economy and the bureaucratic state) and Wolfe's account of the invasion of civil society (where people exist as rule-makers) by the market and the welfare state (where they exist as rule-followers) combine with Durkheim's understanding of the powerful tensions between society and liberal modernity to yield a generally good map of the terrain on which this work walks.

My intention is to improve the map by adding detail to locales already identified, by charting new ways of getting from one place to another, by investigating heretofore unexplored regions, and by resolving inconsistencies found among its makers. Moreover, and most importantly, I wish to make more accessible the argument in whose terms the map is framed. The sociological voice, never very strong to begin with, speaks today in a barely audible whisper even as its words—trust, mutuality, and obligation—are shouted loudly by the various participants in America's politics of social breakdown. But the words, like the concrete things to which they refer, are distorted by the liberal individualism that infuses the political Right and the political Left alike. For the words to mean something, for them to guide an effective effort to reverse the forces of social breakdown, their sociological context and substance have to be restored. At this moment, the rhetoric of solidarity employed by the sociological voice needs to become as popular as the market rhetoric perfected by economics and advanced by the political Right and the rights rhetoric polished by political science and promoted by the political Left.

As initially formulated by Durkheim nearly a century ago, the sociological understanding of the social crisis of modern society distances itself from conventional right-wing and left-wing political views by recognizing that the market economy and the welfare state alike expand in ways that detract from the social settings most congenial to the growth of trust, gratitude, mutuality, and social and personal responsibility. This view does not stand as a rejection of liberal modernity or of the market economy and democratic welfare state that reside at its core. Nor does it call for the restoration of traditional institutions and communal attachments. Instead, it argues for the creation of social institutions and communitarian interdependencies appropriate to liberal modernity and the realization of its major promises—individualism, freedom, and democracy. This is the goal of Durkheim's call for the development of moral individualism. I revise and update Durkheim's proposed solution to social breakdown in modern society to take into account the particular circumstances of the United States at the end of the millennium, and place the social conditions supportive of moral individualism at the center of a sociologically conceived notion of civil society.

The first two chapters introduce the book's primary theme through a concrete examination of the two major forms taken by social breakdown, deinstitutionalization and the weakening of social control. Chapter 1, "Bad Parents," looks at the weakening of family, marriage, and parenthood, and assesses two well-known proposals for reviving the current dwindling sense of parental obligation, one drawn from the rhetoric of the marketplace, the other from the rhetoric of individual rights linked to the welfare state. Both proposals are critically appraised against a sociological understanding of family, marriage, and parenthood as institutions whose character is subverted by the principles offered by the rhetorics of the market and individual rights. Chapter 2, "Bad Neighbors," examines the deterioration of neighborhoods, the primary examples of which are drawn from studies of the inner-city underclass. Two different accounts of neighborhood collapse are presented, the right-wing explanation that fixes primary blame on the rights-protecting welfare state and the left-wing view that relates neighborhood decay to an insufficiently regulated market economy. Both accounts are assessed with reference to the sociological view that the communitarian interdependencies on which vital neighborhoods rest are damaged by both the market economy and the welfare state. Chapter 3, "In the Absence of Society: Liberal Individualism and Anomie," makes explicit an underlying assumption of the first two chapters by identifying the tension between liberal modernity and society, and outlines the sociological criticism of liberal modernity's defining principle, namely, that which is most valuable—individual freedom and happiness—is achieved only outside the oppressive restraints of society. This chapter portrays life in the absence of society as it has been characterized by several sociological, anthropological, and psychological studies; it shows specifically how the main carriers of liberal modernity separate people from society's institutions and communitarian interdependencies, and it uses Durkheim's notion of anomie to describe America's liberal individuals who dwell on the outskirts of a society diminished by the forces of liberal modernity.

The next two chapters look at what comes to people in society in order to rebut the liberal claim that there is a conflict between society and the individual, and to demonstrate that vigorous social life is essential to efficient market economies and effective democratic welfare states. Chapter 4, "Moral Individuals: In the Presence of Society," updates Durkheim's sociology of morality, in part by linking the development of social sentiments and moral sensibility to the institutions and the communitarian interdependencies discussed in Chapters 1 and 2. The moral individual, attached to society, is contrasted to the liberal individual who defines himself or herself largely in terms of market-satisfiable preferences and state-protected rights. Chapter 5, "Social Capital: Gifts and Sacredness in Society," examines a relatively new but increasingly important sociological concept, social capital, which refers to the trust, cooperative habits, social networks, and norms of reciprocity that arise from ongoing social interaction and are indispensable to economic efficiency and governmental responsiveness. Although social capital is most often regarded as a kind of commodity, I understand it, more properly I think, in terms of the gift-giving character and sacred qualities of elemental social relations.

Chapter 6, "The Politics of Social Breakdown: Revitalizing Civil Society," closes the book with a consideration of the various proposals for resurrecting civil society generated by America's increasingly rightward-turning politics. Each draws from an understanding of civil society that was fashioned during liberal modernity's formative period as part of the effort to protect the possibility of the free individual against allegedly uncivilizing societal pressures and constraints. In its place, I offer a sociological conception of civil society as a place hospitable to the development of moral individuals, and point to some of the conditions necessary for its attainment.

1

Bad Parents

Parents have an obligation to raise and care for their children in ways that enable them to become competent and responsible adults and productive members of society. This age-old obligation is difficult to discharge, requiring as it does continuous, massive investments of attentive involvement and financial resources. Good parents recognize, take seriously, and strive to meet this obligation. In so doing, they make an indispensable contribution to the sustenance of a tolerable social existence. If a society is to endure, it must be capable of assuring that the parental obligation, the most basic and fundamental social obligation of all, is carried out effectively.

A large and growing number of parents in the United States fail the test of good parenting. The damage this has done to children and to social life is enormous. There is a long list of impressive reports and studies that support these claims. A 1994 Carnegie Corporation report, "Starting Points: Meeting the Needs of Our Youngest Children," found that "millions of infants and toddlers are so deprived of medical care, loving supervision and intellectual supervision that growth into healthy and responsible adults is threatened" (Chira 1994). The report gives substance to Barbara Dafoe Whitehead's (1993) claim that the current generation of American children is the first "in the nation's history to do worse psychologically, socially, and economically than its parents" (p. 84). David Hamburg (1992:34) identifies a "generation in crisis," a generation marked by rising rates of educational failure, delinquency, suicide, homicide, and teen pregnancy, fueled in part by "the decreasing commitment of parents to their children. Two-thirds of parents now report that they are less willing to make sacrifices for their children than their own parents would have been." Mihaly Csikszentmihayli (1993), a leading student of childhood development, concludes his survey of the recent literature by noting that

> the condition of our children seems to be getting worse from year to year, decade after decade. More of them live in poverty, fewer grow up in homes under the protection and guidance of two parents—and if they do, they seem to be getting less and less attention and comfort. More children are

killed or commit suicide, are sexually or physically abused, become addicted to deadly substances, fall into chronic depression. Those who survive
learn less in school than do their peers in most comparable countries, and
are, therefore, less well prepared for a productive adulthood. (p. 31)

Propelling these developments, according to Whitehead (1993), is a shift
in attitudes that started in the 1970s. As adult well-being took precedence
over child well-being, what "had once been regarded as hostile to children's best interests was now considered essential to adults' happiness"
(p. 52).

Currently, there are twice as many American children in substitute care
as there were ten years ago, one sign that parents are relinquishing responsibility for their children (Ingrassia and McCormick 1994:53). There
are other signs as well. In response to the growing incivility, unruliness,
and violence unleashed by children of bad parents, towns and cities
throughout the country have been implementing curfews; schools have
installed armed security guards, electronic monitoring systems, and dogs
trained to search out drugs; the federal government has threatened to
regulate the television young people watch and the music they hear.
Parental support for these and like measures is strong. "Feeling thwarted
in trying to rear their children and enforce standards of behavior that at
one time seemed clear and universal," the *New York Times* (November 19,
1993, p. E4) reports, "parents are increasingly reaching out for help and
welcoming any help that is volunteered. Many appear willing to subcontract a portion of their role to government, schools, and whatever
communal vestiges remain in a mobile and complex society."

Social problems in the United States tend to be addressed in terms of the
"great divide" that has for so long characterized American politics, and the
social problems attendant upon inept parenting are no different. On one
side of the divide is the political Right, deriving solutions from the principles of the capitalist market economy; on the other is the political Left,
resting its solutions on the extension of the principles of the democratic
welfare state. The two views and the solutions they propose have real and
significant differences, which often obscure what the two have in common.
Both views embrace liberalism's celebration of the individual, and both
solutions have the same consequence, namely, the weakening of the social
contexts within which people learn how to meet their obligations to others,
to take those obligations seriously, and to develop the social control and
self-control that enable them to regulate their interactions without the
assistance of government-imposed curfews, armed security guards, and
trained dogs. This is demonstrated by two representative and reputable
proposals for dealing with the problem of bad parenting. The first is a
market-based solution offered by James Coleman, who until his recent

death was one of the most prominent and influential sociologists in the United States. The second solution draws on the principles and the resources of the democratic welfare state, and is advocated by Hillary Clinton, a lawyer and long-time activist in the children's rights movement and an advisor and wife of President Clinton.

TWO SOLUTIONS

Working with market principles, James Coleman (1993) attributes the growing frequency of cases of bad parenting in modern society to the deterioration of the once-powerful self-interested motives parents had for devoting themselves to the resource-consuming tasks of effective child-rearing. This, Coleman argues, is the primary force driving the steady decline in parental attention to and involvement in the lives of their children, especially over the past quarter-century. In this context, increasing numbers of children never adequately develop their capacity to take responsibility for themselves and others, nor cultivate their skills and desires for working cooperatively in pursuit of common goals. Psychologically if not socially abandoned by the time they reach adolescence, they perform poorly in school, fuel ever-climbing rates of criminal and delinquent behavior and alcohol and drug abuse, and reach adulthood lacking both the social competencies that permit people to live together civilly and the technical skills and knowledge demanded by the modern world.

Forced to incur the steadily mounting costs of the welfare dependency, the unemployment, the antisocial behavior, and the general social decay that accompany the diminution of parental obligation, the state, Coleman claims, has a particularly strong interest in reversing this development. To do so effectively and efficiently, he argues, the state should establish a system of economic incentives designed to motivate more responsible parenting. The system would work by means of a bounty placed on the head of each child in society. Social scientists would make a statistical prediction of each child's costs and benefits to the government, factoring into the prediction conditions such as the income level and family structure of the child's household so that the bounty's value would be higher "for the 'difficult' child than for the average child, because the potential gains for the state would be greater. It would be at least as strong for bringing a child from a prospective future of crime and drugs to self-sufficiency as it would be for bringing a child from a prospective middle income to a higher income" (Coleman 1993:14). At some future point, the prediction would be assessed against the person's actual costs and bene-fits to the government up to that time. A percentage of benefits beyond the predicted amount and a percentage of savings from the expected costs would go to make up the value of each person's bounty. The right to each child's bounty would be vested in his or her parents, who would be free to transfer it contractually to others.

In Coleman's view, the bounty system would elicit two responses, both of which would promote a more serious undertaking of the childrearing practices demanded by the parental obligation. First, the prospect of the bounty would have many parents conclude that it is in their economic self-interest to promote the care and involvement necessary for their chil-dren to become socially competent and productive members of society. Second, the recognition that many other parents would find the promise of future reward too distant or too meager would spur the growth of a market in childrearing. Private vendors would step forward in sufficient numbers to assume the all-important responsibility of raising children in ways that lower their costs and increase their benefits to the state, having purchased from parents their rights to the children's bounties. With the proper enticements in place, Coleman insists, the parental obligation to raise children to become capable, competent, cooperative persons once again would be taken seriously, if not by parents themselves than by the profit-making sellers of good parenting to whom they have contractually transferred their children's bounties.

Coleman's proposal is couched in the rhetoric of the market. It pre-sumes that the market offers the most effective way of regulating human behavior. If the state, or for that matter any agent, wishes compliance with a preferred form of conduct it simply needs to make that option economi-cally attractive enough so that the benefits of compliance outweigh the costs. Drenched in the language of the market, Coleman's solution sees parents as maximizers of utility, it portrays parental obligations as heavily dependent on selfish interests, it characterizes parent-child relations in terms of opportunity costs, and it is designed to facilitate the com-modification of parental responsibility. The market principle, deemed "dollars for deeds" by *Time* magazine (May 16, 1994, p. 51), already operates in a variety of ostensibly nonmarket settings: An East Baltimore health clinic entices pregnant women to come in for monthly checkups with ten-dollar vouchers; a Massachusetts high school offers discounts at local businesses as a way of motivating students to pursue high grades; teenage girls in Leadville, Colorado, are promised one dollar for each day they avoid getting pregnant. The message is the one heralded by the market: people will meet their obligations to others only when it is in their own interests to do so.

A second solution to the problem of bad parenting draws from a rhetoric of rights, and in contrast to Coleman's call for the expansion of market principles, demands the extension of the judicial and administrative principles of the welfare state. Currently, the two best-known proponents of this solution are Hillary Clinton and Penelope Leach, one of the world's most influential experts on child care and development. Clinton and Leach have been long active in the effort to give children and adolescents the same rights as adults, so they too may have access to the protections afforded by the legal system and benefits provided by the welfare state.

"Human rights must include children, because they are human," Leach (1994:204) argues. "Children's rights must therefore, by definition, be the same as everyone else's," and thus should include the right to protection against physical punishment and the right to have a say in matters affecting one's well-being. In the absence of these rights, Leach (1994:211, 213) avers, parents "can imprison children, extending time-out to hours spent locked in a bedroom or worse, or 'grounding' to days of house arrest, with virtual impunity," and can commit bodily indignities on their children, ranging from corporal punishment to changing a toddler's diaper and wiping her nose without asking for her permission and cooperation. As rights-bearing individuals, children would be accorded the protection of the state against arbitrary authority—including, and perhaps most especially parental authority, the exercise of which would be more tightly regulated and more subject to due process procedures. The force of law presumably would lessen the frequency of bad parenting by compelling parents to take more seriously the rights of their children.

Additionally, children as rights-holders would become entitled to state-provided benefits and programs deemed necessary for the satisfaction of their right to healthy development. The welfare state as guarantor of individual rights would assume ever-greater childrearing responsibilities—ranging from prenatal care to day care, to pre- and after-school programs, particularly where those rights-satisfying responsibilities were abridged by parents, and thus would bring more areas of childrearing under the control of legal regulations and administrative procedures. In the name of individual rights, the state would have an easier time intervening in the parent-child relation.

To facilitate this, Hillary Clinton (cited in Lasch 1992:78) opposes the existing "rebuttable presumption of childhood incompetency," which requires "children and their allies" (namely, lawyers and state protective agencies) to prove the need for state interference in the exercise of parental authority, in favor of a "presumption of childhood competency," which would give parents the burden of proving the wrongfulness of any state interference requested by their child. Leach endorses Clinton's argument that children should be presumed competent unless proven otherwise, and thus have the right to be consulted on all matters involving their welfare. "If children's human rights are to be respected and their childish needs met, they themselves must decide when, and if, it is in their best interests to be removed from their home and/or parents, and their care and protection must then be provided for accordingly" (Leach 1994:20). A demonstrably abused child should not be compelled to leave her parents and home if she prefers to stay. "Instead, the resources needed to deal with the current emergency or chronic situation should be taken to her" (p. 21). At the other extreme, courts should grant the request of a child to be removed from her parents and home "even if the parenting adult objects and abuse is not apparent and is denied" (p. 21). In both cases, the children's right to decide is defended by the legal system, and their right to care and protection is met by services administered by the welfare state.

The title of Clinton's recent book extols the village, not the welfare state, as the indispensable friend of parental obligation. Yet, underlying the book's celebration of attentive parents supported by grandparents and friends, churches, PTAs, and grassroots community organizations is Clinton's continued conviction that responsible parenting ultimately depends on the welfare state and its professional, legal, and therapeutic experts as the most reliable allies of children. Indeed, early on the village becomes the welfare state: "In the terrible times when no adequate parenting is available and the village itself must act in place of parents, it accepts those responsibilities in all our names through the authority we vest in government. That means our city, county, and state social welfare services . . . intervene in families to protect children on our behalf" (Clinton 1996:46). The increased frequency of inadequate parenting demands both an expansion of resources that permit child protective agencies to monitor suspect families, remove children if necessary, and counsel or decide to prosecute parents, and the "recruitment of qualified citizens to share with overworked social workers, lawyers, and judges the burden of moving children's cases through the courts" (p. 49). In addition, the village as welfare state provides all parents "expert 'coaching' in children's development" to allow them to base their practical childrearing decisions on the latest research (p. 54).

None of this, Clinton insists throughout, is designed to discourage the structures of mutual reliance and the systems of informal control that prompted responsible behavior in the village of old. There is much to be said for counting on kin and neighbors and peer pressure, but after it is said, we must conclude that "informal means of monitoring care are no substitute for formal systems" maintained by the welfare state (Clinton 1996:76). Dressed in village clothing, the welfare state not only supplies benefits and defends children's rights, it also protects the family "from influences that threaten to undermine parental authority" (p. 313), most of which, in Clinton's view, are promoted by the market—"consumer culture's assault on values," downsizing corporations, greedy executives, and the debilitating consequences of turbocharged capitalism (p. 293).

The road established by the Clinton-Leach argument takes us not to the village, but to the legalization and administrative oversight of the parent-child relation. This is recognized by Jack Westman, child psychiatrist and proponent of the effort to legally guarantee the basic civil rights of children. Westman advocates a national parenting policy, implemented by child advocacy teams comprised of well-trained professionals. Such a policy would give legal recognition to a child's right to adequate parenting by establishing parent licenses that certify the childrearing competence of their holders. Currently, Westman (1994:217) notes, the government's regulation of parenting is limited by child abuse and neglect laws, and the result is that "children now must suffer from incompetent parenting until they are damaged," before they can be rescued by child protective teams. "With a licensing process the question of parental fitness would be faced before rather than after damage to a child. Licensing would hold a parent responsible for being competent rather than forcing children to endure incompetent parenting. The responsibility for demonstrating parental competence before a child is damaged would be with the parent, rather than the responsibility being with the state to demonstrate parental incompetence . . . as now is the case" (p. 239). Parental licensure thus would both shift the burden of proof from the state to the parents and make it easier for the state to intervene in families for the purpose of satisfying the rights of children.

In short, according to this view the problem of bad parenting is resolvable by extending to children the civil rights now possessed by adults. Such rights would circumscribe the exercise of parental authority, and parents, sensitive to the coercive power of the courts and the state responsible for defending these rights, would honor them more regularly. If the marketplace assumptions underlying Coleman's proposed solution imply that people will meet their obligations only when it is in their self-interest to do so, the rights assumptions informing the Clinton-Leach solution suggest that people most likely will satisfy their obligations to others when pressured to do so by some coercive power or authority. Fear of reprisal, not economic incentive, plays the motivating role. When the state's promise or threat to defend the rights of children fails to correct bad parenting, the state is obliged to honor these rights to respectful treatment and healthy development. In consultation with the affected children, the state, through its welfare programs, provides the resources required for their well-being and growth into competent and productive rights-bearing adults.

COMMODIFICATION AND JURIDIFICATION

Users of market rhetoric, like Coleman, find market principles and the market calculus at work in all areas of life. Coleman is very much influenced by the Chicago school of economics, home to the most articulate speakers of market rhetoric, the Nobel Laureates Milton Friedman and Gary Becker among them. They tell us, Alan Wolfe writes,

> that marriage is not so much about love as about supply and demand as regulated through markets for spouses; . . . people should have the right to sell their body parts, after they are dead, to any willing buyer; . . . the best solutions to the problems of surrogate mothering is to allow parties to contract freely on the market with no government regulation; and a man commits suicide "when the total discounted lifetime utility remaining to him reaches zero." (1989:32)

In market rhetoric, people, whether they are buying used cars or considering marriage or wondering what to do with their children, are moved by their selfish preferences, and thus are ever alert for the best deal or the best way to get the highest return on their investments.

Market rhetoric promotes commodification—the transformation of everything people need and want (and thus are willing to buy), including education, women's reproductive capacity, human tissue and organs, and effective parenting, into commodities produced and exchanged in accordance with market principles. In market rhetoric, Margaret Jane Radin (1987) writes, "everything that is desired or valued is an object that can be possessed, that can be thought of as equivalent to a sum of money, and that can be alienated. The person is conceived of . . . as the possessor and trader of these goods and hence all human interactions are sales" (p. 1861). This way of thinking and talking about social interactions places a premium on cost-benefit analysis, a method of decision making that has people weigh the anticipated costs and benefits of the choices before them, a task made easier and more precise by placing a monetary value on preferences and goods. Thus, the technique of cost-benefit analysis applies the market calculus to ostensibly nonmarket choices. In this way, it encourages "the construction of a market . . . where none naturally exists. To create such a fictive market requires one to set a price on everything, from human lives to scenic vistas, so that trade-offs among these goods can be calculated as costs and benefits" (Bellah et al. 1991:28).

Underlying all this is a conception of the person as a maximizer of utilities, a rational, self-interested chooser, directly responsible for himself but no one else, and bound to others not by obligations that bear the force of shared moral understanding but by voluntary exchanges calculated to further personal advantage. This conception of personhood grounds Coleman's proposal to remedy the problem of bad parenting by extending market principles. The intended effect of Coleman's proposal is the commodification of parental responsibility. The market deals only in commodities, and, where its principles operate, goods and services, including the attention and involvement necessary for children to become competent adults, are bought and sold. The commodification of social life Coleman endorses both presumes and helps to foster individuals who, in the words of Robert Nisbet (1988) are "loose from marriage and family, from the school, the church, the nation, the job, and moral responsibility" (p. 84). In the absence of economic incentive, loose individuals make bad parents.

If the market deals in commodities, the welfare state which stands at the center of Clinton's and Leach's proposal deals in rights. If the market is home to the rational maximizer of selfish interests, the welfare state gives comfort and safety to the rights-bearer, "a self-determining, unencumbered individual, a being connected to others only by choice" (Glendon 1991:48). If the market seeks commodification, the welfare state pursues juridification, the extension of formal, positive, and written law to spheres of human activity once regulated informally by social norms, moral codes of conduct, or public opinion (Habermas 1989a:357). Like market rhetoric, rights rhetoric adulates the individual while both encouraging her to advance her own interests and providing her the means to insulate herself from others in the privacy which rights create.

Users of rights rhetoric, like Clinton and Leach, premise their arguments on the long and widely held view that preservation of the bases of individual freedom is the defining responsibility of the liberal welfare state. This responsibility requires the state to remain neutral, to distance itself from particular conceptions of the right way to live, to favor no particular ends or preferences over others, to respect the individual's freedom to choose for himself or herself what is good. The neutrality of the liberal state, as Michael Sandel (1984) notes, rests on a

> distinction between the "right" and the "good"—between a framework of basic rights and liberties, and the conceptions of the good that people may choose to pursue within that framework. . . . What justifies the rights is not that they maximize the general welfare or otherwise promote the good, but rather that they comprise a fair framework within which individuals and groups can choose their own values and ends, consistent with a similar liberty for others. (p. 16)

The political Right (users of market rhetoric) and the political Left (users of rights rhetoric) accept this distinction but disagree over which rights are most essential to the realization of the chief goal of the neutral state.

The former defend "negative rights," those that leave the individual alone and permit him or her to do something without interference. The political Right argues that "property rights and the efficient functioning of the market economy will best allow individuals to choose their own conception of the good" (Sandel 1988:14). In contrast, the political Left favors "positive rights," which entitle the individual to have provided for him or her those goods and services required for developing and exercising the capacity to choose a preferred way of life. That the individual be free to live as he or she sees fit—the liberal ideal of the neutral state—goes unquestioned by both the Right and the Left.

As rights and entitlements triumph, the neutral state becomes a welfare state wherein the judiciary and government bureaucracy, the primary dispensers and defenders of rights and entitlements, triumph as well. Shielded from the force of democratic politics and deaf to the voices of particularistic communities, the judiciary and bureaucracy promote a shift "from a public philosophy of common purposes to one of fair procedures, from a politics of good to a politics of right" (Sandel 1992;26–27). As this happens, impersonal judicial and bureaucratic administrative principles designed to defend and satisfy individual rights come to regulate more extensively the conduct of human affairs.

The structure of liberal law, writes Jurgen Habermas (1989a), "dictates the formulation of welfare-state guarantees as *individual* legal entitlements under precisely *specified* general legal conditions" (p. 362). The juridification of social life that accompanies the multiplication of rights and entitlements thus defends the individual—the individual citizen against the state, the individual employee against the firm, the individual student against the school, the individual child against the parents—and does so with reference to formally specified conditions and procedures that have family members, citizens, students, and teachers "encounter each other as legal subjects" (Handler 1990:75). Such encounters invite, indeed often demand, constant vigilance and frequent intervention by administrative and judicial authorities charged with securing rights and satisfying entitlements.

In the United States, the process of juridification gained force in the 1970s as the civil rights movement and, later, movements in support of the rights of women, the handicapped, gays and lesbians, and children demanded legally secured protections and benefits. As the responsibilities of the welfare state grew and as the areas of life it set to regulate expanded, a panoply of due process procedures was erected to defend and to meet the newly established rights and entitlements. In their relationships with the larger, more powerful governmental regulatory agencies responsible for administering the new rights-enhancing entitlement programs, "citizens were given the right to invoke the rule of law . . . to challenge government action in administrative and judicial proceedings. The extent of the spread of these two phenomena—substantive regulatory law and procedural due process rights," according to Joel Handler (1990:2), "was truly remarkable." The increase in due process procedures was justified as necessary to protect individual rights in the face of the more intrusive forms of bureaucratic administration brought by a more expansive regulatory state which was itself justified by the need to protect individual rights.

Infused with rights rhetoric, Clinton's and Leach's proposal to deal with the problem of bad parenting by extending to children the same rights afforded to adults would further the reach of juridification. Recognizing the child as a competent, self-determining subject legally entitled to the conditions of healthy development, the courts would issue rulings and the welfare state would establish administrative directives that would regulate family life, most particularly parent-child relations, in a way designed to secure individual rights. As this happens, Christopher Lasch (1978:229) argues, the family and its individual members would be made more dependent on "professional services over which [they have] little control" and more reliant on the judicial and bureaucratic ensurers of those services. This, of course, is the irony of the Clinton-Leach solution. Once granted the right to self-determination children become legal subjects dependent on the courts and entitled clients dependent on welfare state provisions. Clinton and Leach, convinced that courts and the welfare state are indispensable to responsible and effective childrearing, appear willing to live with this paradox.

At first glance, the self-interested loose individual promoted by market rhetoric seems to be at odds with the rights-bearing dependent individual (Siegel 1988) advanced by rights rhetoric. Close up, however, it is clear that not only are the loose individual and the dependent individual closely related, they often are one and the same. Individuals loosened from intimate, sentimental, communal, and motivational ties cannot count on family members, friends, neighbors, and fellow parishioners for support. Accordingly, they become increasingly dependent on the commodities provided by the market and the protections and benefits supplied by the welfare state. Indeed, this premise is shared by Coleman's solution and the one proposed by Clinton and Leach. As more children are unable to rely on their parents to meet their obligations to them, we need to arrange matters so they can rely on market principles or welfare state principles. Both sets of principles give rise to laws and rules that regulate human interaction impersonally and in a way that defends the freedom of individuals to live as they see fit. Market rhetoric and rights rhetoric derive from the same source: liberalism and its celebration of the individual. Market rhetoric portrays the individual as a bearer of selfish preferences, and thus defends the market where those preferences are freely pursued. Rights rhetoric understands the individual as a bearer of rights, and thus defends the welfare state which safeguards those rights.

Like the liberalism that spawned them, neither the market nor the welfare state "puts its emphasis on bonds that tie people together because they want to be tied together without regard for immediate self-interest or for some external authority having the power to enforce those ties" (Wolfe 1989:12). Guided by liberalism, both minimize social (as distinct from contractual and legal) obligations, weaken people's sense of personal responsibility for the fates of others, and diminish their capacity to rely on one another. Both detract from those social settings in which people acquire the habits and cultivate the sentiments that enable them to care for and count on one another. If more parents today are bad parents, they are so in part as a consequence of the commodification and the juridification of social life. To the extent that this claim is correct, Coleman's proposal to commodify parental responsibility and Clinton's and Leach's seemingly contrary proposal to bring parental responsibility under greater legal and administrative regulation will reach the same end through different routes. Each will make worse the problem it purports to solve, and each will do so in the name of guaranteeing individual freedom.

A SOCIOLOGICAL VIEW: THE IMPORTANCE OF SOCIAL INSTITUTIONS

In the modern world, socially competent persons exhibit trustworthiness, industry, initiative, cooperation, and autonomy, qualities they come by, students of child development tell us, thanks to responsible parental care. The key elements of such care, according to Csikszentmihayli (1993:42), include "the means and the willingness to provide for the physical needs of the children . . . [to] love them—i.e., express genuine pleasure in their existence and hold their well-being to be as important as their own." Responsible and effective parents, write Felton Earls and Mary Carlson (1993), demonstrate "loyalty, responsibility, honesty, and moral courage . . . the capacity to elicit trust and security from other human beings, to cooperate without regard for immediate personal benefit, to make sacrifices, and to accept enduring responsibilities" (p. 102). Responsible parental care requires, in addition to parents who possess these qualities, "a human context ruled by face-to-face interactions and the weight of public opinion. . . . [W]ithout manageable face-to-face groups which take responsibility for the common welfare," Csikszent-mihayli (1993:49, 52) insists, "it is unlikely that the conditions for optimal childhood growth will be attained." Note that the traits, dispositions, and qualities that make for good parenting—the capacity to love and express genuine pleasure in the child, to sacrifice for the child, to cooperate without concern for personal gain, to elicit trust and security—are not the same as those that drive the pursuit of selfish advantage or those that compel compliance with court-mandated, state-enforced requirements. To believe that parents and parent surrogates can be enticed into responsible and effective parenting by the prospect of personal gain or by fear of reprisal for violating individual rights is to misunderstand responsible and effective parenting. Note as well that the extension of impersonal market principles and impersonal legal rules centered on individual interests and rights does nothing to advance and much to diminish the small-scale, personal social contexts within which people learn to take responsibility for the common welfare.

The principles of regulation applied by the market and by the welfare state are inappropriate to the practice of good parenting. The commodification and juridification those principles promote are destructive to the conditions on which good parenting rests. Elizabeth Anderson (1990) makes this point in part, in her argument against commercial surrogate motherhood and the commodification of women's reproductive labor it represents. To treat something as a commodity, Anderson (1990) notes, is to assume that market principles "are appropriate for regulating its production, exchange, and enjoyment" (p. 72). The application of market principles to a good is inappropriate when as a consequence that good is degraded or prevented from being valued in ways appropriate to it. Thus, the commodification of a judge's verdict would distort the meaning and practice of justice; the buying and selling of votes would degrade the meaning and practice of citizenship, just as the buying and selling of children would corrupt the meaning and practice of parenthood. For justice, citizenship, and parenthood to be properly valued, their "production, exchange, and enjoyment must be removed from market norms and embedded in a different set of social relationships" (Anderson 1990:73).

Commercial surrogate motherhood contractually relates three persons, the intended father, the lawyer, and the surrogate mother. The lawyer secures an acceptable surrogate mother and makes the medical and legal arrangements necessary for the conception and birth of the child and the transfer of legal custody of the child to the father. The intended father agrees to pay the lawyer, the mother, and medical expenses, and supplies the sperm with which the mother agrees to become impregnated. The surrogate mother consents "to carry the resulting child to term, and to relinquish her parental rights to it. . . . Both she and her husband (if she has one) agree not to form a parent-child bond with her child and to do everything necessary to effect the transfer of the child to the intended father" (Anderson 1990:74). Commercial surrogacy applies market principles to women, to children, to the relationship between mother and child, and to the process and experience of human reproduction. And, in so doing, Anderson shows, it degrades each.

By transforming children into objects of profit-making, commercial surrogacy devalues them and undermines parenthood as a social practice whose norms, values, and virtues run counter to those of the market. The fundamental obligation of parents is to love their children. "Children are to be loved and cherished by their parents, not to be used or manipulated by them for merely personal advantage" (Anderson 1990:75). Commercial surrogacy, of course, replaces this social obligation with a contractual obligation that has the surrogate mother treat her child as a commodity that, like other commodities over which she retains property rights, she can exchange for individual gain. The market principles at work here debase not only the child and the social practice of parenting but the surrogate mother as well, reducing her from a person "worthy of respect and consideration to [an] object of mere use" (p. 80). In accepting the contract, and thus rejecting the norms of parenthood, the surrogate mother loses her claim to the special treatment—to the respectful and sensitive consideration—accorded to those who undertake the often self-sacrificing obligations embedded in deep emotional attachments. The introduction of market criteria and attitudes transforms the mother into a producer, the father into a buyer, the child into a commodity, and the mother-child relationship into a property relation, eliminating the special social significance that made each worthy of reverential regard.

Anderson's argument is not that commodification is bad in itself. It is, rather that certain goods—childrearing, mothering, parenting, and family—can exist and can be valued properly only when beyond the reach of the market. The preservation of these goods requires that they be set apart from market considerations. By injecting market considerations into the bloodstream of parent-child relations, the bounty system proposed by Coleman would destroy the responsible and effective parenting it is designed to encourage.

Matters would hardly be different if surrogate mothering were regulated by the principles of the welfare state. Women drafted by lottery, would serve their country by carrying to birth children who would be redistributed to childless couples in order to satisfy their legally established right to a child, and the consequence would be the same sort of degradation of the parent-child relation brought by commercial surrogacy (see Atwood 1985 for a fictional account of state-controlled surrogacy). Embedded in legal structures and administrative procedures, mothers, children, and fathers would be transformed into legal subjects bound to one another through precisely specified obligations. The juridification entailed by Clinton's and Leach's proposal to extend rights and entitlements to children would mark a move in this direction.

The obligation parents have to care for and raise their children in ways that enable them to become competent adults is a social obligation. The love, affection, and selfless involvement required for the effective discharge of this obligation can be neither spurred by economic incentives nor compelled by legal rulings. What is the ground of social obligation? How is social obligation recognized, accepted, and undertaken? Daniel Callahan (1987) seeks to answer these questions in his assessment of the parent-child relationship. While Callahan's focus is on what children owe their parents, his observations hold as well for the obligations parents have to their children.

At the center of any important social obligation, Callahan (1987) argues, "is the vulnerability and ultimate neediness of another and, in the context of family life . . . a vulnerability that often can fully be responded to only by a family member" (p. 101). The vulnerabilities associated with illness, old age, and childhood most require a "response from someone who deeply cares, someone who will remain faithful—but faithful to us as a special and distinctive person, not as a mere object of moral duty or universal love" (p. 101). Social obligation, in this view, is anchored in interdependence and in "the recognition that others are dependent on us, and are especially vulnerable to the courses of action that we choose" (Regan 1993:96). The close interdependencies that constitute family, marriage, and parenthood create the mutual reliance and the mutual vulnerability that give rise to special responsibilities. Being a spouse or a parent means "assuming an obligation to honor that reliance and to refrain from exploiting that vulnerability" (p. 96).

If the key to social obligation is the vulnerability of others in a context of close interdependency so that only we as particular parents, spouses, or adult children of elderly parents are able to supply the care needed by those dependent on us, then it is essential to secure both inner meaning and external support for that obligation. Recognizing the obligation and possessing a willingness to honor it often are not enough. In addition, Callahan (1987:97) writes, people need to "find the necessary strength, endurance, and stability to sustain their commitment and, no less important, to make moral sense of it." The burdens and difficulties of social obligation, Callahan (1987:105) continues, "must be pooled and shared. I can conceive of myself making a radical sacrifice for another if I live in a community, and am part of a way of life, that understands the interrelationship of our mutual needs and vulnerabilities and creates social institutions to respond to them." Thus, significant, difficult, time-consuming obligations that call for some degree of self-sacrifice are more likely to be met when the effort to meet them is both assisted by friends, neighbors, community associations, and a collective commitment to provide basic economic and medical support, and honored as socially significant. To achieve this we need, not more economic incentives or more individual rights, but a shared, coherent understanding of the moral significance of key social obligations, one that transforms the care of another "from a stark and unpalatable moral demand borne in isolation to a satisfying moral vocation . . . respected by the community" (p. 106).

A vocation, Lawrence Blum (1990:179) notes, "invokes a general place and purpose within society and carries with it certain values, standards, and ideals . . . that speak specifically to the individual in question. There is a personal identification with the vocation, with its values and ideals, and a sense of personal engagement that helps to sustain the individual in carrying out the activities of the vocation." Good parents regard parenting as a vocation, a life project, and they define themselves, in part, in terms of the obligations of that vocation. For them, the effort to satisfy the parental obligation is an opportunity to express and affirm an important part of their identities. Good parents, then, meet their fundamental obligations to their children, even in the absence of material incentive and legal coercion, because this is how they constitute themselves as persons. The fact that fewer parents are willing to act on this obligation—or, that more parents will act on it only if it is in their self-interest or the state requires it—is a sign of the dissolution of the vocational character of parenthood that once gave inner meaning to, and made moral sense of, the many and enduring burdens and sacrifices entailed by responsible and effective parenting. More specifically, it is an indication of the weakening of the institutional foundations on which vocation rests.

Family, marriage, and parenthood are institutions. Institutions provide the basic framework, the underlying architecture, of social life. They order human activity, govern individual behavior, and regulate interaction in ways that give coherence and continuity to human life. In institutions people are able to step out of themselves and into a shared social life. Institutions offer guidelines and criteria of right and wrong that lie beyond the self-interested preferences of the individual as utility-maximizer/rights-holder. The web of understandings, the rules of cooperation, the established conventions, the tacitly shared conventions, and the positive and negative sanctions that make up an institution are ongoing, culturally reproduced, human creations, sometimes deliberately and reflectively designed, other times simply emergent from social interaction. Institutions are arrangements of mutual support centered on activities that are essential to human development and the satisfaction of important human needs. In part collective responses to human vulnerability, institutions regularize and justify by making moral those cooperative activities that help assure the orderly provision of the basic requirements of human existence and coexistence (Bellah et al. 1991). A viable institution, Arnold Gehlen (1980:162) notes, is overdetermined in that it is both necessary and functional and a source of higher ideals in whose terms good—a good life, a good spouse, a good parent, a good teacher, a good citizen—is defined. Thus, an institution must be useful in a practical sense; the forms of cooperation it imposes on human activity must effectively enable people to meet their needs. It also must bestow social significance on those rules and expectations. To institutionalize a segment of human activity is not simply to order and regularize it but also to infuse it with moral value so that "this is how things are done" becomes "this is how things should be done" (Berger and Luckmann 1966:59). So moralized, the rules and expectations acquire greater force.

A viable institution, in short, is authoritative, regarded as legitimate and worthwhile by most whose lives are directed and disciplined by its conventions and sanctions. Its authority is grounded in its practical usefulness—compliance with its conventions brings palpable benefits— and in its moral standing, the ideals it expresses are taken seriously, and the effort to live the good life entails, in part, a life lived in accordance with these ideals. As long as the moral grounding of institutional authority remains secure, that is, as long as the conception of the good signaled by the institution's values is upheld, the practical benefits the institution brings to individual participants will be of secondary importance. In this context, satisfying institutional obligations becomes intrinsically valuable, an end in itself, an act undertaken for its own sake, not for the sake of some external good or benefit. People who are integrated into authoritative institutions strive to be good. Being good, living up to the institution's ideals and expectations, often means acting contrary to the selfish preferences celebrated by the rhetorics of the market and of rights.

Institutions connect people to one another. Participation in institutional life takes place within roles that define the particular responsibilities people acquire in their connections to others. These responsibilities, or role obligations, express the expectations that must be met if institutional ideals are to be achieved. Institutional roles are constituted by such obligations—the role of teacher or citizen or parent is defined by particular sets of responsibilities. Being a parent means doing what parents do, namely, committing oneself to the obligations of the institutionally defined role of parent. Taking on an institutional role is not a matter of blind and rigid conformity to specified expectations. Rather, it is "largely a matter of finding an interpretation that fits one's own temperament and character. There are different ways of being a [parent]. Part of what it is to become a good [parent] is to find a way of carrying out the responsibilities

. . . which suits one's particularities" (Hardimon 1994:355). Thus, the experience and meaning of role responsibilities may be deeply personal and highly varied, and should entail, as Katherine Barrett (1988:299) reminds us, "more than fulfilling some precise set of pre-defined role requirements. A responsible person cares not only about doing her part in a limited sense, but also about outcome, and is disposed toward expanding or perhaps redefining the demands of role as necessary to accomplish that outcome." Responsibility rests on a personal commitment to the role obligations and to the institutional ideals that define outcomes with reference to particular conceptions of human flourishing or good. To the extent that these obligations and ideals are valued as socially significant, the effort to meet them may become a vocation, and as such an important source of identity. For those for whom being a good parent or a good teacher is an essential part of their self-understanding, measuring up to the demands of this role is a way of being who they are, an important source of respect and well-being.

Seen in this light, obligation is rooted in more than vulnerability, and includes among its aims not only the provision of caring assistance in times of need and weakness but also the achievement of the good for both self and others. Social obligation, Philip Selznick (1993) writes, is rooted as much in

> our own sense of identity and relatedness. . . . To be sure, many specific obligations are triggered and defined by vulnerability and dependency. What children need, and to whom they must turn, tells us what parents must do if they are to fulfill their responsibilities. But the *ground* of these obligations lies in the parental role, not in the child's needs. It is their commitment to relevant roles that governs how people should respond to the dependencies they create or accept. (p. 204)

Thus, while the vulnerabilities born of interdependence give rise to many parental obligations, it is the institution of parenthood that gives significance and weight to these obligations, and so "transforms a discretionary act of benevolence into a binding duty" (p. 204). In seeking to honor this duty, good parents act not from the hope of reward or the fear of punishment but from the disposition to be a good parent. This disposition is the best guarantee that parental obligations will be respected, and it is a guarantee anchored in part in a vital institutional life.

Bad parents, according to this view, proliferate alongside the deinstitutionalization of parenthood, marriage, and family. Over the past thirty years, the social significance of each has diminished considerably. The social approval and legitimacy they confer on human activity do not matter as much as they once did. Their rules of cooperation are widely contested, and their sanctions are fewer in number and weaker in force.

The ideals they embody have been deconstructed and are less likely to inspire devotion and commitment. The obligations they place on people are taken far less seriously. These processes of deinstitutionalization show themselves in the rising divorce rate (a rate that in recent years has risen most quickly among couples with children), in the increasing rate of out-of-wedlock births, and in the decreasing amounts of time, attention, and involvement parents devote to childrearing responsibilities. The activities associated with sexual relations, childbearing, and childrearing are less institutionalized—less regularized, less moralized, and thus less stable and certain—than they were before. As a consequence, the obligations entailed by each are taken more lightly, and with increasing frequency are abrogated when they conflict with personal preferences.

In important ways, this deinstitutionalization has been promoted by market rhetoric and the rhetoric of rights, users of which are more likely to subordinate the claims of social obligation to those of personal preference and individual rights. Market rhetoric's "logic of self-interested rational calculation," Alan Wolfe (1989:54) finds, more powerfully now than before, "is reflected in such areas as family size, arrangements for child care, patterns of marriage and divorce, and relations among grandparents, children, and grandchildren."

Increasingly, Milton Regan (1993:49) notes, "the legitimacy of self-interest as the decision criterion" is acknowledged in determining whether or not or the degree to which spousal and parental obligations should be met. With market rhetoric as a guide, institutional obligations are viewed as potential impediments to the exercise of individual choice that makes us most human and happiest. Thus, they lose much of their moral force and become more easily revocable.

Rights rhetoric has had similar effects. As Whitehead writes,

> Increasingly, political principles of individual rights and choice shape our understanding of family commitment and solidarity. Family relationships are viewed not as permanent or binding but as voluntary and easily terminable. Moreover, under the sway of [rights rhetoric] the family loses its central importance as an institution in the civil society, accomplishing certain social goals such as raising children and caring for its members, and becomes a means to achieving greater individual happiness—a lifestyle choice. (p. 84)

Like market rhetoric, rights rhetoric challenges institutional authority, finding in deinstitutionalization greater opportunity for individual self-determination.

The significant increases in divorce, out-of-wedlock births, and parental abandonment of childrearing responsibilities can be—indeed, in the United States they frequently are—celebrated as signs of expanded individual freedom, the consequences of more and more individuals deciding for themselves, and on the basis of their personal preferences how they will live their lives. Yet, the triumph of the rationally self-interested, self-determining individual over institutions has led to the decay of important social obligations, most especially the fundamental parental obligation. America's children currently pay an exorbitantly high price for this.

Solutions to the problem of bad parenting derived from market rhetoric and rights rhetoric will only facilitate and extend the processes of deinstitutionalization that have been at work over the past thirty years. The problem requires for its resolution not further commodification and juridification but the reinstitutionalization of parenthood. We need, according to Barrett (1988), "a society in which parents share the highest norms of what the parent-child relationship should be" (p. 297). Those norms and ideals need to be clarified, their authority has to be restored, and the sanctions lying behind them have to be strengthened. Parental obligations need to be privileged, and the social significance of parenthood must be highlighted so that taking these obligations seriously becomes a source of self-respect and public honor. Alone, valued institutional ideals and the prospect of honored status are not enough to assure good parenting. Good parents also require resources—the emotional and physical support provided by neighborhood face-to-face groups and community voluntary associations, and the material and medical support supplied by collective agencies designed to meet society's commitment to responsible childrearing. To reach this point, we need to appeal to people as social beings, not as rationally self-interested individuals or rights-bearing legal subjects. We need to scale back the principles of the market and the welfare state to re-create that social space within which cooperative forms of human connectedness grow.

2

Bad Neighbors

Pedro Pagan has lived in the Bronx for nearly half a century. Beset by repeated break-ins to his home and increasing acts of vandalism on his block, Mr. Pagan recently "has shunned his neighbors and fenced himself behind window gratings and wrought iron gates backed by wire mesh and topped by gleaming coils of razor ribbon. For good measure, a clump of razor ribbon lies on the second-floor balcony, just in case invaders try to jump over from the fire escape of the adjoining building" (Gonzalez 1993). Not far away Ralph Montes has enclosed his front porch with a wrought-iron cage to protect himself against the young men who regularly loiter around his house and occasionally rifle through his mail. Mr. Pagan and Mr. Montes neither socialize with their neighbors nor invest themselves in their neighborhood, a placed marked by "the architecture of fear—churches have no windows, restaurant counters are protected by bullet-proof glass and libraries seal their windows and place razor ribbon atop their roofs" (p. 1). In a bad neighborhood, surrounded by bad neighbors, both withdraw to the tenuous security of their heavily fortified residences.

Drawing from a long-established sociological literature, John Logan and Harvey Molotch (1987:108) define neighborhood as a "shared interest in overlapping use values . . . in a single area . . . a shared experience of an agglomeration of complementary benefits." Among the most important use-values people gain from the neighborhood are the following (Logan and Molotch 1987:103–8): The daily round—the integrating routines centered around the neighborhood-based goods, services, and facilities with which "concrete daily needs are satisfied." Informal support networks that "provide life-sustaining products and services"—ranging from "friends and neighbors who baby sit, do yard work, or shovel snow, to friends, neighbors, and acquaintances who offer aid that can alter a way of life, such as referrals for an available job, a political connection to solve a problem, or a welfare benefit." The sense of security given by known, dependable, and trustworthy people in a familiar, predictable environment supported by shared symbols, kinship ties, and personal reputations. "Neighborhood can provide the benefit of *membership* in a social space that is viewed as orderly, predictable, and protective." Finally, neighborhood serves as a source of identity for its residents, providing both the physical location and the symbolic meaning that distinguish them from their counterparts in other neighborhoods.

Misters Pagan and Montes would be hard-pressed to find even a trace of one of these use-values in their neighborhood, assuming they could work up the courage to leave their secured houses for a look around. Theirs is a neighborhood fraught with danger and filled with unpredictable, untrustworthy, uncivil, often violent strangers. Insecurity and fear, not a daily routine, loitering gangs, not informal support networks, await them beyond the razor wire and wrought iron cages. Incivility and disorder—the two most significant signs of neighborhood deterioration according to Wesley Skogan (1990)—lie outside their fortifications.

Skogan's meticulous examination of forty cases of neighborhood decline reveals a process of deterioration in which incivility and disorder feed on themselves. Incivility grows as once-accepted standards of polite behavior and good manners lose their hold on more and more residents. Disorder takes root as the moral reliability of the neighborhood declines so that residents believe there are fewer trustworthy people among them, fewer people, that is, who can be relied upon to uphold neighborhood values, meet neighborhood expectations, and take seriously neighborhood sanctions. In the face of lessening moral reliability, many begin to experience a weakened sense of personal responsibility to the neighborhood.

Invariably, Skogan (1990:21–46) finds, incivility and disorder initially are expressed in potentially serious but still manageable forms. Vacant structures are vandalized, streets are littered, housing and building stock become dilapidated, street corner gangs grow in number and boldness, street harassment takes place, and public drinking and drug use become more common. If left unchecked, these conditions rapidly multiply, eliciting in the residents of Skogan's forty neighborhoods a remarkably consistent set of responses, including anger and demoralization.

> The anger came from being crowded out of community life. Residents . . . find it uncomfortable or even dangerous to be in parks, in shopping areas, or even on the streets near their homes. . . . Residents also often noted . . . that "no one cares" and expressed a certain degree of hopelessness about their situation. (p. 47)

Fear was an equally common response to the mounting physical decay and social unpredictability of the environment. "Abandoned buildings may harbor predators; corner gangs can be menacing, especially for women and the elderly." Rising intergroup conflict, sometimes racial, other times "between generations, or between homeowners and renters, landlords and tenants" (Skogan 1990:47), added to both the sense of fear and the pessimism over the neighborhood's future.

These responses, Skogan shows, fuel further incivility and disorder. Residents withdraw from neighborhood life in greater numbers. Those who can afford to move, leave. Those who cannot, seek the safety of their homes. Neighborhood decay deepens as cooperative activities dwindle, responsibility for monitoring the behavior of young people and strangers erodes, and hostility, distrust, and fear for the safety of children mount. At some point in this process the residents relinquish their responsibility to the well-being of their neighborhood. This is the point at which bad neighborhoods find their source of sustenance. Since 1970 the number of bad neighborhoods in the United States has risen by over 300 percent (Mincy, Sawhill, and Wolf 1990:452). Most of this increase took place in the poor inner-city areas that are home to America's underclass.

BAD NEIGHBORS AND THE UNDERCLASS

In his 1962 book *The Challenge to Affluence,* Gunnar Myrdal introduced the term *underclass* to describe the very bottom of the American system of inequality. There he found long-term poor African-Americans, poorly educated, unskilled, unemployed people denied the benefits of postwar economic growth. Myrdal defined the underclass structurally, relating their material deprivation and persistent poverty to a lack of access to the structure of mobility opportunities offered by education, training, and jobs. In the 1970s, this structural definition was popularized by journalists as they sought to get a handle on both the rapidly growing underclass population and the ways its poverty differed from that of the traditional lower class (Auletta 1982). In the 1980s, as part of the right-wing turn in American politics that brought Ronald Reagan and conservative Republicans to power, the underclass was reconceptualized to highlight the alleged cultural and behavioral deficiencies of its ever-growing population. Persistent poverty, according to this view, results less from structural impediments than from deviant and criminal behaviors and cultural values that promote resignation, apathy, and helplessness and dull aspiration and initiative. Material deprivation, rooted in cultural deprivation, prevents people from making good use of available opportunities (Katz 1989). Poverty thereby becomes self-perpetuating.

Careful investigation of the underclass began in the late 1980s with the groundbreaking work of William Julius Wilson (1987) who locates the underclass in ghetto neighborhoods . . . populated almost exclusively by the most disadvantaged segments of the black urban community, that heterogeneous grouping of families and individuals who are outside the mainstream of the American occupational system. Included in this group are individuals who lack training and skills and either experience long-term unemployment or are not members of the labor force, individuals who are engaged in street crime and other forms of aberrant behavior, and families that experience long-term spells of poverty and / or welfare dependency. (p. 8)

In Wilson's formulation, structural factors are combined with cultural and behavioral ones to incorporate into the underclass residents of ghetto neighborhoods exhibiting high levels of both long-term poverty and anti-social behavior. In their effort to construct more precise measures of the underclass, Ronald Mincy, Isabel Sawhill, and Douglas Wolf (1990) have specified these points. They first identify a persistence-of-poverty measure that defines underclass members as "that subset of the poor who have chronically low incomes [for] eight or more years" (1990:450). Second is a behavior-based measure that conceptualizes the underclass as a group of people who violate generally accepted normative expectations, most particularly, those "that young people will complete their education, at least through high school; that they will delay childbearing until they are able to support their offspring; that adults who are not old, disabled, or supported by a spouse will work; and that everyone will be law abiding" (p. 450). Finally are location-based measures that pertain to neighborhoods, not individuals. Poor neighborhoods are those where the overall incidence of poverty is over 40 percent. Bad neighborhoods are those where the "incidence of nonconformity with existing social norms is high" (p. 451)—that is, where the rates of school dropout, single parenthood, welfare dependency, male joblessness, and crime are high. Underclass neighborhoods are poor and bad. "Not all of the residents of underclass neighborhoods are poor and not all of them are engaged in dysfunctional behaviors, but all are living in neighborhoods where such conditions are commonplace" (p. 451). These conditions—Wilson calls them "neighborhood effects"—play a key role in transforming poor people into an underclass.

The underclass is a relatively recent development. Forty years ago most urban black neighborhoods were stable and secure, and, even more so than white neighborhoods, displayed a high degree of class integration. Black adults at all class levels shared the same neighborhood, and their children went to the same local schools, played in the same parks, and worshiped in the same churches. The racial discrimination that kept middle-class African-Americans from moving to more prosperous areas also made it enormously difficult for their less well off counterparts to get the better-paying jobs. Yet, the overwhelming majority of adult males worked regular jobs, married the women who gave birth to their children, and lived with and supported their wives and children (Lemann 1991). All this started to change in the early 1960s. Since that time, Carl Nightingale (1993) observed, "key relationships within families especially between adult men and women, and between fathers and their children, have undergone extreme stress, highlighted by the virtual disappearance of marriage as an institution among poor black people. Also an extraordinary surge in levels of fatal violence has threatened to overwhelm not only the traditions of cooperation rooted in African-American extended families, active neighborhood organizations, and churches but also mainstream institutions of social control operating in inner-city communities—like schools, social welfare services, police, and the courts" (p. 16). Starting in the late 1960s and continuing through the 1970s and 1980s, the proportion of poor black children born to women neither married to nor living with the children's fathers rose precipitously, as did the incidence of crime in general and homicidal violence in particular. Initially related to gangs and drugs, by the 1980s the rising rate of violent death had cast its shadow on young and middle-aged women and on children under the age of four whose only sin was to live in poor and bad neighborhoods (Nightingale 1993:22). According to most estimates there are about two million Americans currently living in neighborhoods characterized by persistent poverty, high levels of unemployment, crime, violence, out-of-wedlock births, and single-parent families, and low levels of neighborly trust and goodwill (Mincy, Sawhill, and Wolf 1990:452; Wilson 1991b:26).

Wilson's account of the development and persistence of the underclass places great weight on family instability, to which he attributes much of the aberrant behavior—crime and delinquency, teenage pregnancy, welfare dependency—that keeps poor people poor. At the base of family instability is the disappearance of the two-parent family, a consequence, in part, of the scarcity of marriageable men in poor black urban neighborhoods. Compared to their counterparts elsewhere, marriage-aged men in these neighborhoods are likely to be jobless, in prison, on parole, or dead. In this context fewer women marry, and those who do get divorced more quickly. The result is unstable, single-parent, female-headed poor families.

Underlying this development, Wilson argues, is increased joblessness among young black men. The deindustrialization of northeastern and midwestern cities began in the late 1960s and early 1970s as manufacturing facilities moved to the suburbs, nonunionized parts of the country, and foreign locations, taking with them the unskilled and semiskilled manufacturing jobs that gave many inner-city adults regular employment (Wilson 1987:chap. 2). A growth in service-sector employment filled the gap, but the large majority of these new jobs offered low wages, few benefits, part-time hours, and little security. Competition for these jobs stiffened as the pool of inexperienced workers—high school students, wives seeking to supplement the family's income, immigrants, displaced employees—expanded. Wages lagged as the supply of unskilled workers outpaced demand, and the chances of being idle rose, particularly for young black men. Wilson attributes the overrepresentation of young black males in the pool of idle workers to a combination of factors: racial discrimination in hiring practices; poorer school performance and less developed reading and math skills; employer experiences of higher levels of unreliability with this group of workers; a growing disdain for minimum-wage, and insecure dead-end jobs among black inner-city males. In the three poorest neighborhoods in Chicago in 1960, there were seventy employed males for every one hundred females aged sixteen or older. By 1990, the number of employed males had plummeted to twenty-three (Wilson 1991b:26).

Joblessness, single parenthood, and the poverty they produce are not enough to create an underclass. Also required is isolation of poor unemployed males, single mothers and their children from the larger society. The social isolation of ghetto neighborhoods began, Wilson (1987:56–57) argues, with the departure of stable working-class and middle-class families. Prompted by both the advantages of better residential areas, made more accessible to African-Americans by the Civil Rights Act of 1964, and the incipient deterioration of inner-city neighborhood life, the out-migration of stable families fueled the abrupt erosion of local businesses, churches, schools, parks, and recreational facilities, and left the area without people whose lives would confirm the message that education is valuable, steady work is superior to welfare, teenage pregnancy is wrong, and honoring family responsibilities is necessary, valued, and meaningful. With their departure, stable families took with them the resources that once helped to sustain the poor during bouts of unemployment and to socialize and inspire their children. In addition, their migration left already deindustrializing neighborhoods with weak labor force attachment.

Poor and jobless people living in a neighborhood that reinforces weak labor force attachment are more likely to encounter the persistent poverty and exhibit the aberrant behaviors that define the underclass, than are poor and jobless people with similar occupational and educational skills who live in neighborhoods that encourage strong labor force attachment. In a neighborhood not organized around regular employment, Wilson argues,

> what is lacking is not only a place in which to work and the receipt of regular income, but also the coherent organization of the present, that is, a system of concrete expectations and goals. . . . In the absence of regular employment, life, including family life, becomes more incoherent. (1991a:10)

In such neighborhoods, job information and contact networks are nonexistent, pressure on the unemployed-unemployable to rely on illegal sources of income is high, chances of marriage to a stably employed mate are slim, and opportunities for children to acquire the disciplined habits and skills necessary for regular employment are few. There is an important difference, Wilson claims, between a poor and jobless family whose opportunities are restricted by the structure of the economy but that live in a neighborhood with strong labor force attachment and a poor and jobless family that "lives in an inner-city ghetto neighborhood that is not only influenced by these same constraints but also by the behavior of other [poor and] jobless families in the neighborhood" (Wilson 1991a:10). Only the second kind of family will be swallowed into the underclass.

The underclass is rooted in bad neighborhoods. As characterized by Wilson and Mincy, Sawhill, and Wolf, bad neighborhoods are poor. They are economically deprived, socially impoverished in the sense that they are unable to sustain basic local institutions and orderly public places, and isolated from the larger society. They exhibit high levels of joblessness, single parenthood, and welfare dependency. Bad neighborhoods are extraordinarily dangerous, beset by crime and violent death and peopled by neighbors whose experiences "decree an edgy mistrust of others and a cynical sense that manipulation and force win out" (Nightingale 1993:23).

TWO ANALYSES

The two most influential accounts of the deterioration of social life in underclass neighborhoods derive from the two sets of assumptions that form the market and welfare state solutions to bad parenting, as examined in Chapter 1. Right-wing or conservative assumptions expressed through market rhetoric give rise to an argument that the expansion of the welfare state is primarily responsible for the development of the underclass. Left-wing assumptions mirrored in the rhetoric of rights lead to an argument that the underclass is primarily a product of an increasingly harsh and unchecked market economy. There is some evidence that both arguments have merit. To the extent that bad neighbors are generated by the extension of both the market and the welfare state, the solutions proposed by the Right—strengthen the market over the welfare state—and by the Left—enlarge the welfare state and constrict the market—are equally wrong. Just as we did with the problem of bad parenting, we need to look for a solution beyond the market and the state.

The Right-Wing Account

Designed in part to counter the development of a permanent under-class, President Johnson's Great Society programs, launched in 1964 in conjunction with his declaration of war against poverty, substantially enlarged government responsibility for providing assistance to those in poverty. Benefit levels were upgraded, new services were established, and eligibility criteria were lowered. Antidiscrimination laws were passed and enforced to assure that blacks had the same access to public assistance as whites. Informational campaigns and legal services were established to aid the poor in securing the goods and services that would enable them to overcome their poverty. As cash payments and in-kind benefits (medical and housing subsidies) increased and enrollment re-quirements were relaxed, the "welfare rolls grew from 3 million in 1960 to 6.7 million in 1969, to 10.9 million in 1972; of single mothers, 29 percent were on welfare in 1964 and 63 percent in 1972" (Lemann 1991:282–83). This is the point at which, according to the right-wing view, ghetto life rapidly disintegrates.

The right-wing argument gained ascendancy in the 1980s when it was used to guide and justify the attack on the welfare state orchestrated by President Reagan. Its central claim is that government poor-relief programs—Aid to Families with Dependent Children (AFDC), food stamps, subsidized housing, and the like—harm the poor. Indeed by demoralizing and devitalizing the poor, by sapping their independence and sense of responsibility, and by undermining families and neighbor-hoods, the welfare state entraps the poor in their poverty. Great Society programs, according to this view, discouraged marriage, enabled poor women to bear children out of wedlock, encouraged reduced work effort, and promoted long-term, often intergenerational dependency among poor single mothers and their children (Roche 1992:104–5; McClelland 1990:212–18). George Gilder (1981), one of the architects of this perspec-tive, insists that these programs undermine the framework of work and family the poor require to overcome their poverty: poor people become otherwise only by working hard, an arduous task spurred on by the obligations of family. The welfare state, he tells us, weakens commitments to work and family not only by replacing hard work as a source of income, but also by making income a right of single mothers and basing the amount of that income on the number of children they have. In the midst of the welfare state, people are able to improve their economic position by leaving work and by not marrying or divorcing the fathers or mothers of their children.

Charles Murray's *Losing Ground*, published in the middle of Reagan's eight years in office, offers the most influential statement of the right-wing argument. Murray finds that despite the substantial increase in welfare expenditures from 1965 on, ghetto life became more desperate as the incidence of poverty and the rate of antisocial behavior increased. In inner-city neighborhoods targeted for welfare programs, unemployment rose steadily from 1966 on as larger numbers of young people, between eighteen and twenty-four, voluntarily withdrew from the labor force, and the number of female-headed families skyrocketed as more young men and young women saw less reason to marry. The higher levels of unemployment and female-headed families, Murray (1984) argues, are the result of perfectly rational responses to the perverse economic initiatives supplied by federal welfare policy after 1965. The new and expanded welfare state ensured that it was

> easier to get along without a job. It was easier for a man to have a baby without being responsible for it, for a woman to have a baby without having a husband. It was easier to get away with crime. Because it was easier for others to get away with crime, it was easier to obtain drugs. Because it was easier to get away with crime, it was easier to support a drug habit. Because it was easier to get along without a job, it was easier to ignore education. Because it was easier to get along without a job, it was easier to walk away from a job and thereby accumulate a record as an unreliable employee. (p. 175)

In this context, Murray reports, the authority of the low-income, independent, working families is successfully challenged, respect for behaviors that enable people to escape poverty—staying in school, working hard, staying married, supporting children, and abiding by the law—turns to ridicule, and the civility and moral reliability of the neighborhood deteriorates.

A decade after the appearance of *Losing Ground,* Murray remains in the forefront of the right-wing opposition to the welfare state. At the center of his strategy for diminishing the underclass is the proposal to drastically cut back and, in some cases, eliminate entirely welfare programs. The overwhelming majority of long-term users of public assistance are young, nonwhite, unwed mothers who had their first child as teenagers, are high school dropouts, and had no work experience prior to receiving AFDC benefits (McClelland 1990:217). On average, these women remain on welfare for ten years, and there is a 40 percent chance their daughters, after age sixteen, will go on to become long-term dependents on the welfare system (Roche 1992:105). Currently, 68 percent of births to black women are out of wedlock. In urban ghettos, that figure rises to 80 percent (Murray 1993, 1994a). Illegitimacy, Murray contends, "is the single most important social problem of our time . . . because it drives everything else"—

crime, drugs, poverty, and welfare dependency. The proper and only response to it is

> to end all economic support for single mothers. The AFDC payment goes to zero. Single mothers are not eligible for subsidized housing or food stamps. An assortment of other subsidies and in-kind benefits disappear [so that] the message is loud and unmistakable: From society's perspective, to have a baby that you cannot care for yourself is profoundly irresponsible and the government will no longer subsidize it. (Murray 1993; also see Murray 1992)

In Murray's scheme, government would continue to provide medical coverage to children and would lavishly fund orphanages and adoption services for children surrendered by single mothers unable to care for them. Murray contends that once state-provided benefits for unwed mothers are eliminated, the high rate of illegitimacy and the social problems it fuels would decline.

Other right-wing analysts see additional gains accruing from the diminution of the welfare state. The state would be made weaker and less capable of intruding on people's lives. The reduction in welfare expenditures would translate into lower taxes. Fewer government regulations and taxes would encourage fuller expression of and greater reliance on market principles, creating a climate more hospitable to the pursuit of self-interest through hard work, investment, and the creation of new jobs, many of which would be made available to unwed mothers and idle boyfriends no longer subsidized by the welfare state. If the welfare state is the problem, the market, according to this view, is the solution.

The Left-Wing Account

Elliot Currie (1993) offers a clear and concise statement of the left-wing argument that the deterioration of ghetto life and neighborhoods is driven by market forces. Changes in welfare policy and programs launched by Great Society initiatives did substantially increase expenditures on public assistance, but even at their most bountiful, the benefits America's welfare state offered the poor were easily the most meager and least generous when compared with other advanced industrial societies, among which the United States continued to have the strongest market and the weakest welfare state. Throughout the 1980s, the Reagan administration sought to make the market even stronger and the welfare state weaker. Influenced by the work of George Gilder and Charles Murray, it slashed many welfare programs, reducing already inadequate benefits. Currie (1993:131–41) supplies a number of examples:

- "Between 1979 and 1986, the average benefit under AFDC fell by 20 percent in real terms while the proportion of poor children actually receiving benefits fell from 72 to 60 percent."
- "By the late 1980s, thirty-five states and the District of Columbia paid average welfare benefits that were less than *half* the federal poverty level."
- The mixture of AFDC, social security, and unemployment insurance that lifted one poor family in five above the poverty line in 1979 was sufficient to raise only one poor family in nine in 1986. This means that "about half a million families remained in poverty who would have ceased to be poor had benefits been maintained at even their already minimal late-seventies levels."
- "Low-income housing construction dropped precipitously from roughly 50,000 units a year in the mid-sixties . . . to less than 25,000 in the 1980s."

Throughout the 1970s, Currie argues, lower-income Americans were hit hard by market-guided corporate decisions to close plants, eliminate jobs, and lower wages. Starting in the early 1980s, they were hit equally hard by a right-wing administration that cut support payments, in-kind benefits, and related forms of assistance exactly at the time they were most needed. The two developments deepened, hardened, and geographically concentrated poverty in ways that solidified the foundations of the underclass. This combination of a more powerful, less restrained and less regulated market, and a weaker welfare state, Currie finds, made an already desperate set of circumstances intolerable. Inequality grew, and poverty increased as the number of poor people rose and the extent of their poverty deepened: Between 1979 and 1984, 8.3 million people "joined the ranks of those living below 125 percent of the federal poverty level" (Currie 1993:135). The capacity of neighborhoods to provide mutual support and effective socialization of the young was damaged by the excessive geographical movement caused by the loss of stable jobs and the unavailability of low-income housing. Many of the desperately poor were driven into homelessness and many others were forced to "move repeatedly in search of an affordable place to live—undermining the social cohesion of local communities and eroding traditional sources of social support" (Currie 1991:256, 1993:141). Families were destabilized by the economic dislocations, losing much of their capacity to support themselves, never mind besieged friends, relatives, and community support associations (Currie 1991:256–57). For those in poor neighborhoods ridden with economic insecurity and bereft of even minimal networks of mutual aid, the withdrawal of public services—preventive health care, mental health services, hospitals, recreational facilities, and fire protection—led not only to an intensification of economic desperation but as well to an increase in delinquency, drug abuse, tuberculosis, infant mortality, and violent crime (Currie 1991:257). In short, Currie argues, a stronger, more callous market joined with a weaker, more callous welfare state to strip people of jobs and income and to create neighborhoods that "lacked not only visible economic opportunities, but also hospitals, fire stations, movie theaters, stores, and neighborhood organizations—communities without strong ties of friendship or kinship, disproportionately populated by increasingly deprived and often disorganized people locked into the bottom of an already deteriorating job market" (1993:141).

In this light, the problem with the welfare state, even before the 1980s attack on it, is that the benefits it supplied and the protections it offered against the harsher consequences of the market economy were too few in number and too thin in substance to effectively counteract the forces of debilitation that overwhelmed inner-city neighborhoods. If the underclass problem is to be handled effectively, a more active, intrusive, and generous welfare state capable of taming the destructive tendencies of the market must be established. Its primary responsibilities, according to Currie (1993:285–319), would include the following:

1. Enhancing the opportunity structure by using state power to create jobs, raise wages, and upgrade skills. A national labor market policy would raise the federal minimum wage, reduce inequalities within and across occupations, and create a system of incentives to reward private firms for improving the quality and skill level of jobs and to penalize them for decisions that lead to the deterioration of the job structure and communities. The government would also assume greater responsibility for employment training and public-job creation. A particularly urgent task facing the United States today, rebuilding the infrastructure—roads, bridges, waterways, and transportation systems—would entail the creation of hundreds of thousands of new jobs.

2. Extending public health care by instituting a national health system and by introducing into poor communities efficient, well-funded prenatal and infant care, drug treatment, and hospital emergency services.

3. Increasing support for families by requiring employers to extend paid family leaves to parents and by expanding both high-quality public child care and the Head Start program for preschool children.

4. Providing adequate shelter by improving and increasing the existing stock of low-income housing.

In undertaking these last three responsibilities, the government would generate massive numbers of new jobs, and thus "would dramatically expand the structure of opportunities for those now denied the chance to contribute to their society. . . . [It also] would deliver critical health and social services to those most at risk. . . . [It] would make people more productive and less dependent. [It] would strengthen families and stabilize local communities" (Currie 1993:321–22). Thus, in the case of the underclass as elsewhere, the Left looks to the welfare state for solutions while the Right keeps its eye on the market.

A SOCIOLOGICAL VIEW: THE IMPORTANCE OF SOCIAL CONTROL AND COMMUNITARIAN INTERDEPENDENCIES

Good neighbors are capable of social control. Good neighbors participate in and are responsive to social control. Social control requires for its effectiveness ongoing communitarian interdependencies that feed the trust, reciprocity, and sense of mutuality on which rest responsible neighborhoods. When neighborhoods are organized more by market or welfare state principles and less by principles of sociability, cooperation, and mutual support, they tend to become bad neighborhoods. When neighbors rely less on one another and more on the market and the state, they tend to become bad neighbors.

Social control refers to the capacity of a group to regulate itself informally and morally by a set of collective principles authoritative enough to counter the unbridled expression of self-interest (Janowitz 1978:27–34). Social control sustains collective goals and values and makes effective the rules or norms that guide their pursuit. Within the group, judgments are made, sanctions, both positive and negative, are administered, and behavior is regulated with reference to group values and norms. In a group that has social control, those who act in accordance with acknowledged values and rules are honored, those who do not are pressured through a variety of measures—shaming, gossip, ostracism, and other threats to their reputation—to change their ways or leave. Effective social control depends on clearly understood values and norms backed by strong and certain sanctions, and these are rooted in sustained, recurrent contact between and among the members of the group. The greater such contact is, the stronger the degree of interpersonal sentiments (Horvitz 1990). In this context, most come to regard the interaction as beneficial and meaningful and to value the good opinion of others in the group. As fewer people find the interaction rewarding and value a good reputation in the group, and as collaborative activities, the basis of clear values and norms and effective sanctions, decline in number and intensity, social control diminishes, and there is little the group is able to do to encourage the good to stay and the bad to leave. At this point, as the residents of the Bronx neighborhood described at the beginning of the chapter know well, civility and moral reliability quickly evaporate. Neighbors retreat to the relative safety of their fortified residences and, no longer capable of regulating neighborhood life themselves through informal, moralizing measures, call for the more formal, impersonal, and repressive modes of regulation supplied by the state's police and courts. Thus, social control, and this is its primary justification, is the opposite of coercive control, which rests on the threat and use of official state instruments of force. Once a group or a neighborhood loses its ability to regulate itself, in John Braithwaite's words, "moralizing social control collapses, a vacuum is created that will attract the most brutal, repressive, and intrusive of police states" (1989:186).

Effective social control depends on what Braithwaite calls "communitarian interdependencies." Interdependencies are established in the activities carried out by people who depend on one another for the achievement of valued goals. Interdependent people to one degree or another have personal attachments, awareness of one another's expectations, and a stake in conforming to those expectations. Interdependencies are communitarian when they "have a special kind of symbolic significance. Interdependencies must be attachments which invoke personal obligation to others within a community of concern. They are not perceived as isolated exchange relationships of convenience but as matters of profound group obligation. Thus, a communitarian society combines a dense network of individual interdependencies with strong cultural commitments to mutuality of obligation" (Braithwaite 1989, p. 85). By making obligations acquired in collaborative activities matters of serious personal and collective concern, communitarian interdependencies accomplish two related tasks. First, they significantly restrain antisocial behavior. Low-crime neighborhoods and societies, Braithwaite (1989:84–86) shows, are neighborhoods and societies enmeshed in communitarian interdependencies. Second, they promote trust.

Indispensable to civility and moral reliability, trust is to society what contract is to the market and coercive authority is to the state. In the absence of formal contract or coercive political authority, we trust others to meet their largely open-ended, unspecified, and nonstipulated social obligations. Trusting others requires people to make the assumption that others are trustworthy. Acting on trust "is to act as if the uncertain future actions of others were indeed certain," and thus entails undertaking a potentially "risky course of action on the confident expectation that all persons involved in the action will act competently and dutifully" (Lewis and Weigert 1985:971). Trust, then, requires the confidence that others will act responsibly, keeping their promises and meeting their obligations. To the extent that this confidence is confirmed and people show they can be counted on to do what is expected of them, trust becomes a more active and powerful force in social life, creating greater opportunities for empathy, mutuality, and solidarity.

Trust originates in small-scale social settings like family, neighborhood, and community where empathy, mutuality, and solidarity already exist. It rests on "unspecific solidarities," and the social sentiments that nourish these solidarities—loyalty, sympathy, empathy, mutuality, and promise-keeping—"well up", according to Alan Silver (1985:63), "from those aspects of society untouched by the explicit spirit of contract—conspicuous among them is the area of personal relations, defined by criteria that stand in contrast to the modalities of market, bureaucracy and formal law." Without the formal stipulations and precise specifications characteristic of contractual and administrative relations, the social relations that are part of communitarian interdependencies draw their sustenance from—and thus are hospitable to—the conditions that further trust. Trust grows most easily in the personal and particular experiences framed by those social relations and settings. When these relations and settings are damaged, people become less trusting and trustful, and more willing to rely on the contractual relations and the coercive state authority that seem to require a far smaller degree of interpersonal trust. As a consequence, social obligations begin to take on the formally specified and precisely stipulated character of contractual and legal obligations. As trust diminishes, people become increasingly less willing to commit themselves to long-term relationships and to join in projects of mutual aid, and they are increasingly more likely to adopt calculative attitudes toward the relationships they enter and to terminate those relationships when they no longer satisfy self-interest (Lewis and Weigert 1985:980). A sense of basic trust "as essential trustfulness as well as a fundamental sense of one's own trustworthiness," the psychoanalyst Erik Erikson (1968:96–97) observes, is the "most fundamental prerequisite of mental vitality . . . the cornerstone of a vital personality." Without it, people become apprehensive of and estranged from others, withdrawing from a world they regard as unsympathetic, if not hostile.

Trust exists to the extent that people regularly meet their social obligations and by so doing sustain a context within which they are able to rely on one another for various forms of assistance. Trust helps constitute what James Coleman (1990a, 1990b) calls "social capital," and neighborhoods and the people in them that possess this social capital, he shows, are able to accomplish more than those without it (Coleman and Hoffer 1987). Capital is a resource people can use to benefit themselves. Economists distinguish physical capital lodged in productive equipment and stocks of goods from human capital found in the skills, talents, and knowledge of individuals. In contrast to physical and human capital, social capital, as Coleman (1990a) describes it, "inheres in the structure of relations between persons and among persons," and, "since it is not the private property of any of the persons who benefit from it," it cannot be exchanged like other forms of capital (p. 302, 315). Social capital is a resource people give one another when their actions are embedded in communitarian interdependencies.

Coleman offers several examples of social capital. A family moves from Detroit to Jerusalem where, the mother believes, "it is safe to let her eight-year-old take the six-year-old across town to school on the city bus and to let her children play without supervision in a city park. . . . In Jerusalem the normative structure ensures that unattended children will be looked after by adults in the vicinity, but no such normative structure exists in most metropolitan areas of the United States" (Coleman 1990a:303). Some first-generation Asian-American families buy copies of their children's textbooks to enable "the mother to better help her child succeed in school. The mother, uneducated, had little human capital, but her intense concern with her child's school performance, and her willingness to devote effort to aiding that, shows a high level of social capital in the family" (Coleman 1990b:334). Outside the family, social capital shows itself as adult interest in the children of others. "Sometimes that interest takes the form of enforcing norms imposed by parents or by the community; sometimes it takes the form of lending a sympathetic ear to problems not discussable with parents, sometimes as volunteer youth group leadership or participation in other youth-related activities" (p. 334). Children with access to social capital, Coleman shows, achieve higher levels of academic performance and engage in fewer incidents of self-destructive behavior than do other children.

Neighborhoods and communities with access to social capital, Robert Putnam shows, achieve much more—including better government and higher levels of economic development—than those bereft of social capital. Neighborhoods and communities capable of sustaining the mutually strengthening interaction of trust and cooperation give rise to norms of reciprocity that, by obligating people to reciprocate in general and unspecified ways for benefits received from others, highlight mutuality of obligation. They also promote networks of social engagement—cooperatives, clubs, neighborhood associations, and the like—held together by ties of mutual benefit (Putnam 1993a:171–77). Through norms or reciprocity and social networks, personal trust—trust in particular, in familiar persons— is generalized into social trust. It is easier to trust someone we do not know very well if that person is embedded in a place hospitable to robust norms of reciprocity. It is easier to trust an acquaintance or even a stranger if that person's trustworthiness is vouched for by people we do know and trust and who happen to be part of that person's social network.

Stocks of social capital—trust, norms of reciprocity supportive of cultural and personal commitments to mutuality of obligations, and dense overlapping networks of social engagement for mutual benefit—constitute a "moral resource . . . whose supply increases rather than decreases through use, and which (unlike physical capital) becomes depleted if *not* used" (Putnam 1993b:37–38). In neighborhoods where this resource is in good supply, social control prevails, and neighborhood life is regulated by the principles of generalized reciprocity, cooperation, and mutuality. Neighbors participate in networks of social engagement, take some personal responsibility for the social and physical well-being of the neighborhood and its residents, and value the good reputation of themselves and their surroundings. Trusting and trustworthy, they are quick to assist one another in time of need and equally quick to join forces to resist people and developments that threaten the neighborhood's civility and moral reliability. Communitarian interdependencies and the social capital they generate sustain the use-values of the neighborhood—the daily round, the informal support, the security and reliability, the identity— mentioned at the start of this chapter, and others as well. Inner-city youth living in neighborhoods with ample stocks of social capital, Putnam notes, "are more likely to finish school, have a job, and avoid drugs and crime. . . . That is, of two identical youths, the one unfortunate enough to live in a neighborhood whose social capital has eroded is more likely to end up hooked, booked, or dead" (Putnam 1993b:39).

Most inner-city youth fall into the "unfortunate enough" category. Their early years are spent in fractured families with parents who devote little time to them and their activities. They come to adolescence in communities where "social capital, in the form of effective norms of social control, adult-sponsored youth organizations, and informal relations between children and adults" (Coleman 1990b:333), has been depleted and where, as a consequence, poverty, drugs, and violence blanket the landscape. Children in these neighborhoods are often denied the experience of orderliness, continuity, and mutuality on which the sense of basic trust depends. Elijah Anderson, a long-time observer of poor inner-city African-American neighborhoods, finds that the "interpersonal trust and moral cohesion that once prevailed" there have been undermined,

> and an atmosphere of distrust, alienation, and crime pervades the area, further disrupting its social organization. One of the community's most important institutions has become a casualty of these changes—the relationship between "old heads" and young boys. Traditionally the "old head" was a man of stable means who believed in hard work, family life, and the

church. He was an aggressive agent of the wider society whose acknowledged role was to teach, support, encourage, and in effect socialize young
men to meet their responsibilities regarding work, family, the law, and
common decency. The young boy . . . had confidence in the old head's
ability to impart useful wisdom and practical advice about life. (1990:3)

As opportunities for meaningful employment dried up, as many of those
who might have become old heads departed the ghetto with the middle
class or withdrew to the safety of their households, and as the conventional advice of the old head met with increased skepticism and ridicule,
Anderson argues, a new role model emerged.

He is young, often a product of a street gang . . . derides family values and
has a "string" of women. He may feel little obligation toward them and the
children he has fathered, but on "mother's day", when welfare checks come
to these single mothers, he expects his share. On the local street corners, his
self-aggrandizement consumes his whole being as he attempts to impress
people through displays of material success. . . . For some [of the unemployed, demoralized young black men] who follow this model, great
though often fleeting financial success may be in store. More often a trail of
unfulfilled dreams, broken lives, jail, and even death awaits. (1990:3–4)

Old heads were good neighbors, and their demise reflects the demise of
good neighborhoods marked by social control, adult involvement, and
informal support networks, supportive of what Anderson calls a "culture
of decency" that valued personal responsibility and respect for authority
and promoted "close and extended families, a low-income family stability, deep religious values, a work ethic and desire to 'get ahead'" (1992:32,
1994:82–86).

The culture of decency stood at the center of these neighborhoods'
once-developed capacity to regulate themselves in accordance with widely held values and norms. With its deterioration, a weaker yet more
dangerous form of regulation emerges, one based on armed apartment-
dwellers, armed gangs, and armed police. In the spring of 1994, Vincent
Lane, head of the Chicago Housing Authority which is responsible for the
high-rise projects that are home to many of the city's inner-city poor,
authorized the police to make regular, unannounced sweeps of the buildings, invading residents' homes at will and without warrants to search for
weapons. The sweeps violated the residents's right, guaranteed by the
Fourth Amendment, to protection against unreasonable and warrantless
searches (see Kramer 1994 and Yarosh 1994). While the American Civil
Liberties Union castigated the action as an infringement on individual
freedom, the housing project residents, long endangered by the warring
gangs that ruled their buildings and playgrounds, overwhelmingly en-

dorsed Lane's strategy, favoring physical safety over constitutional rights. Incapable of social control, they demanded the formal control supplied by police officers, police dogs, identification checks, and surprise searches of their private belongings. Here as elsewhere the loss of social control and social capital is accompanied by the diminution of individual freedom.

The key to social capital resides in the degree to which people call on one another for assistance and the extent to which they are able to rely on one another and their interdependencies for the aid they need. "When, because of affluence, government aid, or some other factor, persons need each other less," Coleman (1990a:32) notes, "less social capital is generated." The market favored by the Right and the welfare state endorsed by the Left expand in ways that either make people need each other less or render them less able to meet each other's needs in stable, ongoing cooperative contexts. As the market commodifies goods and services for which people once depended on the goodwill of others to provide, those able to afford them get them, those who cannot often go without. Moreover, as Currie shows, when left to its own devices, the market generates inequality, deepens poverty, and brings into poor communities instability, dislocation, and insecurity while sapping them of the basic resources that allow their residents to assist one another. As the welfare state makes available more goods and services in the form of entitlements, people increasingly count on it more than on those with whom they share family, neighborhood, and community. Furthermore, as Charles Murray shows, the welfare state, even as inadequate as that found in the United States, reduces some people—especially young, unmarried mothers who started receiving benefits as single-parent teenagers and their children—to the condition of long-term, helpless dependency and enables others to shirk their responsibilities. The neighborhoods that house the underclass are the creation of the market and the welfare state. In different ways, the expansion of each has led to the depletion of social capital.

It is important to recognize along with Jennifer Hochschild (1991) that the underclass mirrors the larger American society, expressing in exaggerated, distorted, and more harmful forms the behaviors and attitudes characteristic of a large and growing number of other, more privileged Americans. This mirroring has its roots in a broad cultural transformation whose development since the 1960s has helped propel the forces of deterioration that reproduce the underclass. The glorification of individual freedom that stands at the center of this cultural transformation was actively promoted by both the left-wing and the right-wing. Pushing for the extension of individual rights that make for greater lifestyle freedom, the Left sought the deregulation of social life. Committed to the extension of market freedom, the Right aimed for the deregulation of economic life. The two efforts combined to produce a popular culture corrosive of social responsibility and communitarian interdependencies. Though economically and socially excluded from the larger society, the underclass is culturally included in, and thus directly and devastatingly affected by the culture of personal freedom in its various forms of expression (Nightingale 1993:52–53).

A culture of lifestyle freedom valuing the right to self-regulation, the right to be happy by doing what one wants, spun off from left-wing efforts in the 1960s and 1970s to advance civil rights, welfare rights, prisoners' rights, women's rights, and gay and lesbian rights, among others. In these terms attitudes toward sex, marriage, divorce, parenting, drug use, and work were altered dramatically as the freedoms to dissolve marriage, have children out of wedlock, use drugs, and reject meaningless work came to be regarded by many as essential to self-realization and by others as inescapable features of modern life. It is in this context, Christopher Jencks contends, that the stable two-parent family began to decline and single parenthood started to rapidly increase throughout society, not only in poor black inner-city Watts, but in rich white Beverly Hills as well. "In the space of a decade, we moved from thinking that society ought to discourage extramarital sex, and especially out-of-wedlock births, to thinking that such efforts were an unwanted infringement on personal liberty" (Jencks 1988:28). For the educated and affluent, among the primary supporters of lifestyle freedom, the costs imposed by these changes are easily borne: abortions are arranged, child support payments are made, separate households are maintained. For the desperately poor, these cultural and attitudinal changes exact a heavy toll. "Divorce is far costlier for women with limited schooling and job skills. . . . Poorly educated ex-husbands can seldom afford to support two households, and they seldom make adequate child support payments. Nor are these women in a strong competitive position if they want to remarry" (Jencks 1988:26). The excessive selfishness, the nonjudgmental attitudes, the diminished sense of personal and social accountability that accompanied the well-publicized and widely supported pursuit of lifestyle freedom were enough to unravel the already weakened fabric of poor inner-city families and neighborhoods. Social control does not survive for long in a culture averse to blame and accountability, and communitarian interdependencies diminish when self-realization takes precedence over obligation to others.

If the Left often downplays the destructive consequences of weak commitment to marriage and parental obligations, refusal to accept unattractive work, drug use, and teenage sex, the Right "wants to divert our gazes from the capitalist economy and self-interest-driven policy [and from the recognition] that the profit motive of the drug seller or the rationality of the welfare mother is the same as the profit motive of the investment banker and the rationality of the salary negotiator" (Hochschild 1991:573).

Though opposed by the Left, the market freedoms and deregulation of economic life advanced by the Right in the 1980s were not all that different from the lifestyle freedoms and deregulation of social life encouraged by the Left. The Right firmly tied the culture of personal freedom to the expanding market and its principles and imperatives. Hippies became Yuppies as lifestyle freedom was interweaved with rational self-interested calculation and the profit motive, and advertised as something one purchases in the market. In the 1980s the popular culture of personal freedom became more heavily consumerist. Working its way through a deregulated television industry, the consumerist ethos had a particularly powerful effect on poor inner-city children.

A Neilson Media Research study found that "black households across the country watched just under 70 hours of television during the average week, some 48 percent more than 'all other' households. In one important subcategory, blacks aged 2 to 17 watched a staggering 64 percent more than all others in that age range" (*New York Times*, October 27, 1991, p. A36). There is good reason to believe that television use among this age group in urban ghettos is even higher (see Nightingale 1993:176–79 and Carton 1991). The consumerist message and its underlying market orientation come to underclass children and teenagers unmediated by family, church, ethnic tradition, community values, and adult involvement. "Because the prevailing culture acts upon them most directly, these children are among its purest products," writes Arthur Kempton (1991:61). "The culture is disclosed to them through a small window, and there is little they can see of it that doesn't suggest to them that the measure of the value of a human being is the value of what he or she can consume. They have inherited one more of our bankruptcies, these most American children of all."

While most immediately destructive of the social capital of poor neighborhoods and the lives of poor children, the lifestyle and market freedoms promoted by the culture of personal freedom affect other neighborhoods and children as well. "Fewer Americans of all races and classes are holding jobs, getting or staying married when they have children, abstaining from illegal drugs," Hochschild (1991:568) notes, and, as a consequence, bad neighborhoods—characterized by a disproportionate number of female-headed families, out-of-wedlock births, welfare recipients, adult males working less than half time, and criminal acts—are proliferating throughout society, taking on a whiter, more suburban tone as they do (Hacker 1992; Didion 1993). "Between 1960 and 1990," Nicholas Eberstadt (1994) finds,

the annual number of white persons arrested in America more than tripled. From 1961 to 1991, the U.S. white illegitimacy ratio quintupled. By 1992 . . .

over a quarter of the country's white families with children under six years
of age accepted some form of means-tested public assistance; in the early
1990s, every seventh white family with young children was taking cash aid
from the state. (p. 16)

Accompanying these developments is what Robert Reich (1991:282–301)
calls the "secession of the successful," the most privileged 20 percent of
the American population. The successful segment that benefited most
substantially from the market-generated increases in inequality in the
1980s, are in the process of seceding from the larger society, ensconcing
themselves in secluded, protected, luxurious, and private communities,
schools, and recreational facilities. Just as the departure of the black middle class weakened African-American urban neighborhoods, so the current secession of the successful fuels the deterioration of what were
recently stable working-class and middle-class, largely white urban and
suburban neighborhoods, leaving them without the resources they need
to resist both the decay of public schools, parks, playgrounds, and common services and the temptations of the culture of personal freedom.

Reich's successful secessionists comprise, in Michael Lind's (1995) apt
term, the American overclass, a national elite that effectively controls the
country's major economic and political decision-making processes. Over
the past generation, Lind argues, the United States has come to be

dominated by the white overclass—a small group consisting of affluent
white executives, professionals, and rentiers, most of them with advanced
degrees, who with their dependents amount to no more than a fifth or so of
the American population. . . . [A]lmost all of the individuals in positions of
responsibility in the major institutions of government, business, philan-
thropy, the media, and education are members of this strikingly homoge-
neous oligarchy. . . . [B]y means of their near monopoly of campaign
finance, members of the white overclass tend to control both the Democratic
and Republican parties; they also provide the overwhelming majority of
political candidates and political and judicial appointees from within their
own ranks. (p. 100)

Unlike earlier American upper classes, the contemporary overclass is
both national in scope and little influenced by the sense of noblesse oblige
which in the past encouraged benevolence directed toward the public
good. Like the underclass, the overclass is separated from the larger society, standing apart from (in this case, far above) the class structure and in
isolation from mainstream institutions and values. In the emerging apartheid economy engineered by the policies its members support, the overclass acts to further its removal from a collapsing social order, and in the
process gives new meaning to the concept of a bad neighborhood.

The overclass's withdrawal of resources for and participation in America's common life constitutes, in Christopher Lasch's (1995:25) view, "the revolt of the elites." For Lind, it represents the culmination of "a generation-long class war" carried out by the overclass in order "to drive down American wages and roll back the New Deal/Great Society social safety net" and to redistribute the tax burden downward and political power upward (Lind 1995:188, 195). Along with widening the income and wealth gap between the overclass and the remaining four-fifths of the population, this effort has placed in jeopardy a host of public amenities—roads, transportation systems, schools, libraries, police protection, and parks. "In the United States—to a degree unmatched in any other industrial democracy—these things are once again becoming private luxuries, accessible only to the affluent few" (p. 211).

All this is symbolized most vividly in the rising number of well-fortified, highly exclusive, and private residential community associations where more and more of America's affluent set up home and hearth. Currently, there are over 150,000 residential community associations in the United States, exceeding the 55,000 that existed in 1980 and the fewer than 500 found in 1962. Thirty million Americans or 12 percent of the population, a figure expected to double within the next ten years, reside in one of these homeowners' or property owners' associations, or gated communities (Kennedy 1995:764–65; Egan 1995:A22). Some indication of what makes the residential association so attractive to so many Americans is given by the following description of Bear Creek, a guarded neighborhood outside Seattle, Washington.

There are no pesky doorbellers, be they politicians or Girl Scouts, allowed inside this community. . . . A random encounter is the last thing people here want. There is a new park, every blade of grass in shape—but for members only. Four private guards man the entrance gates 24 hours a day, keeping the 500 residents of Bear Creek in a nearly crime-free bubble. And should a dog stray outside its yard, the pet would be instantly zapped by an electronic monitor. The streets are private. The sewers are private. There is gun control. Residents tax themselves heavily, dictate house colors and shrubbery heights for their neighbors, and have built in the kind of natural buffers and environmental protections that are the envy of nearby middle-class communities that remain open to the public. (Egan 1995:A1)

Closed off from what its residents take to be a decaying social order by means of gates, moats, or private security forces, Bear Creek, like other residential associations, presents itself as the only alternative to bad neighborhoods.

The legal framework of residential associations is suggested by the above characterization. Ownership deeds require membership in a nonprofit property owners' association that supplies services and facilities to residents funded by mandatory homeowners' dues. In addition, the deeds bind residents to a set of private laws—"covenants, conditions, and restrictions"—which precisely defines what is and is not allowable within the association's borders (Kennedy 1995:762; Bell 1995:27). With dominion over parks, lakes, recreational facilities, roads, and police protection, and authority to determine how many pets, if any, residents may have, and whether or not they may hang basketball hoops on their garages, and with de facto taxation power, residential associations, writes David Kennedy, "enjoy a degree of power virtually equal to that of municipal governments but assume none of the corresponding liabilities" (Kennedy 1995:768). Within these private governments, neighborhood becomes a canine-patrolled enclave dotted by motion-detectors and surveillance cameras set in place to maintain property values by protecting residents from outsiders and one another. On the rare occasions when civic engagement occurs, it takes a narrow, self-interested form in which, as Daniel Bell (1995) observes, "participants learn to act in opposition to the interests of the wider community and to evade their responsibility for a fair share of the burdens" (p. 33).

The increasing withdrawal of the overclass into separate, exclusive, well-protected residential community associations is clearly a response to social breakdown, and more particularly in Kennedy's (1995) words, "to the widespread feeling that crime has spun out of control and that the state has allowed the social fabric to unravel and is impotent to stop this decay" (p. 767). Underlying the arrogance and scorn of the overclass, Lasch (1995:28) reminds us, is a pervasive insecurity, the result, in part, of a growing apprehension that the masses, following the lead of the underclass, will do whatever it takes, however irresponsible, to survive their worsening circumstances. The overclass, of course, enacts its own, more luxurious brand of irresponsible survivalism. In their pristine fortifications, the secessionist successful establish strict gun control and environmental regulations and heavily tax themselves to support their private parks, recreational facilities, and roads. Yet, they also endorse those right-wing political policies that make easier gun possession and environmental damage in the world outside the residential association, and that reduce the taxes necessary to support the public parks, recreational facilities, roads, and schools used by those on the other side of the gates.

Fleeing from a world of bad neighborhoods whose badness their revolt helped to create, the overclass has managed to produce its own bad neighborhoods, shaped as much by the logics of commodification and juridification as is any poor inner-city underclass neighborhood. Designed and marketed for their ability to secure personal safety and property values, the residential associations of the rich display their badness not in rising rates of male joblessness, welfare dependency, crime, and school dropout but in their failure to achieve the communitarian interdependencies that permit both informal social control and a sense of attachment to the larger community. As incapable of regulating themselves informally as their underclass counterparts, the residents of overclass neighborhoods rely on highly restrictive rules and an extensive private security apparatus to order their interactions. Showing the same disregard for the public good that is nourished by poverty, joblessness, and crime, the gated-community rich turn out to be bad neighbors to those on the outside.

CONCLUSION

Bad neighborhoods are created by an unregulated, destabilizing market economy, a welfare state that allows dependency and the denial of personal accountability, and a culture that heralds both the lifestyle freedoms evoked by a left-wing rights rhetoric and the market freedoms articulated by a right-wing market rhetoric. It makes no sense then, to take either the Right's road to market expansion or the Left's to the extension of the welfare state in search of a solution to bad neighborhoods in general and the underclass problem more specifically. Just as good parenting cannot be prompted by appeals to selfish interest or by fear of coercive state authority in the service of individual rights, good neighborhoods cannot be organized around the principles of the market or the welfare state. People become good parents in strong institutions. They become good neighbors in strong communitarian interdependencies organized by the principles of social control, cooperation, reciprocity, and mutuality. Institutions are refashioned and communitarian interdependencies are revitalized in social spaces where people must rely on one another to get much of what they need, where they must depend on each other's trustworthiness and cooperation to achieve valued ends, and where they are able to develop their social dispositions for belonging, attachment, and solidarity. Minimally, rebuilding institutions and communitarian interdependencies requires the cultivation of these social spaces, a task that begins by cleansing them of, and protecting them against, any future invasion by the market economy and the welfare state.

3

In the Absence of Society:
Liberal Individualism and Anomie

The celebration of the individual that stands at the center of the modern world carries with it a precisely defined, often hostile, suspicion of society. Society restrains, according to this view, and what it most restrains is the development of the individual. In the eighteenth century, as the modern world struggled to be born, most Enlightenment thinkers portrayed society as a source of ignorance, a constellation of oppressive customs, superstitions, prejudices, and traditional institutions that blocked the development of an individual reason whose presence would launch the journey to a more humane existence. As the modern world took decisive shape in the middle of the nineteenth century, John Stuart Mill polished the liberal defense of liberty by specifying the principles that would protect the individual from society (here conceived as the pressures to conform to communal or majority standards). Currently, contemporary theories of morality equate moral agency with individual autonomy and explain to us that people mature as moral beings to the extent that their cognitive capacities permit them to assume a standpoint outside society. The authors of a highly acclaimed study of middle-class Americans find their subjects speaking a "first language of individualism," by which they regard society as a constraint on both freedom of personal choice and the opportunity for individual success and happiness (Bellah et al. 1985). Speakers of the first language, middle-class Americans, among the purest embodiments of modernity's individualism, know they can realize their true selves only away from the distorting encumbrances of social obligation. Reason, liberty, morality, happiness, and a true self—these are what the modern world promises the individual, along with the warning that the security of each requires protection against society.

Both the Right and the Left, both the market economy and the welfare state, both market rhetoric and rights rhetoric draw from the liberalism that glorifies the individual and locates individual freedom away from the obligations of authoritative institutions and the social control of communitarian interdependencies. The liberal individual as carrier of selfish interests and preferences and a holder of individual rights is most at home in the market and in the welfare state, each of which safeguards the individual—in her pursuit of personal pleasure or in his exercise of individual rights—against the tyranny of society. This view, so broad in reach and with so very powerful an impact, is mistaken, and destructively so. With the assistance of several portraits of life in the absence of society, some of which in places recall the description of life in the underclass, we will see that away from society people acquire not liberty but a morbid restlessness that passes for liberty, not a moral stake in the fate of others but a distrust of them, not happiness but an abiding sense of anxious unfulfillment, not a true self but a truncated, shallow, and unreliable self. Some of these portraits suggest a link between the modern liberal world and the dissolution of the institutions and communitarian interdependencies that make up society, and this connection deserves our careful examination. Each of these portraits confirms an important sociological truth; society does indeed constrain; living with others, after all, requires restraint. But societal restraints in the form of institutional obligations and social control can and often do enable people to become morally responsible individuals, and as such good parents and good neighbors. Liberal individuals have a difficult time being either.

PORTRAITS OF LIFE IN THE ABSENCE OF SOCIETY

Four of the best descriptions of what characterizes people when society exists, if at all, in a diminished state are provided by Thomas Hobbes's portrayal of the state of nature, Colin Turnbull's anthropological study of the Ik, Kai Erikson's sociological analysis of a disaster-induced breakdown of community, and investigations of the narcissistic personality. Formulated in 1651 amid the social breakdown produced by the English Civil War, and regarded as one of the foundation stones of liberalism, Hobbes's "state of nature" is a conceptualization of the manner of life as it exists prior to society. The accuracy of many of its descriptive details is confirmed by the lives of more recent victims of social breakdown— Turnbull's Ik, Erikson's West Virginia coal miners, and the narcissistic personalities promoted by the conditions of liberal modernity.

The State of Nature

As Hobbes ([1651] 1963) depicts it, the state of nature is a harsh, forbidden, hostile environment populated by threatening, untrustworthy, amoral individuals. Humans, in this view, are selfish by nature, inclined to take advantage of others in order to satisfy their personal interests. Human selfishness is on full display in the state of nature where laws are unknown and common rules unformed. Life is lived in accordance with the fundamental right of nature, which gives each the liberty "to use his own power, as he will himself, for the preservation of his own nature; that is to say, of his own life; and consequently, of doing anything, which in his own judgment and reason, he shall conceive to be the aptest means thereunto" (p. 145–46). Having no obligations to others and no duties to common projects and shared purposes, people are driven solely by the interest in self-preservation, and thus they come to regard one another as invaders willing to destroy and to subdue for personal gain, safety, and reputation.

This, Hobbes tells us, is the natural condition of humankind, a condition that knows only force and fraud, not justice. At its mildest, it assumes the form of an aggressive competition where one gains only by depriving others. At its worst, when the ever-present fear and danger intensify, it sustains the climate of war wherein "every man is enemy to every man" and insecurity and mistrust reign supreme. "In such condition there is no place for industry . . . no culture of the earth . . . no knowledge of the face of the earth; no account of time; no arts; no letters; no society; and which is worst of all, continual fear, and danger of violent death; and the life of man is solitary, poor, nasty, brutish, and short" (p. 143).

The overriding goal of the solitary individual is survival, and one's survival requires two things—first, the ability to deprive others before they deprive him, and, second, the capacity to defend one's possessions against invaders who "may probably be expected to come prepared with forces united, to dispossess, and deprive him, not only of the fruit of his labor, but also of his life, or liberty" (p. 142). The manner of life in the absence of society, Hobbes argues, allots "no pleasure, but on the contrary a great deal of grief" (p. 144). Expressing no need for belonging or for deep, committed emotional relationships, incapable of sympathizing with and showing respect for others, bereft of moral codes of conduct, the self-interested invader among self-interested invaders knows he cannot rely on others just as they know they cannot count on him.

The Ik

In the mid-1960s, Colin Turnbull (1972) traveled to the mountainous northern region of Uganda to study the Ik. Consisting of nearly 2,000 people, the Ik were once nomadic hunters and gatherers living off a large stretch of land covering parts of Uganda, Kenya, and Sudan. As national boundaries were firmly established after World War II, the Ik's movement was restricted. Having lost access to their hunting grounds, they pursued the more settled routines of farming. Persistent drought assured the failure of this effort. When Turnbull arrived, the Ik had been living on the verge of starvation for some time. They had adapted to severe environmental deprivation by becoming "as unfriendly, uncharitable, inhospitable, and generally mean as any people can be" (p. 32).

Like the occupants of Hobbes's state of nature, the Ik regarded individual survival as their primary task, and they undertook it in isolation from one another, regarding cooperation, mutual support, and willingness to sacrifice for the other as impediments to self-preservation. Interpersonal affection was in extraordinarily short supply. Envy, acrimony, suspicion, and mutual distrust abounded. Children regularly denied their elderly parents food, water, and shelter. Parents neglected and, not uncommonly, mistreated their young children. Social relations, formed on the principle of self-interest, were temporary and expedient. Marriage partners cooperated rarely and only when necessary (for instance, in building their hut). They obtained food and water separately, ate alone, and made no provisions for their children over the age of three.

The birth of a child held no special significance. The mother breast-fed her child for three years. During the last of these years, she regularly and sometimes maliciously teased and taunted the child and responded with indifference to the child's pain and fears in an effort, Turnbull (1978) argues, to prepare the child for the realities of Ik life. "She knew that after three years, if she and the child both survived, there would be no possibility of her continuing to nourish the child. She also knew that in adult life the child would spend much of his or her time away from all others on the solitary quest for food and in difficulty or danger, or in cases of accident, there would simply be nobody nearby to help [and] that even if anyone were nearby he or she would not care" (p. 62).

At the age of three, the child joined a gang of children ranging in age from three to eight. Age groups existed not to foster the cooperative pursuit of collective goals but to safeguard "the solitary purpose of protection against predators—including adult Ik." In this predatory context, Turnbull continues,

> any adult who found a child with food and could take the food and eat it was a "good" adult. . . . But since adults normally pursued their food quest alone, only a solitary child was in danger. Hence, the [gangs were] an adaptive response to wider threats in the population. . . . The gangs roamed the ravines and when food was seen, the first child to reach it, consumed it instantly. . . . The fastest and strongest survived; the others died. When a child reached the age of seven or eight [he] was thrown out of the junior age gang and joined a senior age gang, becoming once again the weakest member, the least likely to get food before the others, and the least likely to

survive. If the child survived until about twelve, he was considered to be an adult and was once again thrown out. The child had theoretically learned all he needed to know at this point: to survive one had to depend on himself, expecting no help from others, except on rare and unpredictable occasions where there might be some mutual profit. He had to want to survive and to be prepared to survive alone, in relative isolation. (1978:63)

The children of the Ik were born into and, if lucky, grew up in not a society, but a system of survival, an affectionless, expedient association of mutually exploitative individuals who learned early on that trust, altruism, and commitment to the demands of social obligation substantially reduced the odds of self-preservation.

Buffalo Creek

On the morning of February 26, 1972, Buffalo Creek, a community of sixteen villages in the coal-mining region of Logan County, West Virginia, was suddenly and without warning destroyed. The collapse of a dam threw 132 million gallons of black water through the narrow mountain hollow that was home to Buffalo Creek. The flood destroyed, in the title of Kai Erickson's study of its social and psychological consequences, "everything in its path," human life, homes, workplaces, schools, church buildings, and long-established social relationships and the spirit of communality that had nourished them.

Amidst the rubble of what once had been their places of home, work, and worship, the inhabitants of Buffalo Creek, as expected, expressed their trauma in the form of a disaster syndrome. They were depressed, anxious, apathetic, and unable to sleep. Drained of emotional resources, feeling alone, their senses numbed, they found it too difficult to grieve for the dead and sympathize with the living. With time, traumatic wounds inflicted by abrupt, sharp blows to the psyche usually diminish. This is not what Erikson found when he visited Buffalo Creek several years after the flood. The "disaster syndrome" continued, and in some regards had even intensified, a sign to Erikson that the healing power of time is effective only when "it acts in concert with a nurturing communal setting" (1976:155). Such a social setting had been washed away by the flood and never replaced.

The federal government responded quickly, creating thirteen trailer camps to house the flood's victims who were placed in vacant mobile homes on a first-come, first-served basis. Intended as temporary shelter, the camps became permanent, and the result, in Erikson's words, was to take a community of people who were already scattered all over the hollow, already torn out of familiar neighborhoods, and make that condition virtually permanent. Most of the survivors found themselves living among relative strangers a good distance from their original homes, and although they continued to be within commuting range of old friends and churches and stores, they felt alien and alone. In effect, then, the camps served to stabilize one of the worst forms of disorganization resulting from the disaster by catching people in a moment of extreme dislocation and freezing them there in a kind of holding pattern. (1976:47)

These circumstances sustained a "collective trauma": wrecked social attachments and a deflated sense of communality, whose robust presence would have helped cushion the pain of—and start the recovery from—individual trauma.

In the absence of society, outside a meaningful community setting and the social supports it sponsors, the Buffalo Creek survivors became increasingly fearful, apathetic, and demoralized. As Erikson (1976) discovered, they felt "emptied of reasons for doing anything, emptied of explanations for their feelings and motives, emptied of love or conviction or pleasure, emptied of self-esteem and an ability to relate to others" (pp. 221–40). Unable to sustain either faith in the comforting rhythms of a reliable social order or their capacity to empathize with, care for, and trust one another, their approach to the world became markedly more self-interested. The post-disaster residents of Buffalo Creek were "very absorbed in their own problems," profoundly uncertain "as to how one goes about 'making' relationships, distrusting of even old neighbors," fearing "those very persons on whom one once staked one's life." Having lost direction, purpose, connection with moral standards, and a sense of mutuality, they existed as isolated selves burdened by an ever-present "sense of vulnerability, a conviction that the world is no longer a safe place to be." Rising rates of drug abuse, theft, delinquency, and family breakup and the severely damaged social fabric from which they emerged had made Buffalo Creek "a strange and precarious place."

Buffalo Creek never became as nasty and as callous as Hobbes's fictional state of nature or the Ugandan home of the Ik. Nevertheless, the flood's survivors came to share with the inhabitants of the state of nature and the Ik the sense that they no longer could rely on one another. In a harsh and dangerous world, made harsh and dangerous in part by the erosion of the spirit of mutual assistance and the trust on which it depends, the arduous task of individual survival comes to be regarded as something best pursued in anxious and vigilant isolation. In the absence of society, the experience of others as hostile strangers "comes to be seen as a natural feature of human life," and "evidence that the world is a place of unremitting danger . . . and [that] a kind of natural malice lurks everywhere" is found wherever people look (Erikson 1991:466–68).

The Narcissistic Personality

Over the past twenty years, narcissistic character disorders have increased substantially in modern society, and, according to some, have become the chief source of complaints tended to by psychiatrists (Cushman 1990; Solomon 1988; Lasch 1978). In desperate pursuit of the goal of psychic survival, narcissists experience life as impoverished, shallow, and without purpose. They bring an aloofness and a keenly developed suspicion of others to their interpersonal relations. The narcissistic preoccupation with the self—relating to objects as extensions of the self, defining others as objects existing to serve the self—rests on and promotes a devaluation of others. The inability to care that is characteristic of narcissism, the powerful sense that there is no one to turn to for support in time of need, advances the effort to create a self-absorption that permits the person to need no one at all. Bereft of conscience and incapable of sustaining significant, emotionally deep social bonds, the narcissistic personality equates psychic survival with the appropriation, exploitation, and even annihilation of others. The "pathological narcissist," James Glass (1980) writes, "is locked into a self-contained, omnipotent world, a personality type incapable of identifying with any principle, choice, or commitment which is not a function of the need to omnipotently control experience or to use the other as fuel for immediate need gratification" (p. 357).

The clinical literature, as summarized by Glass, includes among the major symptoms of narcissistic pathology the following: a need to devalue others, often expressed in an inability to relate to others in ways other than those that promote self-gratification; an incapacity to empathize and thus to love, the result of a "precarious inner condition that is unstable, envious, raging, and insecure"; a grandiose sense of self that feeds a feeling of emotional separation from others; the virtual absence of internalized values; and an exploitative approach to interpersonal relations, driven by an "insidious set of psychological dynamics; the rational manipulation of the other, the demand to be admired and loved, the view of the other as 'fuel' or 'supply' for egoistic needs, and ruthless and unfeeling behavior toward others the self perceives as necessary for its own interests" (p. 338, 349).

Resembling those who dwell in Hobbes's state of nature and the Ik, modern narcissists, according to the analyst Otto Kernberg, bear an "image of the world as being devoid of food and love" and a "self-concept of the hungry wolf out to kill, eat and survive." Like them, they struggle to survive, unrestrained by conscience or commonly held ethical principles. In each case, an empty self, alert to the dangers represented by others, moves through the world devouring the necessities of survival "without any inner feeling of constraint, without any sense of principle or commitment to anything other than" self-preservation (Glass 1980:348; also see Levin 1987). Like the traumatized residents of Buffalo Creek, narcissists live for the moment, fear what the future holds in store, seek protection against an unreliable and unsafe world, and lack the capacity to trust. Like them, and like Hobbes's natural people and the Ik, narcissists exist in the absence of nurturing social settings. Pathological narcissism "derives from the absence at an early age of pivotal feelings and experiences of gratification, certainty, trust and gratitude. The needed supplies are withheld . . . and the infantile self reacts with . . . rage, anger, and hurt. . . . The consequence is a severe blow to the infant's self-esteem, to its capacity to trust the others" (p. 350–51). Where warm, close, committed, trustful, enduring social relations and the sense of community they sustain are fragile and in short supply, this narcissistic wound never heals.

Over the past decade, many have seen in the narcissistic personality an exaggerated version of the personality traits possessed by the self in the contemporary United States. Philip Cushman (1990) characterizes it as an empty self, and argues that fundamental changes since the end of World War II have "shaped a self that experiences a significant absence of community, tradition, and shared meaning. It experiences these social absences and their consequences . . . as a lack of personal conviction and worth, and it embodies [them] as a chronic, undifferentiated emotional hunger. . . . It is empty" (p. 600). For Robert Bellah, this self is unencumbered, detached from and not securing its identity in social obligation and institutional or moral ideals. It is a self guided by feelings and thus an arbitrary and isolated self. "A self free of absolute values or 'rigid' moral obligations can alter its behavior to adapt to others and to various social roles. It can play all of them as a game . . . because [its] identity depends only on discovering and pursuing its own personal wants and inner impulses" (Bellah et al. 1985:77). Robert Nisbet describes the loose self, detached from institutions and communitarian interdependencies "and playing fast and loose with other individuals in relationships of trust and responsibility" (1988:84). The self set loose from family, community, and social obligation exists outside the social contexts that cultivate both the practices of mutual aid and the competencies that enable people to rely on one another as parents, neighbors, and citizens. The loose self then, is at the same time, as Christopher Lasch emphasizes, an incompetent and helplessly dependent self, dependent on the impersonal structures of the market and the state for goods and services once made available by friends, relatives, and neighbors, and dependent on others for the validation of his self-esteem. "His apparent freedom from family ties and institutional constraints does not free him to stand alone or to glorify in his individuality," writes Lasch (1984:10). "On the contrary, it contributes to his insecurity, which he can overcome only by seeing his 'grandiose self' reflected in the attentions of others, or by attaching himself to those who radiate celebrity, power, and charisma." In line with recent fashion, Kenneth Gergen celebrates the rise of a postmodern self from "the demise of personal definition, reason, authority, commitment, trust . . . sincerity, belief in leadership, depth of feeling, and faith in progress. In their stead, an open slate emerges on which persons may inscribe, erase, and rewrite their identities as the ever-shifting, ever-expanding, and incoherent network of relationships invites or permits" (1991:228). Fragmented, decentered, discontinuous, the postmodern self—which, as Gergen admits, is really "no self at all"—moves in and out of confused and disconnected relationships, able to rely on no one at all, not even itself. The empty, unencumbered, loose yet helplessly dependent, postmodern self expresses in muted form the characteristics shared by the pathological narcissist, Hobbes's natural being, the Ik, and the victims of Buffalo Creek's flood. It lacks moral conviction, is self-centered, unreliable, untrustworthy, and distrustful. It regards the world as hostile, cold, and uncaring, and takes survival as its primary goal.

Kai Erikson (1976) concludes his study of Buffalo Creek by proposing that "instead of classifying a condition as *trauma* because it was produced by a disaster, we would classify an event as *disaster* if it had the property of bringing about traumatic reactions" (p. 254). In these terms, liberal modernity legitimately could be added to the roster of disasters, he suggests, "for there are ample indications that [it] can become a principal cause of traumatic reactions [as it] distance[s] people from primary associations and [separates] them from the nourishing roots of community" (p. 258). Like shockingly abrupt and disruptive disasters, liberal modernity erodes the ground of meaningful relationships and shakes until they break the bases of confidence in others, in order, and in the future. Modernity and disaster—each washes away the social supports of individualism, freedom, morality, and the personal happiness that so many believe are to be found only away from society. Each leaves the survivor alone amidst the rubble of the damaged human relationships found in the absence of society.

LIBERAL MODERNITY

Liberal democratic capitalism stands at the center of the modern world. Challenged throughout the twentieth century by various forms of fascism, state socialism, and religious fundamentalism, it enters the twenty-first century bruised and bleeding, but still standing as the world's most powerful force. Rooted in liberalism's three-hundred-year long defense of liberty and in two hundred years' worth of democratic movements, and resting on an often uneasy combination of the dynamics of capitalism and the principles of the welfare state, liberal democratic capitalism defines and structures modernity in the name of the individual. The liberal principles that frame it and the two major manifestations and carriers of these principles—the capitalist market and the liberal democratic welfare state—defend the individual while at the same time, and often quite deliberately, desiccating the wellsprings of social life.

Liberalism

Over the past three centuries, liberalism has emerged as one of history's most powerful ideologies. Its appeal is easily understood for it ties together individual freedom and the possibility of unlimited material gain and defends the two against the arbitrary imposition of external, most especially, governmental powers (Bellah et al. 1985:66–70). Rooted in John Locke's opposition to the absolutist state, liberalism began by offering a basis for denying "the historical legitimacy of unfree commonality (feudalism, ancient slavery, traditional tyranny)," and developed by expanding that basis to include both a denial of "the future possibility of a free commonality" (Barber 1989:60) and a warning that individual freedom is often among the earliest casualties of the search for common ground, common purpose, and common ideas of the good.

Liberalism emphasizes the priority of the individual over the social. Individuals are said to antedate society. They exist before society. Indeed, they are the makers of society, making it the same way they make contracts between and among themselves, and for the same purpose, namely, to preserve their individual freedom. Thus, society—social institutions and communitarian interdependencies—has no existence apart from the individuals who compose it, "and therefore no claims, beyond or above those individuals. Its function is to serve individuals, and one of the ways it should do this is by respecting their autonomy, and not trespassing on their right to do as they please so long as they can do so without harm to others" (Arblaster 1984:45). Individuals then are morally superior to society. The preferences, interests, demands, and rights of the individual take priority over the interests and demands of the group or society.

Liberalism's individuals are self-contained, self-sufficient, and self-motivated. They are, as Anthony Arblaster (1984) describes them, "driven actively from within by the natural energy of innate desires and appetites

. . . which are fundamentally selfish, in that the individual naturally seeks his or her own happiness, pleasure, and gratification" (p. 28). Naturally self-interested and antisocial, regarding others as real or potential helps or hindrances to the maximizing of self-interest, and entering into relations with them only to further personal advantage, this individual is, in the words of C. B. Macpherson (1962:263), a possessive individual, "the proprietor of his own person and capacities, for which he owes nothing to society," the owner of himself, whose self-reliance, freedom, pleasure, and happiness are grounded in his separateness from others.

Liberal individualism, Benjamin Barber (1984:81) aptly notes, distrusts the individual it idolizes, and with good reason. Sparked into action by egotistical desires, rationally calculating the best way to satisfy these desires, selfish, acquisitive, possessive, the individual exists primarily for himself. Recognizing this, liberalism advances social, political, and economic arrangements designed to keep people "safely apart rather than to bring them fruitfully together, [arrangements] capable of fiercely resisting every assault on the individual—his privacy, his property, his interests, and his rights—but far less effective in resisting assaults on community" (p. 4). Assuring that the individual is left alone is the defining task of liberalism, and when "it must interfere or interdict it does so in the name of leaving alone. Protection, preservation, and the security of private interests . . . are the whole of the liberal agenda" (p. 91). Only when left alone, when shielded from the intrusions of others, liberalism insists, is the individual free.

Liberalism takes individual freedom as its highest, most uncompromisable end. From the beginning, liberalism defined freedom negatively, as the absence of restraint, force, and interference, that is, as being left alone. "The only freedom which deserves the name," John Stuart Mill ([1859] 1978:12) insisted, "is that of pursuing our own good in our own way, so long as we do not attempt to deprive others of theirs, or impede their efforts to obtain it." Freedom consists in the individual's right to choose for himself how he will live his life, to believe, worship, think, and live the way he finds good. Freedom, then, is a private affair, a matter of personal fulfillment. Judgments of the human good, of the proper way of living, are subjective. They reflect personal, private, inherently arbitrary opinions, none better or worse than, morally superior to or inferior to, the others. Freedom demands the individual be able to define the good for himself and to seek personal fulfillment or happiness by selecting a manner of life consistent with that definition. These demands, according to liberalism, take absolute precedence over the demands of the social.

Liberalism's search for places in which to ground individual freedom settled on three—the capitalist market, the state (protective of individual rights), and democracy. Together they gave decisive shape to modernity in the form of liberal democratic welfare state capitalism. The liberal market is valued as an arena of free choice. Therein individuals are free to express their preferences and to seek their satisfaction. Free from the coercive power of others, they do what they do in the market because they find the benefits of such action attractive. The liberal state, like all other states, does rest on coercive power—the power to tax, to punish, and to conscript. Liberalism limits the use of state power to the protection of the bases of individual freedom, including the market. Committed to the doctrine of individual rights, the liberal state is obliged to use its power to assure that the individual's right to live as he or she sees fit is secured. Democracy adds a political dimension to individual freedom, allowing individuals as citizens to determine for themselves how they shall be governed. Democracy came late to liberalism. It was accepted reluctantly at first and only after safeguards had been established for the protection of the individual against the democratically expressed will of the people or preference of the majority (Macpherson 1977). The liberal solution to the problems posed by democracy consists of two strategies, first, defining the market as private and thus beyond the reach of political democracy (the owners of a business firm, not the citizens of the community or nation where that firm is located, decide with an eye on their self-interests how the firm's profits will be allocated and its labor force deployed), and second, extending the range of individual rights the state is required to protect (the right of a woman to have an abortion is defended by the courts and, if necessary, by the police even when it clashes with the clearly expressed opinion of the majority). In these ways, democracy is liberalized, subordinated to the liberal market and the liberal state committed to the preservation of individual rights. While their operating principles are different—indeed, as we have seen, so different that they underlie the great divide in American politics between the Right and the Left—the two are equally animated by liberalism's effort to save the individual from society.

The Capitalist Market

"The natural effort of every individual to better his own condition, when suffered to exert itself with freedom and security," wrote Adam Smith ([1776] 1910:12), "is so powerful a principle, that it is alone and without any assistance . . . capable of carrying on the society to wealth and prosperity." According to Smith and the many defenders of the capitalist market who followed him, the market, relying on neither coercion nor goodwill, simply has people be what they are—self-interested, and it coordinates the selfish pursuits of individuals efficiently and in a way that substantially increases the odds that more people will have their preferences satisfied more often and more completely than otherwise would be the case.

For the market to regulate behavior in this way, several conditions must be present. Individuals must be free to undertake the selfish pursuit of personal gain. Rationally calculating the costs and benefits of the various transactions available to them, individuals meet in the market as sellers, intent on maximizing their profit, and as buyers, striving to maximize their personal satisfactions. These encounters generate the increased wealth and prosperity that enable more individuals to gratify more of their interests only when competition prevails. There must be enough sellers so that no one or any group of several are able to set prices independent of the individual preferences expressed in supply and demand. This requires that there be no insurmountable barriers (for instance, monopoly control over resources or distribution channels) to market entrance. The greater the number of sellers, the more competitive the market, which makes it easier for buyers to leave one seller for another thus allowing them to satisfy their preferences more cheaply or at a higher level. Ease of entrance makes for ease of exit. Both promote competition, which places a premium on self-interested rational calculation (Best and Connolly 1976:4–11). To that extent these conditions are met, the market exists as a basis of individual freedom. It is open to all, and the transactions that take place are strictly voluntary. Thus, the obligations people incur are freely chosen with a view toward selfish advantage. Employees are free to choose their employers. "Consumers are free to choose among products and sellers; sellers are free to choose which product markets to enter" (Best and Connolly 1976:5). The market brings together self-maximizing, rationally calculative individuals in impersonal, contractual relations that do little to nourish, and much to discourage, the sentimental bonds and moral attachments that make for long-term meaningful social ties.

The market is not simply an arena for self-interested exchanges, it is also a psychological environment characterized by anonymity, indifference to others, lack of commitment and minimal levels of communication, trust, compassion, and benevolence. For many, this is the strength of the market: individuals who are indifferent toward or lack compassion for others satisfy their personal interests in ways that allow others to satisfy theirs more easily. "By economizing on valuable traits—feelings of solidarity with others, the ability to empathize, the capacity for complex communication and collective decision making, for instance—markets are said to cope with the scarcity of these worthy traits," Samuel Bowles (1991) writes. "But in the long run markets contribute to their erosion and even disappearance" (p. 13). The market, Bowles argues, rewards some personal traits and penalizes others, and thus influences not only what individuals get but also what they become. It not only reduces the need for compassion, benevolence, belonging, and solidarity, it discourages their expression and cultivation as well, and in this way actively develops in people the kind of traits its defenders presume them to have by nature.

What are some of the psychological effects of the market? Robert Lane (1981:5, 1991) identifies five. The market, he shows, has people become more cognitively complex, that is, it fosters their "capacity to understand abstractions, to hold preferences in abeyance while . . . judging the self and others . . . to change concepts to fit reality rather than fitting reality to fixed conceptions, to hold several ideas in one's head at once and to 'shuffle them around' . . . to arrive at original solutions." The market lessens people's respect for custom and traditional authority, encourages a high degree of self-reliance, and continuously has people make choices that require them to calculate their interests. In this way it furthers cognitive development and promotes the idea that the individual controls his or her destiny. Thus, the market also inculcates in people a sense of autonomy, "the desire and ability to remain independent of environmental stimuli, to master one's environment, and to avoid stimulus-boundedness."

Market relations are impersonal, generally attaching people to one another superficially and for limited and specific purposes, and thus they require little in the way of mutual understanding and sympathy for the other. The market, Lane shows, subordinates sociocentrism to egocentrism. It does little to advance people's capacity to empathize with others and much to improve the individual's capacity to rationally pursue personal satisfactions. In addition, the market makes it difficult for people to achieve a stable and integrated identity, an essential basis of consistency, reliability, and respect for self and others. "The market's indifference to the whole person, its instrumental character, the very complexity of choices it requires—all leave the individual with a sense of uncertainty about his place, his role, his person. He has trouble finding a secure and satisfying identity" (Lane 1981). Finally, the market dilutes people's identification with moral values. Advancing the view that the individual's primary obligation is to him- or herself and rewarding rationally self-interested behavior, the market does nothing to reinforce—indeed, it often discourages—the altruistic concern for the well-being of others and the disinterested point of view central to moral action.

The market inclines people to orient their behavior toward individual advantage. As its influence expands, the sentiments, habits, and practices necessary to sustain a common life diminish. In their study of changing American values, a group of psychologists found that when

individual happiness becomes the criterion by which all things are measured, when the ability to withstand, strength of character, position in a
community, the good of the group, exemplary and responsible adult behavior, and / or the welfare of one's children are all subjugated to individual
happiness and "self-realization," then social arrangements weaken. And the
calculus assumes a market quality. (Veroff, Douvan, and Kulka 1981: 140–41)

The market calculus—ease of entrance and exit based on the rational
calculation of self-interest—is a poor system for the achievement of good
parenting and good neighborhoods.

Generally, Albert Hirschman (1970) finds, there are two reactions to
dissatisfying arrangements—exit, or withdrawal from them, and voice,
the effort to repair or improve them. Exiting a relationship that serves an
important purpose requires the availability of other relations capable of
satisfying that purpose. "Exit is therefore often predicated on the availability of choice, competition, and well-functioning markets," and exit
decisions, like market decisions, "are usually made only on the basis of a
short-run private-interest calculus" (Hirschman 1986:78, 81). Exit is a considerably easier undertaking than voice, which requires those in a relationship to communicate, cooperate, and work with one another in an
effort to remedy the problems that threaten it. Take, for example, the
options available to residents of a neighborhood increasingly beset by the
unruly behavior—petty crime, street harassment, vandalism, public
drinking and drug use—of several street corner youth gangs. They can
undertake the difficult task of voice, working together as neighbors, and
parents and friends to exert informal social control. Alternatively, those
who can afford it are able to exit by moving to a less troubled neighborhood (usually assuring the further deterioration of the area left behind).
Hirschman's point is that as the market becomes more powerful and
influences more strongly people's attitudes and perceptions, the exit option expands and becomes more attractive, the voice option recedes and
becomes less appealing. As the exit option of just walking away becomes
more common—corporations walking away from communities, spouses
from marriages, parents from children, neighbors from neighborhoods—
people lose access to opportunities for developing the social competencies that allow them to create and sustain the trust and the mutuality that
give life to the common projects and shared purposes indispensable to
enduring and satisfying social arrangements.

The Liberal Welfare State

The liberal state, as liberals from Locke on have insisted, is a limited
state, one whose exercise of power is confined to the protection of "life,

liberty, and property." Its defining responsibility is to preserve the bases of individual freedom. As noted in Chapter 1, this requires the liberal state to remain neutral on questions of the good or the right way to live, questions answered most properly by individuals exercising their freedom to choose for themselves how their lives will be arranged. The task of the liberal state is to erect and defend the basic rights that ensure the individual's freedom to so choose. If the responsibility of the liberal state is to protect and promote what individuals are able to do, the "modern welfare state is important because . . . it promotes autonomy by offering to its citizens a broad range of choices and the necessary resources for them to exercise those choices" (Jacobs 1993:381). The liberal welfare state not only secures an arena of noninterference within which the individual is able to do what he or she has a right to do, it also supplies the resources that enable him or her to do it.

The welfare dimension of the liberal state arises, Alan Wolfe (1989) explains, in response to a recurring question in liberal society: "Who is responsible for others when people are expected primarily to be responsible for themselves?" (p. 109). If people are as self-seeking as liberals assume, there exists a "need for some authoritative instrument capable of providing the direction and steering necessary to account for the needs of all" (p. 107). When the liberal state employs its authority (and, when necessary, its power to coerce) to secure the "compulsory, collective provision for certain basic needs as a matter of right" (Goodin 1985:784), it becomes a welfare state. Unlike private, voluntary charitable forms of giving, the welfare state, under the compulsion of law, uses the collective resources at its disposal to assure that its citizens get what they are entitled to as a matter of right, namely, the satisfaction of their basic needs.

Which basic needs is the welfare state obliged to satisfy? The weak answer to this question (the answer that has helped shape the American welfare state, especially since 1980) defines basic needs generally in terms of subsistence requirements, and mandates the state to make minimal provisions to the neediest and most vulnerable members of society, sustaining them until they are able to sustain themselves and at a level that doesn't discourage them from taking personal responsibility for the provision of their needs. The strong answer to this question (the consequences of which are evident in the Swedish welfare state) defines basic needs as those whose satisfaction is necessary if people are to live their lives with dignity, that is, in a way they freely choose. In contrast to the first answer, this one makes the state responsible for providing for more of its citizens' needs and at a higher level, and this requires a larger, more active, powerful, and resource-laden welfare state.

The welfare state, in both its weak American form and, to a far higher degree, its strong Swedish form, uses its authority to bring greater equality to society by redistributing income and to professionalize the provision of human services, assigning that task to social workers, therapists, and other government-employed professionals (Poponoe 1991:72–73). In both cases, it does this in a way consistent with the liberal ideal of neutrality, justifying its activities not in terms of "mutual obligations we owe as fellow citizens who share a common life" but with reference to "the idea of public provision of rights and entitlement for the sake of freeing people to pursue their own interests and ends" (Sandel 1988:13). In the name of individual freedom, the coercive liberal state, like the noncoercive liberal market, remains detached from a shared conception of the common good. In addition, the liberal welfare state, like the liberal market, tends to diminish social capital by lessening people's need and capacity to rely on one another for assistance and by deadening their sense of personal responsibility for the fates of others.

The welfare state moves in this direction by assuming more of the responsibilities once accorded parents, families, kinship and religious groups, neighborhoods, and communities, and thus by having people become increasingly dependent on the state. Right-wing critics, as we saw in Chapter 2, insist that the American welfare state has spawned a helplessly dependent inner-city underclass whose members are quite accustomed to letting the state meet their obligations to one another as parents, children, friends, and neighbors. If such a relatively meager welfare state could have this effect, one would expect to find at least something similar being produced by stronger, more generous and comprehensive welfare states, like the one developed in Sweden. Indeed, critics of the strong Swedish welfare state argue that its extensive policies and well-funded programs, designed to assure the independence of every adult citizen, have seriously undermined the interdependencies that sustain family, neighborhood, and community, and that give weight to the obligations people have to those with whom they share society.

The logic of the liberal welfare state is expressed more clearly and powerfully in Sweden than in the United States. As the Great Society reforms were being instituted in the United States in the 1960s and 1970s, the Swedish welfare state grew in more substantial ways, a process that continued in the 1980s, at a time during which its American counterpart was reduced. Sweden's high taxes translate into high public expenditures used to support extensive welfare programs. Thanks in good measure to their active, resource-laden welfare state, Swedes can boast of being among the most personally economically secure people in the world. Their cities are safe and clean; poverty, violent crime, and drug abuse are comparatively rare; the resources available to the most vulnerable among them—children, the elderly, and the sick—are unsurpassed. Almost equally unsurpassed has been the erosion of the familial institution and related neighborhood interdependencies.

In the 1970s, the Swedish welfare state switched from the principle that the obligation of government was to transfer money from those who needed it less, to those who needed it more to "the principle that government could build the institutions and carry out the services that the family itself had once provided" (Wolfe 1989:135) with the assistance of kin, friends, and neighbors. Welfare state legislation and policy generated a panorama of programs and entitlements—pre- and after-school programs, public day care, housing and care for the elderly, social work, nursing, psychological, and home helping assistance carried out by civil service professionals—designed both to upgrade and equalize access to basic necessities and to advance individual autonomy by making people less dependent on parents, spouses, children, kin, and neighbors for these necessities. In this context, David Poponoe (1991) argues, there is "a strong likelihood that the family has grown weaker [in Sweden] than anywhere else in the world" (p. 65).

Sweden's marriage rate is the lowest in the industrialized world; its rate of nonmarital cohabitation is among the highest. Sweden's divorce rate is the highest in Europe, but just below the American rate. It combines with the rate at which unmarried couples (nonmarital cohabitators) with at least one child break up to give Sweden the highest rate of family dissolution in the developed world. Sweden is among the world's leaders in single-parent families, out-of-wedlock births, single-person households, and smallest average household size (Poponoe 1988:116–75). The waning of the institutional authority of the family suggested by these developments is buttressed, according to Poponoe (1988:182), by a cultural message that society "holds the couple (as an agent of society) less responsible for both each other and their offspring," a message reinforced by a welfare state assuming more responsibility for each partner and their children.

The welfare state contributes to family decline in Sweden in more direct ways as well. As Poponoe shows, it has circumscribed parental authority and made it considerably easier for social workers to intervene in and remove children from the family. The entitlements it provides have reduced both the family's responsibility for its elderly members and the economic interdependence of spouses. Government-subsidized medical and dental care, public transportation, education through college, and, for those sixteen and older, jobs and social welfare benefits have substantially minimized the economic dependence of children on their parents. Within the developed world, Poponoe writes, individual family members

are the most autonomous and least bound by the group, and the group as a whole is least cohesive. The family carries out fewer of its traditional functions; these have shifted to . . . the state and its agencies. . . . The family is smallest in size, least stable, and has the shortest life span; people are therefore family members for the smallest percentage of their lives. (1991:69)

In achieving greater individual autonomy for spouses, parents, and children, not only has the welfare state weakened familial interdependencies and institutional authority, it has also made individual spouses, parents, and children more dependent upon it.

Interdependencies of neighborhood and community and the sense of mutuality and spirit of cooperation they nurture also were diminished as the magnitude of the welfare state grew. Reliance on kinship and community altruism and on friends, neighbors, and informal social networks declined as the sense of entitlement to public welfare as a matter of individual right strengthened. Mutual support in the form of charitable giving and voluntary acts of helping have come to be viewed, in Alan Wolfe's (1989:168) words, "through unfriendly eyes—as threats, and niggardly ones at that, to the idea that social benefits ought to be a right guaranteed by government and delivered to all rather than a feeling dependent on individual whim." It seems that another cost of Sweden's welfare state–generated individual autonomy is a weaker sense of personal responsibility for the fates of others. In times of need, Swedish individuals are more likely to seek and receive assistance from their welfare state than from family, kin, neighbors, and informal community networks of support. This, after all, is why they pay higher taxes!

Sweden's powerful welfare state often is contrasted to the powerful market economy of the United States, and presented as a superior way of organizing social life. In many important respects, this presentation has merit. A child born to a young, unmarried, unemployed, and disadvantaged mother has a greater chance of a tolerable life in Sweden than in the United States. Yet, it is important to recognize that the powerful welfare state is as antagonistic toward society as is the powerful market economy, and it is so because it shares with the market liberalism's commitment to individual freedom.

The liberal market and the liberal welfare state often are presented as devices that enable modern people to meet their obligations to strangers efficiently and without imperiling their individual freedom. Operating without coercion and conscious deliberation, the market channels the selfish pursuit of private gain in a direction that benefits the public good. Consciously, and if necessary, coercively, the welfare state uses collective resources to assure the minimal well-being of all its citizens. Neglected by this presentation is a key point. The people most likely to meet their distant obligations to strangers are those who regularly meet their intimate obligations to family, kin, friends, neighbors, and fellow community members, those who are attached to institutions and communitarian interdependencies (Silver 1985:52–67, Wolfe 1989:20). By breaking these attachments, powerful market economies and powerful welfare states undermine those social settings wherein people learn to be responsible for and care about one another. Unrestrained, intrusive liberal markets and liberal welfare states make it more difficult for people to acknowledge and take seriously their intimate obligations, and in turn it becomes more difficult for them to acknowledge and take seriously their distant obligations to strangers.

ANOMIE AND THE SOCIOLOGICAL CRITIQUE OF LIBERAL MODERNITY

Formulated in the nineteenth century as liberal modernity began to take root, early sociology took as its defining object of study that which modernity most seriously threatened, namely, civil society. Devalued and neglected for the most part by the liberal celebration of modernity, civil society, as it was regarded by early sociologists, is a moral order whose cooperative principles and mutual self-help serve as a counterweight to the demoralizing tendencies of the modern market and state. Seeking an alternative "to the atomization of a competitive market society, on the one hand, and to a state-dominated existence on the other," Alvin Gouldner (1980) writes, sociology defended "civil society as a haven and support for individual persons, i.e., as de-atomizing; as a medium through which they can pursue their own projects in the course of their everyday lives; and as a way of avoiding dependence on the domination of the state" (p. 370). The presence of a strong, vibrant civil society, according to this view, significantly diminishes the possibility of both state coercion and the human misery brought by a market driven only by rational self-interest.

Rejecting the liberal view that in the absence of coercive political authority people will meet their obligations to others only when it is in their selfish interest to do so, early sociology argued that in the families, communities, friendship, religious, kinship, and work groups, voluntary associations, and neighborhoods that constitute civil society, people learn how and cultivate in themselves a desire to satisfy their social obligations. They meet their obligations, even when self-interest must be sacrificed, not from fear of state power, but because doing what is right matters a great deal to them. In civil society, people generate and sustain rules of solidarity by which they regulate their lives together. Unlike the impersonal rules of the market and the state, the moral rules people create and sustain as members of civil society enhance their sense of personal responsibility for the fate of others and foster the development of the sense of communality that keeps alive all those obligations that are "inspired neither by a rational quest after self-interest nor by a fear of coercive external authority" (Wolfe 1989:188). Should civil society continue to be invaded by modernity so that social life comes to be regulated less by the principles of cooperation and solidarity and more by the principles of the market and the state, the result, early sociology warned, will be the erosion of the institutions, practices, sentiments, and capacities that protect us against the isolating and disunifying forces of the market and the totalizing, centralizing, and potentially tyrannical forces of the state.

This sociological understanding of modernity was articulated best by the French sociologist Emile Durkheim. At the center of Durkheim's ([1893] 1947, [1897] 1951) sociological critique of liberal individualism is the notion of *anomie,* a term used by sixteenth- and seventeenth-century theologians to describe the experience of disorder and displacement associated with sin (see Mestrovic and Brown 1985; Orru 1987). Liberal individualism sinned, Durkheim suggested, not because it helped to kill the old gods—the harsh, repressive, stifling institutions and groups so powerfully opposed to the rise of the individual—but because it failed to replace them with new ones appropriate to modernity's promise to respect the worth and dignity of the individual. In their absence, we find anomie, expressed in part as an unbridled, undirected, excessive individualism. The road that takes people away from society, Durkheim knew, leads not to individual liberty and happiness but to a chaotic meaninglessness that makes people fearful, distrustful, and more receptive to the imposition of tyrannical measures of control.

Durkheim attributed the anomie of turn-of-the-century Western societies to a collection of related developments nearly one hundred years in the making: rapid, extensive, seemingly continuous social change and technological transformation; the erosion of intermediary associations and informal practices of mutual aid; the devaluation of collective purpose encouraged by liberal individualism; and the strengthening of egoistic dispositions fueled by "the almost infinite expansion of the market" (Durkheim [1897] 1951:255). Freed by these developments from the regulating force and moralizing influence of society, modern people possess only a confused and transient understanding of what they want, where they are going, and how they should go about getting there. Bewildered and without firm purpose, they live their lives amid a declining sense of social accountability, for the rules that ostensibly govern their relations with others are enforced less frequently, less severely, and more arbitrarily. As more breaches of these rules go unpunished, either because, in Ralf Dahrendorf's (1985) words, "they are too numerous or too many people are involved in them at one time" (p. 20), the rules begin to lose their validity. One response is to define the boundaries of acceptable conduct more broadly, so that what was once deviant (out-of-wedlock

births, teenage pregnancy, parental abandonment of childrearing responsibilities, for instance) now becomes normal (Moynihan 1993). A second
response is the emergence of what Dahrendorf calls "no-go areas," deregulated, demoralized, and thus dangerous places where nothing very
much matters and just about anything goes. If the normalization of deviance often is misinterpreted as a step toward liberalization (as it is in the
culture of personal freedom, discussed in Chapter 2), anomie in the more
developed form of "no-go areas" underwrites the demand for the coercive presence of metal detectors and security guards in schools, police
helicopters in the skies, and unannounced, warrantless searches of private dwellings. In each case, Richard Hilbert (1986) notes, Durkheim
wants us to see anomie as the simultaneous "withdrawal of reality and of
the possibility of objective experience" (p. 1).

With the emaciation of reality and objective experience, anomie, Durkheim ([1925] 1961) wrote, appears as the "malady of infiniteness which
we suffer in our day" (p. 430). In the boundaryless state of infinitude,
undisciplined passions continuously pour forth demands that defy satisfaction and that underlie the constant agitation, sense of excitement, and
restless pursuits of the eternally dissatisfied so much admired by the
defenders of the unregulated market. Liberal individualism normalizes
anomie, and as a consequence

> greed is aroused without knowing where to find ultimate foothold. Nothing
> can calm it, since its goal is far beyond all it can attain. Reality seems
> valueless by comparison with the dreams of fevered imaginations; reality is
> therefore abandoned. . . . A thirst arises for novelties, unfamiliar pleasures,
> nameless sensations, all of which lose savor once known. Henceforth one
> has no strength to endure the least reverse. The whole fever subsides . . .
> and it is seen that all these new sensations in their infinite quantity cannot
> form a solid foundation of happiness to support one during days of tri-
> al. . . . What blinded [anomic man] to himself was his expectation always to
> find further on the happiness he had so far missed. Now he is stopped in his
> tracks; from now on nothing remains behind or ahead of him to fix his gaze
> upon. Weariness alone, moreover, is enough to bring disillusionment, for he
> cannot in the end escape the futility of an endless pursuit. (Durkheim [1897]
> 1951:256)

The abandonment of reality for the infinite is the road to nowhere. For
some on this road, weariness, disillusionment, and futility give way to
"anomic terror," an often suicidal panic stoked by the prospect of unabated confusion, uncertainty, and meaninglessness (Hilbert 1986:10).

Durkheim treated anomie as an attribute of social structure. Today,
thanks in part to work done a quarter of a century ago by Herbert Mc-
Closkey, John Schaar, and Charles Hampden-Turner, many view anomie

as a psychological condition, a state of mind, a collection of attitudes, beliefs, and feelings expressive of an inner moral emptiness. At the core of the anomic personality, McCloskey and Schaar (1965:19) found, "is the feeling that the world and oneself are adrift, wandering, lacking in clear rules and stable moorings. The anomic feels literally *de*-moralized." Unable to relate events and ideas clearly and to organize observations and experiences into understandable wholes, anomic persons display a marked indifference to a world they regard as complex, ambiguous, and precarious. Into this world they carry a generalized aggression fed by an often-present combination of rage and fear. Anomics anticipate rejection and loss, and thus fail to invest themselves in the social environment of institutions and communitarian interdependencies. Fearing failure, having little faith in the outside world and in others in it, anomic persons alternate between moving away from and moving aggressively against other people, all the while remaining incapable of making and meeting commitments. The key to the anomic personality, according to Hampden-Turner (1971, 1975), is its inability to both confirm and transcend the self in a social context. This prevents anomic people from developing the competencies that would enable them to assume personal responsibility for both their lives and the lives of those made vulnerable by their actions.

McCloskey and Schaar (1965) argued that anomie is highest among certain groups of people:

> persons of low education, those with low incomes and low prestige occupations, people experiencing downward social mobility [and others who] are outside the articulate, successful, prosperous sectors of the population. Anomic feelings appear most frequently and most strongly among those who . . . are stranded in the backwaters of the symbolic and material mainstream, those whose lives are circumscribed by isolation, deprivation, and ignorance. (p. 19)

Among the highly anomic, McCloskey and Schaar prominently included, as did Hampden-Turner, poor inner-city African-Americans. This at a time—between the mid-1960s and the early 1970s—when persistent poverty was combining with rising rates of antisocial behavior to fuel the rise of the underclass. Indeed, the psychological concept of anomie gains in significance during this period precisely because its proponents claim that it affords insight into and remedies for overcoming the psychological dynamics of the newly recognized underclass.

Quite clearly, the underclass is a good place to look to discover the social conditions and psychological traits of anomie (Buffalo Creek and Hobbes's state of nature are equally good). Yet as we saw in Chapter 2, the anomie so widely displayed in the underclass offers a powerful reflection of the anomie present in the United States at large. This claim is at odds with McCloskey and Schaar's insistence that poverty, bad education, and stunted cognitive abilities serve to isolate people from a cultural mainstream replete with coherent and meaningful values and norms. The evidence we have, as previously noted, is that while members of the underclass are economically isolated from job markets, "the twentieth-century history of black inner-city culture has not been, overall, one of increasing isolation, but one that has proceeded from relative isolation to greater participation in the larger American culture" (Nightingale 1993:11). Contrary to McCloskey and Schaar, it no longer makes sense to assume that stable values, norms, institutions, and communitarian interdependencies exist "out there" among the "articulate, successful, and prosperous," waiting to be grasped by those whose improved education and elevated cognitive capacities will enable them to escape their state of isolation. Out there, and this is reflected clearly in the larger American culture, is the debris of the broken institutions and the damaged communitarian interdependencies left in the wake of the stampede by liberalism's market and state. While it sits most destructively on a group of poor people who even in the best of times found it difficult to sustain the moral order that is the antidote to anomie, it also leaves its stench on those who lead more privileged lives in America's market economy and in Sweden's welfare state.

Underclass anomie draws its animus from the same liberal individualism that shapes what the philosopher Charles Taylor calls "the modern self." Suffering from "an acute form of disorientation" and "a radical uncertainty of where they stand," modern selves, in Taylor's account, "lack a frame or horizon within which things can take on a stable significance, within which some life possibilities can be seen as good or meaningful, others as bad or trivial. The meaning of all these possibilities is unfixed, labile, or undetermined. This is a painful and frightening experience" (1989:27–28). Bereft of identity-creating moral spaces that require people to take positions on significant questions of value, modern selves have no firm place on which to stand. For them, anomic terror or panic is experienced, in the words of Kroker, Kroker, and Cook (1990), as a "two-fold free-fall: the disappearance of *external* standards of public conduct . . . and the dissolution of the *internal* foundations of identity" (p. 444). Infinitude expressed as free-fall places a premium on the ethic of individual survivalism. Yet, panic-stricken modern selves, never certain of who they are and what they stand for or what is demanded by an ephemeral social reality, often question their survival capabilities. A sense of catastrophe often accompanies the anomic's effort to survive (Kroker, Kroker, and Cook 1990:445–47).

Among the desperately poor in America's inner cities, the destructive rhythms of catastrophe are played out daily with dispiriting effect.

Among more privileged modern selves, particularly those who regard themselves as postmodernists, the anomic sense of catastrophe and the disintegration of society and identity that fuels it are embraced as signs of advancing personal freedom. Postmodernism celebrates the collapse of the stable, ordered, permanent arrangements and identities on which modern structures and selves rested. It affirms that which, by rupturing boundaries, breaching conventional roles and rules, and breaking through the repressive restraints of gender, race, and other traditional markers of identity, brings us more quickly to the fluid and chaotic world of the contingent, the impermanent, and the uncertain—a liberated world where people are free to reinvent themselves at will. Postmodernism sees "in the destruction of humankind's social bonds, the chance for an extension of . . . freedom," Axel Honneth (1992) writes. In these terms, "human subjects are . . . beings whose possibilities for freedom are best realized when, independent of all normative expectations and bonds, they are able to creatively produce new self-images all the time" (p. 166–67).

If, as Durkheim argued, liberal individualism normalized anomie at the end of the nineteenth century, presenting its characteristics as the traits that make for success in the market economy, then postmodernism normalizes anomie at the end of the twentieth century, working hard to portray the anomic terror generated by the chaotic, volatile, no-guarantee world of the global market economy as the liberating experience of continuous self-realization. Postmodernism is little more than the intellectual equivalent of rap music. Just as rap music often glorifies the brutal irresponsibility that flows from the social disorganization of the inner city, the postmodernist finds freedom in the panic and disorientation promoted by ever-changing, uncommitted, temporary relations and selves. In the rap musician and the postmodernist intellectual alike, liberal individualism's hostility toward society and its affinity for anomie live on.

CONCLUSION

What awaits us in the absence of society, Durkheim insisted, are the insecurities of anomie, the distrust that accompanies unbridled egoism, irresponsible corporations, spouses and parents, abandoned towns, husbands, wives, and children, and the coercive agencies of the state ready to step in when the market falters. In the absence of society, we find Hobbes's state of nature, the Ik, the trauma-stricken survivors of the Buffalo Creek flood, the pathological narcissist, and the anomic personality. Increasingly, we find there as well modernity's liberal individuals, not luxuriating in their freedom but struggling to survive an unfriendly and unreliable environment. Fluent only in the languages of liberal individualism, they are able neither to name their unease nor to understand that its remedy requires them to relearn the practices of mutual assistance and social obligation and to rebuild their social institutions and communitarian interdependencies.

Recognizing that the restoration of the harsh, repressive, rigid, anti-individual values of traditional society would be an entirely inappropriate and ineffective response to anomie and to the moral crisis of modern liberal society it reflected, Durkheim argued for the creation of a morality appropriate to the individual freedom, equality, and democratic government promised by modernity. Indispensable to this, he thought, is a vigorous social life centered around morally dense relations and secondary groups rooted in "a spirited sentiment of common solidarity on the consciousness of all" their members (Durkheim [1893] 1947:10). Moral ideals arise from such relations and groups to signify what matters most in society. What matters most to modern society is the individual. Durkheim's argument, then, is that the moral crisis of modern liberal society requires for its resolution the morality of individualism that can come only from a revitalized society insulated against the market and the state.

4

Moral Individuals:
In the Presence of Society

Seeking satisfaction and realization away from society, the liberal individual, according to Émile Durkheim, is an anomic individual and, as such, amoral, for, Durkheim argued, morality is acquired only in society, in the very institutions and communitarian interdependencies diminished by the driving forces of liberalism. For liberals, the liberal individual is the quintessential moral individual. For them, morality, like freedom and happiness, is found in the individual standing outside society. This premise underlies the two dominant liberal views of morality, utilitarianism and Kantianism. Utilitarianism, proposed early on by Jeremy Bentham and John Stuart Mill, offers an account of morality consistent with the principles of the liberal market and the conception of the person as an aggregate of desires and personal preferences. The deontological view of morality developed by Immanuel Kant regards the person as an autonomous and reasonable individual respectful of and protected by the rights enshrined in the liberal neutral state. Durkheim locates morality in individuals attached and committed to the social, that sphere of human activity most jeopardized by the ongoing expansion of the liberal market and the liberal neutral state.

LIBERAL VIEWS OF MORALITY

Defining people as infinite desirers and maximizers of utility, utilitarianism regards as morally correct those arrangements and actions that produce the greatest happiness for the greatest number of people (see Kymlicka 1990: chap. 2). The rightness or wrongness of arrangements and actions is to be judged or, more accurately, calculated on the basis of their consequences. Arrangements and actions that increase the amount of happiness over unhappiness are morally right. In calculating this amount, utilitarianism emphasizes, no one's happiness should be weighted more than others. Thus, at first glance, the moral actor is a calculator of utilities, carefully assessing the probable utilities or the likely consequences of his or her actions, and undertaking that action only if it seems that its usefulness to people seeking to satisfy their various desires will result in raising the balance of happiness over unhappiness. While such a cost-benefit approach to decision making may increase the likelihood of morally right actions, it is no guarantee. It is entirely possible for actors to miscalculate the utilities of their actions, and for the right reason undertake a morally wrong act, one that elevates the level of unhappiness for most people. It is equally possible for people to engage in morally correct acts for the wrong reasons. Volunteering time to help children in a homeless shelter is morally right even when the effort is carried out in order to improve one's image, promotion prospects, or opportunity to meet an attractive volunteer. Given this, utilitarianism insists that the motive or intention of the actor not be considered when determining the moral worthiness of actions. Only the consequences of those actions merit evaluation. In this light, utilitarianism inclines toward a favorable view of commercial surrogate mothering and, as examined in Chapter 1, the market in women's reproductive labor it creates. To the extent that commercial surrogacy adds to the amount of happiness by increasing the number of happy people, by supplying children to childless couples and fees to surrogate mothers and lawyers, it is a morally worthy practice whether or not those engaged in it are motivated purely by selfish concerns.

According to the Kantian view, the rightness or wrongness of acts is determined not by their consequences, but by the imperative or rule by which they are guided. Acts are moral when they conform to moral imperatives, impersonal, universally valid rules whose "oughts" and "should nots" define morally worthy actions. These moral principles are given by reason. Since the faculty of reason works the same way in all people in whom it exists in developed form, these people, despite the vast differences in historical time and cultural space that may separate them, will select the same principles or rules. Moral persons are reasonable, and they use their reason to discover the rules by which they conduct their lives. These moral rules give individuals both rights and duties to respect the rights of others.

Kant ([1785] 1950) illustrates this point in his discussion of the moral imperative that obliges us to treat other people as ends in themselves. Every rational being, he writes,

> exists as an end in himself, not merely as a means for arbitrary use by this or that will; he must in all his actions, whether they are directed to himself or to some other rational being, always be viewed at the same time as an end. . . .

The practical imperative will therefore be as follows: Act in such a way that you always treat humanity, whether in your own person or in the person of any other, never simply as a means, but always at the same time as an end. (pp. 95–96)

Accordingly, helping needy children in a homeless shelter is a moral duty, recognizable as such by all reasonable individuals. Only when carried out in fulfillment of this duty is it a moral act. Thus, the utilitarians who assist the needy as a means to job promotion are not acting morally. Similarly, the moral imperative to respect others as ends requires the rejection of commercial surrogate mothering, a practice that has fathers use mothers, and mothers use their children and their reproductive capacity as means to achieve desired ends.

Lawrence Kohlberg's (1981, 1984) detailed psychological analysis of the stages of moral development is one of the most influential and most concrete representations of the Kantian understanding of morality. Drawing from Kant, Kohlberg presents morality as a matter of rights and of abstract reason—the developed cognitive capacities of an autonomous self capable of grasping the abstract principles that bestow rights and duties. The development of the cognitive capacities on which moral maturity depends takes place through three levels, each of which comprises two stages. In the lowest or preconventional level, at which children and younger adolescents operate, right action is defined initially as deference to superiors, and later as action that satisfies the needs of the self and those supportive of the self. Most older adolescents and adults are at the middle or conventional level of moral development. At this level, people adopt the moral view of the "person in society," the person who is sensitive to the judgments of such significant others as peers, parents, and teachers from whom acceptance is sought, and who acquires respect for the authority of the conventions that maintain the established social order. At the preconventional and conventional levels then, moral guides are drawn from external forces—from older, stronger, or more esteemed others, from peers, friends, teachers, and parents, and from the established conventions of the group or the society. Only at the highest or postconventional developmental level, attained by a small minority of adults, do we find the exercise of principled moral reasoning and what makes this exercise possible, the morally autonomous individual who adopts the view of the person beyond society. Beyond society, that is, beyond the pressures to defer to the powerful, to please significant others, and to abide by established convention, the autonomous individual draws on considerable cognitive powers to define right action in accordance with self-chosen, universal, logically consistent, abstract principles that command respect for individual rights, justice, and the dignity of others. Outside society, according to this view, we find not the anomic nightmare described by Durkheim but cognitively sharp, morally mature, postconventional, autonomous individuals whose reason gives them access to the universal moral principles first described by Kant. A closer look reveals that the overwhelming number of autonomous moral individuals are men.

In Kohlberg's developmental model, women appear as morally deficient. Disproportionately few rise to the postconventional level. Most remain fixed at the lowest stage of the conventional level where morality is defined in interpersonal terms, as a matter of helping and pleasing others. Stuck in society, women rarely achieve the autonomy and cognitive development necessary for principled moral judgment. Carol Gilligan (1982) agrees that women are much more strongly attached to fundamental social relations than are men, and as a consequence more inclined to define morality in terms of care than in terms of abstract rights and universal ethical principles. Gilligan argues, however, that care morality is not inferior to the morality of abstract rights. It offers a different but equally worthy moral perspective.

The morality of care is the morality of the person in society, the person squarely situated in ongoing social relations, the maintenance of which is a primary moral task. For the women Gilligan studied, morality has to do with responsibilities created by connections to others. The resolution of moral dilemmas requires not the discovery of correct abstract principles and the logical derivation of concrete moral rules from them. Instead, it depends on the presence of people whose capacities for sympathy and caregiving sustain the social attachments essential to human dignity. Dignity, therefore, depends less on the assertion of rights and duties than on the presence of people who care and are attentive to the needs of others. For the moral person, the coherence of the social world rests on the fulfillment of responsibilities bestowed by relationships, not on adherence to abstract principles; and morality requires the development of those qualities that sensitize people to, and encourage them to meet, these responsibilities, not the development of cognitive complexity. In this light, the moral person assists homeless children not as an acknowledgment of their right to be treated as ends but because she sympathizes with their plight and is disposed to show them the personal care that is both responsive to their needs, and conducive to the creation of the kinds of social ties that nourish human dignity. From this perspective, commercial surrogate mothering is found morally objectionable for it transforms the fundamental relation between mother and child as an enduring relation based on care into a temporary, expedient relation whose contractual provisions explicitly discourage the disposition to care. For Gilligan's women, moral maturity rests on the development of moral dispositions more than on the development of the cognitive capacity to reason. These dispositions, and not knowledge of abstract principles, are what make people moral.

In part, Gilligan (1982) suggests that women are more oriented to the care morality than are men as a result of differences in the achievement of gender identity. Unlike boys, girls need not sever attachment to their primary caregivers, their mothers, in order to establish their gender identity. They sustain this original and strong social and emotional tie, remaining powerfully attached to the relation. Girls discover the importance of close social bonds and cultivate the capacities—sympathy, empathy, and care-giving—that enable them to sustain, repair, and strengthen social relationships. Boys, in contrast, do break the attachment and separate from their mothers in the process of forming gender identity. For them, the value of sustaining close ties is diminished as are opportunities to develop the capacities that promote the endurance of significant social relations. More than girls, boys learn the importance of standing alone, as autonomous individuals beyond society.

The care morality characterized by Gilligan is grounded in the dispositions to sympathize, empathize, and care cultivated by women in society, women who in part are defined by the social relations they seek to sustain. In these ways, care morality differs from utilitarianism and Kantianism, both of which locate morality in the individual who, existing outside or beyond society, is better able to rationally calculate utilities or reasonably discover universal moral imperatives, and thus act in accordance with principle, not disposition. In these ways as well, Gilligan's care morality resembles in important places the sociological view of morality offered by Durkheim. For Durkheim, however, the dispositions that constitute care morality are not gender-specific. Their cultivation ensues not from the dynamics of gender identity formation but from the experiences of living in society. Men and women alike, Durkheim argues, become moral in society. If women are more moral than men, it is because their attachments to society are more numerous and stronger. If there are fewer moral people today, it is because the social contexts within which moral sensitivity is honed and moral codes are created have been reduced and weakened.

DURKHEIM'S SOCIOLOGY OF MORALITY

Liberal democratic capitalist societies, Durkheim claims at the end of the nineteenth century, are threatened by moral crisis, the most telling sign of which is the already prominent and still growing presence of anomie. "The old gods are growing old or already dead, and others not yet born," Durkheim ([1912] 1965:475) observes. The old gods, the traditional morality of premodern society, have been discredited or destroyed by the forces of modernity. In their absence, the disorders of anomie—lawlessness, morbid restlessness, discontent, incivility, uncertainty, and suicide–reign. The remedy, Durkheim ([1893] 1947) insists, "is not to seek to resuscitate traditions and practices which, no longer responding to present conditions of society, can only live an artificial, false existence" (p. 408). Harshly punitive and repressive, traditional morality imposes rigidly fixed, unquestioned moral boundaries that promote the tyranny of the group over the individual. Distrustful of all that threatens the stability and cohesiveness of the group—strangers, innovative ideas, and most especially, values and behaviors that would distinguish one member of the group from the others—traditional morality obstructs the development of the individual. Since the individual is key to modern society—here Durkheim agrees with liberalism—traditional morality either could not take root or, if it did, would further disrupt the already chaotic ground of modern society. Not the restoration of traditional morality, but the creation of a morality appropriate to the conditions of modernity, a morality of individualism, is the foremost task of the age. In his effort to advance moral individualism, Durkheim proposes a third way as an alternative to the two dominant views, both of which assumed an irreconcilable tension between the individual and society. Liberals opposed society as an oppressive constraint on individual freedom. Conservatives repudiated individual freedom as the force most corrosive of the moral control on which society rests. The shared assumption of the two views, Durkheim claims, is incorrect. Society and the individual, morality and freedom, stand best when they stand together. Based on this recognition, moral individualism avoids both the socially destructive, anomie-generating excessive individualism encouraged by liberalism and the anti-individualism of the excessively tyrannical moral codes favored by conservatism.

The effort to construct a morality appropriate to modern society, Durkheim argues, cannot be guided by either the utilitarian or the Kantian view of morality, both of which are infused by the liberal misunderstanding of society. Utilitarianism and Kantianism alike consist "in determining the form of moral conduct from which one could afterwards deduce the content. One began by establishing the principle of morality as . . . duty or utility and then from this axiom one drew out certain maxims which constituted applied or practical morality" (Émile Durkheim, quoted in Hall 1991:94). For both, morality is a matter of isolated, autonomous individuals deducing prescriptions from abstract principles.

Given the notion of an absolutely autonomous individual, depending only on himself, without historical antecedents, without a social milieu, how should he conduct himself either in his economic relations or in his moral life? Such is the question which they pose themselves and which they seek to resolve by reasoning. . . . If man . . . has no other objective than the development of his moral personality (Kant) or the satisfaction of his needs with the least possible effort [utilitarians], society appears as something against nature, as a violence wreaked upon our most fundamental propensities. . . . [I]t is in their eyes . . . a machine of war against individuals, a remnant of barbarism which is maintained only by the force of prejudices and which is destined sooner or later to disappear. (Durkheim [1890] 1973:37–40)

Neither view admits that the individual it champions—the autonomous reasoner or the calculator of utility—has nothing in common with "actual man [who] partakes of an age and a country; [who] has ideas and feelings which come not from himself but from those around him; [who] has prejudices and beliefs; [who] is subject to rules of action which he did not make but which he nevertheless respects" (p. 38). Equally important, neither view recognizes that people become moral individuals only as social beings. "Society," Durkheim ([1893] 1947) writes, "is the necessary condition of [morality's] existence. It is not a simple juxtaposition of individuals who bring an intrinsic morality with them, but rather man is a moral being only because he lives in society. . . . [L]et all social life disappear, and moral life will disappear with it" (p. 398).

Society for Durkheim is not merely an aggregation of individuals sharing a particular place. Rather, "it is above all a composition of ideas, beliefs, and sentiments . . . which realize themselves through individuals. Foremost of these ideas is the moral ideal which is its principal *raison d'etre*. To love one's society is to love this ideal, and one loves it so that one would rather see society disappear as a material entity than renounce the ideal which it embodies" (Durkheim 1974:59). The central moral ideal of modern society, a reflection in part of both the complex, highly specialized, and differentiated, and thus individuating division of labor, and the traditions and grand events that gave modern society birth and decisive shape, commands respect for the individual. This ideal, Durkheim notes, is captured in the Kantian moral imperative that we respect others by treating them as ends in themselves. Yet, Kant's mistake is to claim that acts are moral only if motivated by impersonal duty. According to Durkheim, such duties and the moral ideals that give them form require for their recognition and fulfillment capacities and sentiments (like the caregiving and sympathy featured in Gilligan's account of morality) that people develop in small-scale social settings as members of vigorous groups and participants in a rich associational life. Directly countering

Kant, Durkheim, as Ernest Wallwork (1985) observes, "links acceptance of impersonal moral principles with the individual's affective relationship to others in society. He believes we cannot understand the *raison d'etre* of obligatory principles unless we are emotionally as well as intellectually tied to others in a social group. We only practically care about [moral] principles . . . if we feel a sense of solidarity with others in the social groups that are held together by such principles" (p. 93).

Indispensable to morality then, are centers of dense social interaction—groups, associations, and social networks—in which people develop the dispositions, capacities, and concrete practices that enable them to live together. At this level, morality grows from "people's efforts to coordinate their behavior for their mutual benefit" (Hall 1987: 219), and to regulate their interactions, not just to ensure the orderly satisfaction of their essential needs but also for the common good, the good of the group as a group, that is, for the sake of solidarity itself. In modern society, the potential exists for a multitude of morally dense groups and associations, many overlapping, many set apart by divergent values. What promises to keep this multitude tied together is the ideal of modern society, moral individualism.

Unlike Kant, Durkheim regards the presence of developed social sentiments as essential to the exercise of duty. Unlike utilitarians, he recognizes that personal desires and preferences motivate morally consequential acts only when they are influenced more by social sentiments than by egotistic ones and when "the good to be advanced is not the greatest happiness for the greatest number, but social solidarity . . . a state of affairs characterized by trust, mutual respect, peace, and cooperation" (Wallwork 1985:94), and to which the individual is affectively committed. These social sentiments essentially are the ones Gilligan identifies as indispensable to sustaining significant social relations—sympathy, empathy, benevolence, mutuality, responsibility, and care. Yet for Durkheim, men are as capable of cultivating these sentiments as are women, and the morality of care sponsored by these sentiments is an important complement to the morality of justice and its emphasis on impersonal duty. All this becomes clearer in the context of Durkheim's elaboration of the sociological account of morality in *Moral Education* ([1925] 1961). There he presents morality as involving three elements—spirit of discipline, group attachments, and autonomy—each of which is found only in society.

By spirit of discipline, Durkheim refers to the experience of morality as a duty or external imperative to act in certain ways. Moral duty prescribes what people ought to do, how they must act, and, when effective, is experienced as a constraining or disciplining force originating in some source outside and greater than oneself. For Durkheim, this source is society, most especially its moral ideal from which duty is generated. To the extent that this ideal comes to be regarded as authoritative and deserving of respect and devotion, moral duty acquires a weightier presence, its power of constraint or discipline receives sharper expression, and its capacity to inspire compliance is heightened.

Morality requires more than the presence and experience of external duty. In addition, the end to which duty directs us must be perceived as a good to which we aspire. Adherence to moral duty undertaken as a means to obtain external reward or to avoid reprisals for disobeying group expectations does not produce moral acts, in Durkheim's view. Moral acts are created by people who desire to comply with duty, who want to be moral because their sense of worth is tied up with doing what is right, and for whom adherence to moral duty is a by-product of adherence to their higher selves. How is it that people want to be moral when very often being moral requires them to sacrifice personal gain and selfish interest for the well-being of others? People acquire this desire, Durkheim argues, in their attachments to vibrant groups and vigorous associational life and amidst the ties of solidarity that feed the social sentiments that occupy the higher parts of the self. Moral feelings are strongest in those who, by virtue of their attachment and commitment to and involvement in social groups, have well-developed social sentiments that constrain egotistic inclinations and motivate fulfillment of those duties whose ends include concern for the well-being of others (see Collins 1988:191).

A disciplined sense of duty and developed social sentiments are components of morality whenever it is found, as essential to the harsh, repressive, anti-individual moralities of premodern societies as they are to the moral individualism appropriate to modern societies. The morality of modern societies, however, has a third element, autonomy, and it, according to Durkheim, distinguishes modern morality from its predecessors. "To act morally . . . it is no longer enough," Durkheim ([1925] 1961) writes,

> to respect discipline and to be attached to a social group. Beyond this, whether it be out of deference to a rule or out of devotion to a collective ideal, we must be conscious, as clearly and completely as possible, of the reasons for our conduct. This consciousness confers on our actions that autonomy which the public conscience now requires of every genuine and completely moral being. Hence . . . the third element of morality is the understanding of it. Morality no longer consists simply in the accomplishment, even the intentional accomplishment of certain specific acts. It is now necessary that the rule which prescribes these acts be freely willed, that is to say, freely accepted, and this willing acceptance is nothing other than enlightened acceptance. This is perhaps the greatest innovation which confronts the moral conscience of contemporary people: intelligence has become and is becoming more and more a matter of morality. (p. 85)

If, to be moral, decisions to act in accordance with moral precepts must be made voluntarily and intelligently, then morality requires autonomous individuals.

Durkheim's autonomous individuals are firmly situated in society, experiencing the constraining power of duty and the solidarity of active group and associational life. Indeed in modernity, it is their involvement in society—their commitment to the collective ideal of moral individualism, their membership in groups that shield them from the anomic forces of the market and the state's tendency toward totalizing control, which by promoting social sentiments, frees them from the blind forces of bodily appetite and passion—that makes their individual autonomy possible. These autonomous individuals are not free from society, but they are free to critically scrutinize and rationally understand how society influences them. "Autonomous agents, then, are those who are aware of the social and historical warrants for moral beliefs and practices, and who are thereby free to embrace and criticize them. Autonomy is an important virtue in modern democracies, for these benefit from an active citizenry that explores present social practices, asks for reasons and pursues just reforms" (Cladis 1992a:205). The autonomous moral individual does not unthinkingly conform to established practices and conventions. Instead, he or she critically assesses those practices and conventions with reference to the collective ideal, and adheres to them only to the degree that they correspond to the ideal, and thus advance those conditions—justice, equality, charity, and cooperation—that are the prerequisites for the respectful treatment of people as individuals.

Individual autonomy is required and encouraged by the decisive features of modern life—a highly specialized division of labor, social and geographical mobility, democratic government, and a market economy centered around contractual relations. Liberalism gives powerful expression to this requirement, but does so only to define individual autonomy in opposition to the societal conditions that, in Durkheim's view, are indispensable to individual autonomy. How, when joined to the features of modern life, do the experience of external duty as constraint and active involvement in robust group life contribute to individual autonomy? The experience of external constraint heightens our awareness that we are in a world different from and greater than our particular selves. When we act in this world, as Ross Poole (1991) writes, "we are aware of resistance; at one level this may be experienced as unfreedom. But at another and deeper level, the fact of resistance is a necessary condition for our awareness of ourselves as agents. Resistance in some form or another is a condition of agency, and thus of freedom" (p. 131). Resistance, often experienced as a tension between personal preference and duty to others, is at the heart of moral dilemmas, the resolution of which awaits the choices made by people. The challenge of modern society is for people to make these choices without damaging their individual integrity, to do what is right without being completely absorbed by the world that is not them. Active involvement in group life, the basis of what Poole calls "intersubjectivity," substantially diminishes the difficulty of this challenge.

The self forged in intersubjectivity is defined in part by its relations with other selves "so that self-awareness involves an awareness of those relations, and the concerns of the self include a reference to the concerns of others" (Poole 1991:87). To the intersubjective self, duty to others and to the responsibilities incurred in these relations is experienced less as a constraint on the pursuit of one's own good than as a way of satisfying that good. Thus, a life that furthers social well-being—and given the conditions of modernity, this means furthering the well-being of independently existing others—is a life found individually satisfying as well. Indeed, Poole argues, individual self-consciousness depends on the "interaction with and recognition by other self-consciousnesses," which constitute intersubjectivity:

> The moment of otherness is crucial: I must recognize and accept that the other has a will and a purpose, thoughts and desires, which are not mine. Ideally, the other will recognize that I too have my own distinct existence. Only through this experience of intersubjectivity—of an otherness which is not other—will I come to have an adequate awareness of myself as an independent self-consciousness. (pp. 142–43)

Consciousness of oneself achieved in these terms is consciousness of self that prizes its intersubjective needs and desires, those whose satisfaction requires ongoing relations between and among independent individuals as interdependent others. In the context of intersubjectivity, we "respect the rights of others, not because it is a commitment that—as rational . . . beings—we cannot help but make, but because it [is] required by our conception of the good. [Here] we have reason, and not just a duty, to respect the rights of others" (Poole 1991:146).

Durkheim clearly endorses the primary objectives of liberalism, the rights, liberties, and dignity of the individual, but contrary to liberalism, insists that their achievement requires a "coherent and animated society [where] there is from all to each and from each to all a continual exchange of ideas and sentiments, like a mutual moral support" ([1897] 1951:210), wherein individuals become social and, hence, moral beings committed to the collective ideal of modern society. Moral individualism encompasses those values and duties that obligate us to respect ourselves and others as individuals, and thus to honor the rights and liberties and acknowledge the worth and dignity of each as an individual. In contrast to traditional moralities whose aim "was to create or maintain as intense a

communal life as possible where the individual would be absorbed"
(Durkheim [1893] 1947:387), moral individualism promotes justice in the
form of equitable rules and relations.

> It only asks that we be thoughtful of our fellows and that we be just, that we
> fulfill our duty, that we work at the function we can best execute, and
> receive the just reward for our services. The rules which constitute it do not
> . . . snuff out free thought, but, because they are rather made for us, and in a
> certain sense, by us, we are free. We wish to understand them; we do not
> fear to change them. (pp. 407–8)

In contrast to liberalism, moral individualism requires us to recognize
that we live for others as well as ourselves and have some responsibility
for their well-being, and to act on this recognition by supporting those
conditions that enable individuals to have a worthwhile, dignified existence. Justice, then, requires not only a system for distributing rewards on
the basis of individual merit, the result of which could be inequality
severe enough to prevent some from obtaining the basic conditions of a
dignified individual life. In addition, justice requires people within whom
the social sentiments of charity, altruism, sympathy, and solidarity have
been developed, and who as a consequence, are disposed to morally
object to the excesses of liberal egoism and the extremes of liberal inequality in the name of common good, in the name, that is, of individual dignity and the conditions that foster it (see Durkheim [1950] 1958; Pearce
1989:137–38, 152–55). Moral individualism highlights what liberalism denies, namely, the worth and dignity of the individual are guaranteed most
securely by a vigorous and moralizing social life, the very kind of social
life liberalism most distrusts.

INSTITUTIONS, COMMUNITARIAN INTERDEPENDENCIES, AND MORALITY

To say, along with Durkheim, that people become moral in society is to
say, in terms of the argument presented in Chapters 1 and 2, that people
become moral in social institutions and communitarian interdependencies. Durkheim's sociology of morality can be reformulated and clarified,
and the characteristics of the moral individual can be further specified, by
examining collective ideals, moral duty, and the spirit of discipline with
reference to social institutions and by understanding group attachments,
moral dispositions, and the development of social sentiments in the context of communitarian interdependencies.

Institutions are neither instruments nor ad hoc creations used by people to facilitate their pursuit of certain goals. Rather, they arise over time, a consequence of people's efforts to make their lives less contingent and more orderly, meaningful, and purposeful. As bearers of ideals and repositories of social wisdom, institutions normatively regulate human behavior in ways that both promote cooperative responses to need and vulnerability and shape individual identity. "An institution," writes Robert Bellah (1991) and his co-authors,

> guides and sustains individual identity, as a family gives sense and purpose to the lives of its members, enabling them to realize themselves as spouses, parents and children. Institutions form individuals by making possible or impossible certain ways of behaving and relating to others. They shape character by assigning responsibility, demanding accountability, and providing the standards in terms of which each person recognizes the excellence of his or her achievements. (p. 40)

From this angle, institutions embody collective codes of honor and discipline that guide the pursuit of institutional ideals or goods by specifying the virtues—the dispositions and character traits—that enable people to undertake the honorable, disciplined, and difficult tasks necessary for the achievement of institutional goods. Institutions thus define the types of virtues, practices, and achievements that are honorable and worthy.

The spirit of discipline is expressed through institutional goods and expectations, and is articulated "in the language of duties and ideals of excellence, rather than in the language of rights" (Moon 1993:131). The institutional language of ideals and duty, honor and discipline, is, J. Donald Moon notes, the language of self-respect. Self-respect, an important component of dignity, is based on "the belief that one lives up to certain standards that define what it is to be a person of worth, a person entitled to respect" (p. 58). To a significant degree, Moon writes, these standards are given by "the institutions and practices of the society [which define] the expectations to which different people are subject, and to which they must 'measure up' if they are to be seen as persons of worth and honor" (p. 58). Self-respect is achieved by becoming the kind of person who lives an honorable and worthy life. Thus, it is not a matter of individual right. In accord with recent fashion, one may have a right to self-esteem or feeling good, though this is doubtful, but being good—being in a way that permits one to realize institutional goods—is an achievement. One earns self-respect only through the disciplined work of performing institutional duties or achieving institutional ideals.

The language of institutions and self-respect does not necessarily breed antagonism toward the language of rights. It simply but importantly brings to the discussion a recognition of the duties and responsibilities we have as participants in a shared life, and does so in a way that enriches the language of rights. It lets us recognize, in Moon's (1993) words, "that a condition of asserting of one's rights depends upon one's having self-respect, that is to say, feeling oneself to be worthy of exercising these rights. And that depends on one being able to live up to certain standards" (p. 58).

If in social institutions we have the experience of constraining ideals and disciplining duties and the opportunity to achieve self-respect, in the group attachments that constitute communitarian interdependencies we satisfy our intersubjective desires—our needs for belonging and solidarity—and cultivate the social sentiments that animate what James Q. Wilson (1993) calls "the moral sense." Wilson, like Durkheim, finds in human beings a natural sociability that, if allowed adequate expression, inclines them to seek out and sustain close, affective, enduring relations of mutual care. In their extensive review of the psychological literature, Roy Baumeister and Mark Leary discover strong evidence for the existence of natural sociability or a need to belong. They conclude that "human beings are fundamentally and pervasively motivated by a need to belong, that is, by a strong desire to form and maintain enduring interpersonal attachments. People seek frequent, affectively positive interactions within the context of long-term, caring relationships" (1996:522).

Moral sensibility, according to Wilson, emerges from the natural sociability of human beings. In the effort to satisfy their need to belong, which, as Baumeister and Leary show, is not merely a need for affiliation or a need for intimate attachment, people, from early childhood develop the capacities, traits, and dispositions—the moral sense—that facilitate close, caring, ongoing relationships. They become sympathetic, sensitive to the feelings and concerns of others, and generous in their response to those feelings and concerns. They cultivate their sense of fairness and become more disposed to sharing, following rules, waiting, and taking turns. Their capacity for mutuality or generalized reciprocity is enhanced, as is their sense of duty or personal responsibility for the obligations incurred in solidaristic relations. In this way, moral sentiments arise from natural sociability. "Because we like the company and desire the approval of others," Wilson (1993) writes,

> we adjust our actions to conform to others' expectations. If that were the end of the matter, we might properly conclude that morality is little more than a popularity contest. But that is not the whole story. Our natural sociability leads us not only to act so as to please others, but also to judge how others act toward us; and in judging them we learn to judge ourselves. We want the approval of others, but—to a degree that cannot be explained by immediate self-interest—we also want to deserve that approval. . . . In other words, we desire not only respect but self-respect. (p. 34)

The moral sensibility and, more particularly, the inclination to achieve mutual and self respect, which naturally sociable people acquire "by their membership in natural social groupings" (Wilson 1993:60), disposes them to do the right thing, to act in less self-interested and more collectively beneficial ways.

Social sentiments, of course, exist in people alongside egotistic sentiments. We are as naturally self-interested as we are naturally sociable. To achieve viability, the moral sense and the social sentiments on which it rests require the hospitable environment offered by the "elemental building blocks of society"—"families, friends, and intimate groupings in which sentiments of sympathy, reciprocity, and fairness" (Wilson 1993:251) receive full expression and active encouragement. In small-scale social settings like this, natural sociability is greeted with affection, nurturance, communication, and in the context of modernity's ideal to respect the worth and dignity of the individual, the result is people with "greater autonomy and confidence, not greater dependence and manipulativeness. . . . This is the great paradox of attachment. . . . [B]onded children will become more independent, not more dependent" (Wilson 1993:147). They also are much more likely to develop a firm moral sense in adulthood than are their unbonded or weakly attached counterparts.

The small-scale social contexts most appropriate to the development of moral sensibility may easily restrict the range of its application to those intimate others with whom the contexts are shared. The result is a moral sense that limits sympathy, generosity, and reciprocity to particular others, one that excludes outsiders from the realm of moral feeling and obligation. Modernity requires a more expansive and inclusive moral sense, one that has its possessors turn their sympathy and compassion outward to distant others, bringing to strangers the concern for the well-being of others they learned in intimate groups. To some degree this is achieved in modernity wherein obligations to distant others are met most frequently by those who take their intimate obligations most seriously. Yet, today there are fewer people meeting their distant obligations, a consequence of the decline of those social contexts wherein people learn how to satisfy their obligations to intimate others. What accounts for both developments—modern people can more easily generalize their moral sense to include strangers, and modern people find it more difficult to sustain the intimate social contexts from which the moral sense grows—is modernity's emphasis on the rights, worth, and dignity of the individual, as that emphasis has been expressed through liberalism and the market economy and the democratic state which embody it. On the one hand, the liberal ideal of the individual, the market's maker of free choices and the state's active citizen, promotes a more accommodating and respectful view of the stranger as the forces of liberal modernity bring us into regular contact with distant others. On the other hand, the market economy and the democratic state, in accord with liberalism's suspicion of society, expand in ways that diminish the social settings required for the exercise of natural sociability and the cultivation of moral sense. The point, and it is Durkheim's point, is that morality requires both society and the respect for the individual so clearly enshrined in liberalism; it requires communitarian interdependencies congenial to natural sociability and moral sense, and social institutions whose goods are compatible with liberal modernity's commitment to the dignified treatment of the individual. Similarly, the promises of liberalism—strong individuals, an efficient market economy, a responsive and effective democratic state, and freedom—require for their realization the moralizing forces of society. This is the point of moral individualism.

This argument defends the social institutions and communitarian interdependencies that constitute society on the grounds that they make indispensable contributions to a morality appropriate to the conditions of modernity. Given by this defense are the standards for assessing particular social institutions and communitarian interdependencies. We are able to distinguish good from bad or better from worse social institutions and communities in terms of how well they meet the test of moral individualism. Good social institutions and communities exist as moralizing enterprises. They afford their participants opportunities to express and act on their need for belonging, to develop their social sentiments, cultivate their moral sense, and create a culture of mutual concern and practices of mutual assistance. While they situate people amidst particular institutional obligations and communal expectations and anchor the moralizing process in concrete relations of particular others, good institutions and communities also dispose their members to generalize moral rules and moral feelings to strangers and other nonmembers, and thus to acknowledge their obligations to distant others.

The test of moral individualism also demands that social institutions and communities satisfy the requirement of autonomy. The moral selves promoted by the ideals and connections of good social institutions and communities exist as autonomous, responsible, and self-respecting individuals. Good social institutions and communities enable their members to achieve their goods, develop their virtues, and meet their expectations in ways that neither violate nor require the sacrifice of the individuals' own sense of worth, dignity, and integrity. Not only do good social institutions and communities contextualize the autonomy of interdependent individuals, they themselves also achieve a degree of autonomy in the sense that they have the capacity for regulating themselves, which is at the core of social control. To the extent that parental authority and informal neighborhood sanctions remain effective, parents and neighbors have less reason to surrender the autonomy of families and neighborhoods to state-provided modes of control that potentially are much more coercive. Good social institutions and communities exercise social control in ways that promote the moralizing process, that are respectful of the autonomy of interdependent individuals, and advance the social ties and practices of mutuality that strengthen their own autonomy. Social institutions and communitarian interdependencies, which in part because of their compatibility with the more inclusive values of modernity, contribute to the development of moral individuals are better than those that do not.

MORAL INDIVIDUALS AND LIBERAL INDIVIDUALS

As participants in the modern world, moral individuals are situated in social institutions and embedded in communitarian interdependencies. From their involvement in the former, they develop an identity and acquire the virtues, habits, and purposes that give depth, coherence, integrity, and continuity to the self. From their participation in the latter, they sustain close ongoing relations with intimate others, which is the environment so conducive to the cultivation of social sentiments and moral sense. Moral individuals possess the personal character and dispositions that make for moral competence. Moral competence is not identical to moral sainthood. Unlike moral saints, morally competent individuals are not confident that they have the morally right answer to every question or even that all moral questions have just one right answer. In addition, morally competent individuals do not consult their moral compass in response to every problem or dilemma. Part of being competent is the capacity to distinguish moral from nonmoral questions and to act accordingly.

A morality appropriate to modernity advises tolerance in the face of the ambiguity and uncertainty given by the pluralism and complexity of modernity. Such a morality acknowledges that "reality does not always lend itself squarely to yes/no judgments and allows practical knowers to say 'perhaps,' 'it depends,' 'who knows,' and to use other indeterminate truth values that help us handle situational indeterminacy" (Shalin 1992:260). Within the boundaries established by this morality, certain possible actions are excluded as clearly wrong, but we often find no ideal answer, only "a number of acceptable answers, among which we are free to choose, provided we can come up with adequate justification" (Zwiebach 1988:86). In this context, the morally competent modern individual is prudent. At the core of prudence is reason, not the abstract reason used to discern universal moral principles, but a reason embedded in character

and in moral sense and attentive to uncertainty. Prudence, as Selznick
(1987) describes it,

> is the will and the capacity to make moral judgments in concrete settings,
> and to do so in ways that take account of what the situation requires, not
> what an abstraction demands. In prudential judgement, rules and principles
> are filtered through the fabric of social life. There is due regard for human
> shortsightedness and unintended effects, for alternative options, competing
> interests, and multiple values. (p. 460)

Prudence is not an excuse for moral relativism or situational ethics. It
counsels not surrender to indeterminacy but a recognition that indeterminacy will be reduced, if never completely eliminated, only through
responsible and cooperative social intercourse. The morally proper responses to the particular dilemmas of concrete situations arise from such
social intercourse as people of character and moral sense seek to reach
agreement on what is good and on what they must or, at least, must not
do to be good. What varies from one situation to another is not the
character and moral sense of moral individuals. What do vary are the
accommodations and adjustments prudent people make in their effort to
create, extend, and enhance those social processes through which moral
rules and expectations are clarified and accorded wider support. In their
commitment to do what is right, prudent moral individuals are ever
mindful of the uncertainties that so often beset the task. This makes them
more reflective of their own moral conceptions, more tolerant of moral
conceptions different from theirs, and more inclined to join with others in
common projects undertaken to figure out what is right and, given the
particular details and conflicting demands of the situation at hand, how
the right course of action might best be pursued.

Morality is called into play most intensely during what Alan Wolfe
(1989:214) refers to as "highlighted moments" of life. For individuals
these moments of moral intensity are sparked by tensions between self-
interest or personal preference on the one hand and obligations to others
or the collectivity on the other, and by the dilemmas generated by conflicting obligations. Divorce, abortion, and serving one's country in a
military capacity during war often are understandable in these terms. For
societies, for institutions and communities, moments of moral intensity
arise when outcast groups—African-Americans, homosexuals, the poor—
seek recognition, respect, and inclusion. For moral individuals, these
highlighted moments constitute moral passages during which they are
asked both "to give account of what they are doing by reflecting on the
moral consequences of their action" and to not only decide but "to decide
how to decide" (Wolfe 1989:215, 236).

Faced with moral dilemmas, moral individuals turn to two sources of counsel, one internal, the other external. Moral individuals look for answers by consulting those parts of themselves that are deeper and more stable than preferences. They look to the social parts of themselves, to the virtues, ethical habits, and institutional identities that constitute character, asking themselves the question, "What must I do to remain true to myself as a good person?" Moral individuals also turn outward to those intimate others with whom they share communitarian interdependencies. Seeking the wisdom, sympathy, compassion, and assistance of those they trust and care about, moral individuals struggle to bring some balance to the obligations they have to others, their collectivities and themselves. At some point, moral individuals meet with those distant others who are their fellow citizens to carry on a public conversation of moral matters. They bring to this conversation a language of social virtue, which has them examine possible responses to particular moral dilemmas in terms of how those responses are likely to affect the kind of people they become, the goods to which they aspire, and the virtues they most admire.

Only superficially attached to institutions and communitarian interdependencies weakened by the great forces of liberal modernity, the capitalist market and the democratic welfare state, liberal individuals as a rule experience fewer tensions between self-interest (for which they have a robust appreciation) and obligations to others (for which they have a diminished sense) than do moral individuals, and they respond to moral dilemmas differently. For answers to moral problems, liberal individuals turn not to character and to those with whom they share communitarian interdependencies, both of which they find in short supply. Instead, they most often turn to personal preferences and impersonal courts.

Preferences dwell at the outer edges of the personality, and they are increasingly volatile, subject to regular change, even reversal, as those who market political candidates and other commodities well know. In the form of political and economic choices, preferences are easily expressed in contexts that require no accountability and justification beyond the claim that "I like what I like." This preference-based approach to moral problems combines the democratic principle of majority rule with the utilitarian principle of the greatest good for the greatest number to argue that, what is right is that which comports to the democratically expressed preferences of the majority.

The second approach to moral problems available to liberal individuals derives from the Kantian commitment to individual rights, and thus relies on impersonal and impartial courts that issue, interpret, and enforce those rights. Accordingly, the morally proper response is that to which the individual is entitled as a matter of legal right, even if that response is contrary to the preferences of the majority. Like the preference-based approach with which it often is in conflict, this rights-based approach forecloses the possibility of moral passage. This point is well illustrated in David Kirp's (1989) study of the response of various American communities to schoolchildren with AIDS in the mid-1980s, a time when most people still regarded the AIDS virus as a threatening unknown, despite the existence of good knowledge of how the disease is contracted and transmitted.

In Kirp's account of the well-known mistreatment visited upon Ryan White, a young hemophiliac HIV-infected by contaminated blood, in Kokomo, Indiana, the inadequacies of the preference-based and rights-based approaches are exposed. When Ryan White's condition became known, the school superintendent and principal, responding to the widely expressed preferences of Kokomo citizens, barred the boy from school. The preferences in whose name Ryan White was exiled were uninformed. Those who stated them were never under any requirement to provide justification, to grapple with the evidence, to confront and take seriously different opinions, or to reflect on and take personal responsibility for the consequences of their views. The White family responded by going to court where it was determined that the boy had a legal right to attend school. While the legal system compelled the people of Kokomo to honor Ryan White's right to attend school, it could not mandate their sympathy and compassion for a child in need. Indeed, the court's decision, handed down by a judge far removed from the confines of Kokomo and endorsed by celebrities like Elton John and Greg Louganis, caused a siege mentality among the townspeople, a sense that their lives were being ruled by outsiders indifferent to their concerns, preferences, and values. Their antagonism to the boy and his family grew. Friendless, the target of frequent teasing and harassment, Ryan White moved from Kokomo shortly before he died.

Several weeks after the events in Kokomo had begun, school officials in Swansea, Massachusetts, were informed that a thirteen-year-old junior high student, Mark Hoyle, a hemophiliac like Ryan White, had AIDS. In their compassionate concern for the boy and his family, the people of Swansea distinguished themselves from their Kokomo counterparts. Mark Hoyle's parents met with school officials and parents of other students and asked for their help in allowing their dying son the possibility of normal life. After consulting medical authorities and learning that the boy posed little if any risk to his classmates, the superintendent and principal, without first tabulating the preferences of the townspeople, permitted the boy to attend school, and they encouraged teachers and students to discuss not only the facts of the disease but also the needs of its carrier. Fearful that the boy's presence would jeopardize their children, many parents preferred that Mark Hoyle be kept from school, and organized a petition drive and letter-writing campaign to this end. In Swansea, however, unfounded preferences did not go unchallenged. In a series of heavily attended community forums, the preferences of frightened parents were confronted by the medical evidence and by the compassion of other parents who, in an effort to come to a moral understanding of the issue,

> could invite empathy with an AIDS-stricken child by relating the young-ster's plight to the cruelties visited on children with hepatitis or polio or physical handicap—or even . . . to the horrors visited on the Jews in Nazi Germany. They could look to their own life histories—as when the woman who founded Friends of Mark in Swansea recalled how, terrified of AIDS, she kept her gay brother away from her home—and vowed to protect a child with AIDS from such destructive passions. They could comprehend the simple human truth, and the relevance, of the testimony of a Polish Catholic woman who at considerable personal risk had rescued Jews during World War II: "What would you have done in my place, if someone comes at night and asks for help?" (Kirp 1989:285–86)

Conversations in these community forums increasingly took a moral turn and brought people face to face not only with each other but with ques-tions of social obligation and social virtue: What are our obligations to those in need? What kind of community do we become, what kind of lives do we create for ourselves and our children, when we refuse to acknowledge and satisfy these obligations? This kind of conversation, Kirp notes, enables people "to situate themselves as givers on the moral landscape [and] builds trust among those who participate by acknowl-edging the gift of their goodness, even as it builds solidarity and commu-nal competence" (1989:282, 284). Rejecting the well-worn paths to the resolution of moral problems represented by preference-aggregation and court-determined rights, the people of Swansea gave Mark Hoyle and his family sympathy, compassion, money to defer medical expenses raised by benefits, child care, meals, and friendship, and they gave themselves a community, a set of expectations, practices, and associations, in which they could and did take pride.

A number of factors combined to make Swansea a friend and Kokomo an enemy of moral passage. Unlike Ryan White who was a newcomer to Kokomo, Mark Hoyle grew up in the schools and on the ball fields of Swansea where his parents and one set of grandparents were long-time residents. In the presence of friends, acquaintances, and those who knew some of the same people they did, Mark Hoyle's parents probably were more comfortable than Mrs. White in asking for understanding and sup-port for their son, an act that afforded the people of Swansea the oppor-tunity to express sympathy and compassion. Swansea's school superintendent had been in the system for thirty years. Well-liked, widely trusted, and authoritative, he took seriously his responsibility to assure the respectful treatment of the students in his charge. Unlike his recently arrived counterpart in Kokomo, the Swansea superintendent looked to his institutional obligations, not the preferences of parents and others, in the process of deciding the right thing to do. Finally, in Swansea, with the exception of the medical authorities brought in for their knowledge of the disease, outsiders were kept at some distance. The Hoyle parents asked school officials, students and their parents, and the community at large to help them shield Mark from the glare of publicity by keeping his name from the local and national media. In making this and other requests, they asked the people of Swansea not to respect their son's individual rights but to acknowledge his needs and to sympathize with his plight. The only effort to have the matter resolved legally occurred early on and was initiated by a group of parents opposed to Mark's attending school. It was rebuffed when the prominent local attorney they asked to represent them successfully encouraged them to give the community forums a chance. In this context, the townspeople themselves would decide, and by focusing on the needs, not the rights, of a vulnerable boy, they did so in a way that called for sympathy, compassion, and reflection.

Moral passages offer people the opportunity not only to be compassionate but to come to an understanding of their compassion in terms of social virtues. The language of social virtue is foreign to most Americans who, as Robert Wuthnow (1991) shows, draw from the languages of liberal individualism to explain their motives for compassion. When asked why they help others, Americans respond most often in terms of the psychological gratification, self-fulfillment, and good feelings they get from their acts of caring. Thus, the desire to help is filtered through the desire to be fulfilled, a desire that finds clearest expression in the vocabulary of personal preference wherein "'should' drops out, choice predominates. To explain why we are involved, it is then easiest to assert simply that it feels good" (Wuthnow 1991:115).

There are, Wuthnow notes, serious limitations to this liberal individualist understanding of compassion. First, it often discourages collective expressions of care and the spirit of mutuality they nourish, promoting instead forms and periods of helping that are chosen individually. Second, the emphasis on fulfillment fails to prepare people for the sacrifices caring demands and for the bad feelings generated by the difficulties, disappointments, and tragedies often encountered when helping others. In addition, caring undertaken for personal fulfillment rarely forges strong social bonds, enduring relations, and mutual obligations. Finally, there is a great deal of evidence that good feelings and fulfillment are relatively weak incentives for acts of compassion. As Wuthnow (1991) writes, the fulfillment we receive from doing things for people does not figure very importantly in our overall happiness. In order of importance, the sources of fulfillment that best predict differences in individuals' levels of happiness . . . are: fulfillment from leisure activities, fulfillment from religion, fulfillment from being good to themselves, fulfillment from doing things for others, and fulfillment from work. Caring behavior does not rank high on the list. (pp. 97–98)

The vocabulary of personal happiness, good feelings, and self-fulfillment that constitutes in part the languages of liberal individualism offers few assurances that care and compassion will be present where and when it is most needed.

Overcoming these limitations and establishing a more enduring and reliable basis for compassion and care, Wuthnow argues, requires a sociological account, one that allows us to locate our compassionate sentiments and acts of caring "in a framework that emphasizes the other, the needy, or community relationships" (1991:88). In this account, compassion and care are understood as gifts, and, offered as gifts, they generate the gratitude and goodwill from which arise ever-widening circles of relations, obligations, and interdependencies, a process examined in much greater detail in the following chapter. Compassion and care are valued not for their contributions to personal fulfillment and good feelings but as social virtues essential to a worthwhile social life. As we offer compassion and care as gifts, Wuthnow writes,

we create a space in which to think about our dependence on one another, the needs that never can be fulfilled by bureaucracies and material goods, and the joys that come from attending to those needs. [In this way,] compassion gives us hope—both that the good society we envision is possible and that the very act of helping each other gives us strength and a common destiny. Part of the sociological case for compassion [is] that compassion is a value that speaks not only to us as individuals but to our sense of living together in society. (1991:304)

The sociological case for compassion emerged in the moral passage that took place in Swansea. There many came to the recognition that in giving of themselves to Mark Hoyle they also were giving something to themselves, namely, a community of care much more conducive to the building of both character and communitarian interdependencies than are the preference-satisfying and rights-defending contexts in which liberal individuals spend most of their time.

The social contexts hospitable to the maturation of moral individuals— character-building social institutions, communitarian interdependencies that feed social sentiments and moral sense, and moral passages—

constitute an endangered species in the United States. They have been substantially weakened, indeed in places entirely destroyed by the extraordinarily powerful forces of liberal modernity. Left standing, or, as is increasingly the case, left wobbling, are liberal individuals with little depth to their personalities, little stability to their identities, tenuous attachments to networks of mutual assistance, and a language devoid of terms capable of giving full expression to solidarity and social virtue. In a poverty-stricken underclass that poisons its own children and, with far greater consequence, in an enormously wealthy overclass hell-bent on getting more no matter the human and social costs, America's liberal individuals pursue the course of moral incompetence. In the middle, increasing numbers of people, no longer certain that the market will hear their preferences and the state will acknowledge their rights, seek to curb the frustrations of anomic insecurity and confusion with the blind acceptance of the rigid, simplistic, often hateful, moral nostrums of old-time religion or old-time, militia-spawning populism, another sign of moral incompetence.

If we are to do better for ourselves, we must relearn the art of doing better for others, and this we do in society. If we are to strengthen and, where necessary, rebuild those social contexts wherein people become preference-seeking, rights-holding moral individuals capable of generating trust and other forms of social capital, we need to examine more carefully the giving of gifts and the sacred qualities on which they rely. This is the task of Chapter 5.

CHAPTER

5

Social Capital:
Gifts and Sacredness in Society

Moral individuals are contributors to and beneficiaries of social capital. As such they exhibit high levels of trust and trustworthiness. Trusting and trustworthy people, Robert Putnam (1995b) notes, "are optimistic about the future, more likely to contribute to charity, to volunteer their time, to entertain strangers in their home, to work on community problems, to vote, and to be willing to serve on a jury. They are more tolerant of social and political minorities and more accepting of differing life-styles" (p. 29). Trust and trustworthiness, and the moral individuals who embody them, arise in communitarian interdependencies and social institutions that instill in people the habits of reciprocity and responsibility and the sense of moral obligation whose presence affords the strongest grounds people have for trusting one another. Social capital, those features of social life such as networks of collaboration, norms of mutuality, and practices of cooperation that enable people to work together in pursuit of shared purposes, originates and becomes abundant only where trust prevails. "Acquisition of social capital," writes Francis Fukuyama (1995), "requires habituation to the moral norms of a community and, in its context, the acquisition of virtues like loyalty, honesty, and dependability. . . . It is based on the prevalence of social, rather than individual virtues. The proclivity for sociability is much harder to acquire than other forms of human capital, but because it is based on ethical habit, it is also harder to modify or destroy it" (pp. 26–28).

Social capital is not the personal possession of the individuals who benefit from it, and unlike other types of capital is not exchangeable for private gain. Rather, as described in Chapter 2, social capital is embedded in the structure of relations between people, receiving expression as mutual expectations, norms of reciprocity, practices of mutual aid, associations, clubs, and social networks that underwrite shared responsibility for collective undertakings and "facilitate coordination and cooperation for mutual benefit" (Putnam 1995c:67). Regular, direct, ongoing association carried out by people with "the proclivity for sociability" is the wellspring of social capital. To Fukuyama this points to the importance of premodern configurations to the effective operation of modern social life. "If the institutions of democracy and capitalism are to work properly," he argues, "they must coexist with certain premodern cultural habits that ensure their proper functioning; they must . . . be leavened with reciprocity, moral obligation, duty toward community, and trust, which are based on habit rather than rational calculation" (Fukuyama 1995:11). Yet, premodern contexts of sociability and association often were rigidly exclusive, and their shared purposes were highly particularistic. Duty to community meant duty to oppose all outside the community; trust among community members was accompanied by distrust of strangers. The effectiveness of modern social life requires modern contexts of sociability and association whose "networks of civic engagement" are home to overlapping multiple memberships which "span underlying social cleavages" and bridge particularistic groups so that social capital is used in the service of the broader interests of the wider community (Putnam 1995a:664). Modern social networks "allow trust to become transitive and spread: I trust you, because I trust her and she assures me that she trusts you," Putnam (1993a:169) observes. By generalizing trust, by transforming direct, personal trust of particular persons into indirect, social trust, modern associational forms promote what Fukuyama calls "spontaneous sociability." A "subset of social capital," spontaneous sociability involves "the capacity to form new associations and to cooperate within the terms of reference they establish" (Fukuyama 1995:27). Animated by the social virtues and by the proclivity to sociability they nourish, moved by the inclination of the members of a group to look to one another and to their associations of mutual benefit for assistance, spontaneous sociability is the key to well-being.

Access to social capital generated by attentive families and by the involvement of family members in extra-familial (e.g., kin-, friendship-, church-, and community-based) groups substantially improves the school performance of children. Particularly important to school success, as Coleman and, more recently, Boisjoly, Duncan, and Hofferth (1995:611) have found, is the achievement of closure of social networks, as, for instance, when "parents of children in private parochial schools have relationships through both church and school," and as a consequence come to know many of their children's friends, the parents of these friends, and the children's teachers. For economically disadvantaged children especially, the availability of social capital in this form substantially increases the likelihood of successful educational performance. Thus, it is not surprising that the presence of social capital significantly improves the chances that poor children have to escape poverty. Frank Furstenberg and Mary Elizabeth Hughes (1995) found that the ability of at-risk youth, children who live most of their lives in or near poverty, to stay in school at least through high school, to enter the labor force, and to avoid illegal activities, teenage pregnancy, and serious depression "was linked to the possession of social capital by the family—that is, the degree to which the parents and children were embedded in a protective social network and were themselves a closely bonded unit with mutual expectations, trust, and loyalty" (p. 589). Specifically, Furstenberg and Hughes note, social capital within the family in the form of involved and supportive parents "results in greater compliance and commitment from the offspring," while the social capital generated by the relationships the family has with other families and community groups give "children . . . a greater probability of achieving conventionally successful outcomes . . . in later life" (pp. 581–82).

Communitarian interdependencies, the strong social bonds, vital social relations, and interdependent networks through which people pursue common purposes, promote the sense of guardianship and the expectations for shared responsibility on which rest informal social control. "Informal social control processes," John Hagan (1995) and his co-authors argue, are a form of social capital that "can shield and protect youth from drifting into subterranean traditions of deviance and disorder during important transitional phases in the life course" (p. 1135). Robert Sampson (1995) agrees, providing evidence that "social networks among adults and children in a community are particularly important in fostering the capacity for collective socialization and supervision. . . . [C]losure of local networks can provide the child with norms and sanctions that could not be brought about by a single adult alone, or even married couple families in isolation" (p. 200). Communities endowed with dense and multiple interpersonal networks make it possible for parents to be more effective and for children to grow up to be more responsible and happier adults. In addition, they sharply reduce the risk of crime, delinquency, and violence encountered by their members, and as Sampson finds, they foster a solidarity that feeds another kind of social capital— public control, or "the capacity of local community organizations to obtain extra-local resources . . . that help sustain neighborhood organization and crime control" (p. 200).

The evidence is that social capital is good for children, for the poor, and for the quality of social life. Thanks to the two most ambitious studies of social capital, Robert Putnam's *Making Democracy Work* (1993a) and Francis Fukuyama's *Trust* (1995), we also know that substantial and continually replenished stocks of social capital are indispensable to effective and responsive democratic government and to efficient and prosperous capitalist economies. The irony, as we have seen throughout, is that these twin pillars of liberal modernity, democratic government and the capitalist market economy, have done their work in ways that have depleted social capital.

Putnam's analysis of the vast regional, political, and economic differences in Italy shows that "[b]y far the most important factor in explaining good government [and economic development] is the degree to which social and political life in a region approximates the ideal of civic community" (1993a:120). Civic sociability and the patterns of civic engagement it sponsors are forms of social capital, and they are more important to effective and accountable government and economic growth than either physical capital or human capital. Those regions with strong societies, with, that is, "a concentration of overlapping networks of social solidarity" supportive of mutuality, habits of cooperation, and a sense of shared responsibility are the very regions characterized by good government and strong economic performance (Putnam 1993a:115). Italy's more democratic and economically advanced regions are civic communities whose members are "bound together by horizontal relations of reciprocity and cooperation, not by vertical relations of authority and dependency" (p. 188). Horizontally ordered civic regions rest on a rich associational life centered around networks of civic engagement—mutual aid societies, literacy circles, athletic clubs, hiking clubs, choral societies, cooperatives, local bands, service clubs, bird-watching groups, neighborhood associations, and the like. These structures of cooperation, Putnam (1993a) shows, create "robust norms of reciprocity" (p. 173) and lessen the likelihood of opportunism and free riding. They "facilitate communication and improve the flow of information about the trustworthiness of individuals . . . allow[ing] reputations to be transmitted and refined" (p. 174); they preserve the lessons of "past successes at collaboration" (p. 167), and offer some good assurance that others will abide by common expectations, and thus they encourage voluntary and spontaneous cooperation. "Networks of civic engagement," Putnam (1993a:173) finds, "are an essential form of social capital: the denser such networks in a community, the more likely that its citizens will cooperate for mutual benefit."

Italy's uncivic regions are low in social capital, vertically ordered, and suffer from the least democratic, least effective governments and the most backward, least efficient economies. Lacking the structures of civic sociability that foster active, trustful, public-spirited citizens, uncivic regions are peopled by "amoral individualists" who "rely on . . . the 'forces of order,' namely, the police" and those who "find themselves clamoring for sterner law enforcement" and the more oppressive state presence each represents (Putnam 1993a:112). Without effective norms of reciprocity, habits of cooperation, and structures of mutual assistance, and thus unable to regulate themselves informally, amoral individualists seek protection from one another in the vertical ties of dependence and exploitation that connect clients to patrons and petitioners to governors. In their uncivic regions, Putnam writes,

> [the] very concept of "citizen" is stunted. From the point of view of the individual inhabitant, public affairs is the business of somebody . . . the "bosses," the politicians—but not me. Few people aspire to partake in deliberations about the commonwealth. Political participation is triggered by personal dependency or private greed, not by collective purpose. Engagement in social and cultural associations is meager. . . . Corruption is widely regarded as the norm. . . . Laws (almost everyone agrees) are made to be broken, but fearing others' lawlessness, people demand sterner discipline. Trapped in these interlocking vicious circles, nearly everyone feels powerless, exploited, *and* unhappy. All things considered, it is hardly surprising that representative government here is less effective than in more civic communities. (p. 115)

In the highly atomized and anomic climate of the uncivic regions, Putnam documents, distrust, narrow self-interest, and political passivity combine to make support for coercively authoritarian horizontal structures of dependency a rational survival strategy. The conditions that force people to place a premium on rational survival strategies are the same conditions that erode the social capital, the structures of reciprocity and social trust, that are indispensable to responsive and competent democratic government.

According to Fukuyama (1995) social capital is equally essential to economic prosperity, or more specifically, to the full and proper functioning of the innovative and wealth-creating dynamics that make the capitalist market economy the most powerful engine of economic prosperity the world has ever known. For Fukuyama (1995), the most significant form of social capital is spontaneous sociability. Spontaneous sociability makes loyalty, reliability, and proclivity to cooperate—which, in traditional society, are confined to long-established groups—portable, so that they work not only to maintain existing groups and associations but also to facilitate the generation of new ones. "In any modern society, organizations are being constantly created, destroyed, and modified. The most useful kind of social capital is often not the ability to work under the authority of a traditional community or group, but the capacity to create new structures of cooperation" (p. 27). Spontaneous sociability replenishes the ground on which grow the voluntary social, political, and business associations intermediate between family and government. Societies, like the United States, Japan, and Germany, with access to a large and vital pool of spontaneous sociability have substantial political and economic advantages over both "individualistic societies with little capacity for association" (like Russia and inner-city neighborhoods in the United States) and "familistic societies in which the primary (and often only) avenue to sociability is family and broader forms of kinship. . . . Familistic societies [like Hong Kong, the People's Republic of China, France, and Italy] frequently have weak voluntary associations because unrelated people have no basis for trusting one another" (pp. 28–29)

Like Putnam, Fukuyama recognizes the indispensability of trust to social capital formation, and recognizes further that the cultivation of trust is threatened by reliance on explicit contractual rules and legal regulations. Trust wells up in communities based on "a set of ethical habits and reciprocal moral obligations internalized by each of the community's members" (Fukuyama 1995:9). The presence of others who possess the social virtues such habits endorse and who share the cultural commitment to reciprocity underlies the expectation that people are trustworthy. Spontaneous sociability requires a high degree of generalized social trust that radiates beyond the narrow confines of family and kinship and long-established particularistic ties.

Generalized social trust and the propensity for spontaneous sociability it subsidizes feed the thriving clubs, groups, and organizations that make for a rich, satisfying associational life and increase the likelihood that government will be responsive, honest, and effective. The two also promote the conditions for economic efficiency, growth, and prosperity. In societies fortunate enough to possess social capital in this form, economic organizations encounter fewer external and coercive regulations and enforcement procedures, and thus operate at a higher level of flexibility, with lower transaction costs, and in a way to allow new enterprises and new forms of existing enterprises to emerge and take shape quickly in response to changing demands. Where individualistic societies rely on the heavy hand of centralized state power for their economic organization, familistic societies depend on family-based economic enterprises whose suspicion of outsiders invites a climate of authoritarian political rule. In contrast to each, high-trust societies achieve well-being by relying on a market economy populated by people whose social virtues and propensity for sociability enable them to work together in maintaining, often by restructuring, established economic forms and in creating new ones.

Most usages of the term *social capital*, including Fukuyama's, derive from James Coleman's formulation that embeds the concept in the rational, self-interested choice vocabulary of market rhetoric. Social capital is another form of capital along with physical, financial, and human capital. "The function identified by the concept of 'social capital,'" Coleman (1988:101) writes, "is the value of . . . aspects of social structure to actors as resources that they can use to achieve their interests." Furstenberg and

Hughes (1995) examine "the investment that individuals create through involvement in social relationships. These investments generate social capital as a resource upon which individuals may draw to enhance their opportunities" (p. 581). Boisjoly, Duncan, and Hofferth (1995) note how this "terminology enables us to think in terms of these assistance networks and resources for children and families much as we think of financial resources. Social capital provides a framework for evaluating the differential investments and accounts of different subgroups of the population and the trade-off between time and money" (p. 612). Fukuyama regards social capital as a commodity, and approvingly cites Kenneth Arrow's claim that "[t]rust and similar values, loyalty or truth-telling, are examples of what the economist would call 'externalities.' They are goods; they are commodities; they have real, practical economic value; they increase the efficiency of the system, and enable you to produce more goods or more of whatever values you hold in high-esteem" (cited in Fukuyama 1995:152). Through the concept of social capital, market rhetoric, with its claim that the assumptions on which we analyze market transactions apply to all social relations, intercedes more deeply into social life, presenting itself as a tool that makes the analysis of social life as rigorous as that of economic exchanges.

Yet, economist Robert Solow, finds analyses guided by the concept of social capital, Fukuyama's especially, to be anecdotally interesting at best and vague and unpersuasive most usually. Although Solow agrees that "cultural imperatives, social institutions and informal standards of acceptable behavior shape and limit what individuals and groups can do in economic life," he concludes that social capital, when compared to the more precise conceptualizations of other forms of capital, is little more than a buzzword (Solow 1995:38). For it to be something more, Solow argues, the social formations to which the concept refers

should be closely analogous to a stock or inventory, capable of being characterized as larger or smaller than another such stock. There needs to be an identifiable process of "investment" that adds to the stock, and possibly a process of depreciation that subtracts from it. The stock of social capital should somehow be measurable, even inexactly. Observable changes in it should correspond to investment and depreciation. Otherwise the analogy to capital is not very useful to the working analyst. A useful way of talking might remain, but without the possibility of distinguishing more from less, causal analysis becomes impressionism. (p. 38)

Resistant to the measurement standards and techniques that admit concepts to the practice of rigorous analysis and policy formation, social capital does not allow us to say much of anything with certainty and precision.

In effect, Solow denies social capital membership in a club that includes human capital, physical capital, and other real—that is, precisely
measurable—commodities, and he is right to do so. This does not mean,
of course, that the material to which social capital refers is less real or less
important than quantifiable forms of capital. It does mean that it defies
complete capture by market rhetoric and the language of measurable
commodities. Consider in this regard the shortcomings of one of the
economists' most celebrated and important measures, the Gross Domestic
Product. The GDP offers a precise measure of an economy's total output,
the value of its goods and services, and the frequency and volume of
market activity. For nearly half a century, the American government,
whether led by Republicans or Democrats, has committed itself to policies
designed to enlarge the GDP, assuming that increases in market transactions elevate the nation's well-being. Yet, as Clifford Cobb, Ted Halstead,
and Jonathan Rowe (1995) show,

> [the] GDP is simply a gross measure of market activity, of money changing
> hands. It makes no distinction whatsoever between the desirable and the
> undesirable, or costs and gains. On top of that, it looks only at the portion of
> reality that economists choose to acknowledge—the part involved in mone-
> tary transactions. The crucial economic functions performed in the house-
> hold and volunteer sectors go entirely unreckoned. As a result the GDP not
> only masks the breakdown of the social structure and the natural habitat
> upon which the economy—and life itself—ultimately depend; worse, it
> actually portrays such breakdown as economic gain. (p. 60)

Thus, the GDP not only fails to register the communitarian interdependencies, institutional virtues, and norms and practices of mutual assistance that constitute social capital, it also incorporates their deterioration
into a concept of economic growth that equates social breakdown with
the nation's well-being. As neighborhoods become more disorganized
and crime-ridden, as communities become less civil and voluntary associations more sparse, as family disintegration proceeds apace, and as
more people find less reason to trust and rely on others, the market steps
in to provide in the form of precisely measurable, rigorously quantified
commodities the goods and services that, unbeknownst to the GDP, once
flowed from social capital. Amid the rubble left by social breakdown, the
GDP rises as more money is spent on divorce lawyers, child care services,
public and private security forces, anti-theft devices, and Prozac.

Given the limits of and the distortions created by GDP, Cobb, Halstead,
and Rowe (1995) propose a broader measure, one that would recognize
and assign values to family and community life. "An approximation of
social and habitat costs would be less distorting and perverse than the
GDP is now; a conservative estimate of, say, the costs of family break-

down and crime would produce a more accurate picture of economic progress than does ignoring such costs entirely" (p. 70). While it makes sense to calculate the costs of the deterioration of social capital and factor them into any measure used to indicate a nation's well-being, it would be a mistake, in part for some of the reasons Solow enumerates, to try to capture the value of social capital in a form comparable to market prices. What is most valuable about social capital defies such operationalization and measurement. Social capital is not a commodity. The material to which it refers is not analogous to physical and human capital. The relationships from which it grows are not at all like market transactions, and the resources it generates are debased when we understand them as if they were financial resources. To properly appreciate social capital, we must separate it from market rhetoric. Indeed, we should stop calling it social *capital* since what it embodies is the spirit of the gift. As we shall see, when gifts are transformed into the things of the market, they lose their capacity to generate the mutuality that is at the heart of trust, cooperation, and ongoing networks of social engagement.

A WONDERFUL LIFE

One of the most popular films in the United States is Frank Capra's 1946 classic, *It's a Wonderful Life* (very helpful accounts of which appear in Luke 1989–1990, Willis 1974, and Maland 1980). Televised frequently throughout the Christmas season, the film chronicles the life of George Bailey in the context of the pressures placed on small-town America between 1919 and 1945. We see George Bailey, portrayed by Jimmy Stewart, as he strives, at times reluctantly, to meet his obligations to family, friends, and community, a difficult task made even more daunting by Mr. Potter, a greedy and ruthless banker determined to extend his already considerable financial control over the town of Bedford Falls. Originally entitled *The Greatest Gift* after the Philip Stern short story from which it was adapted, the film uses the conflict between George and Potter to examine the tension between society and the market. In the film, the greatest gifts—trust, mutual assistance, and communality—are those people give to one another in society, and their sacred character, that which makes them special and worthy of respect and sacrifice, is threatened constantly by Potter's efforts to have more and more aspects of the townspeople's lives organized by market principles. I want to look briefly at some of the film's highlights as a way of introducing the gift-giving and sacred qualities that underlie the creation of those resources of communality that appear as social capital.

"I'm going to shake the dust from this crummy little town and see the world," George announces after graduating from high school. Bags packed and travel itinerary in hand, he plans to visit exotic places and then enroll in college to become an architect and builder of the sky-scrapers, airports, bridges, and roads that would modernize America's then quickly expanding cities. The unexpected death of his father, how-ever, keeps George in Bedford Falls. To enable his brother to attend col-lege, to provide security for his widowed mother, and most importantly to prevent the Building and Loan Society his father founded and ran from falling to the unscrupulous Potter, George agrees to take over. Drawing on his talents, funds, and the good will he and his family had accumu-lated over the years, George keeps the Building and Loan afloat during bad times, allowing it to grow to become a major source of community development. Bailey Park, a collection of small but pleasant and afford-able houses, arises as a successful and attractive alternative to Potter's ill-kept, overpriced rental properties.

Over time, the Building and Loan becomes the focal point of the town's resistance to Potter's encroaching market. Emphasizing mutuality and solidarity—"We've got to stick together. . . . We've got to have faith in each other," George reminds the depositors after one of Potter's attacks—the Building and Loan brought together the resources of Bedford Falls's common people and used them to improve the lives of those people. In this way, he had people rely on one another, and from such reliance was built both low-cost affordable homes and a thriving sense of community. Neither the world traveler nor the master builder of his youthful dreams, George lives his life as a good and responsible father, husband, son, community leader, and local lender.

All this is upset one December 24th when George's kind but bumbling Uncle Billy misplaces (with Potter's "help") $8,000 of the Building and Loan's funds. With an outside audit scheduled for that day, George seeks out Potter and pleads for a loan. Potter's response is to swear out a warrant for George's arrest for misappropriation of funds. Despondent and angry, George heads for a local bar, and after several drinks and a fight decides to commit suicide, convinced that the insurance money would save the Building and Loan and secure a better life for his wife and children.

Preparing to jump from the town's bridge, George encounters Clarence, an angel sent to rescue him. Clarence does this by showing George the "Pottersville" that Bedford Falls would have become without him. Main Street is transformed into a seedy world of tawdry hang-outs, cheap ho-tels and dance joints, sleazy bars, places of prostitution, and pawnshops. Bailey Park is a cemetery surrounded by Potter's dilapidated rental dwell-ings. Uncle Billy is in an insane asylum; brother Harry is dead. George frantically runs through a town that has no place for him. He is not known to his best friends, his mother, and his wife, who in "Pottersville" have become unhappy, lonely, guarded, and suspicious people. Governed by market principles alone, Bedford Falls as "Pottersville" is devoid of human decency. Appalled, frightened, and pursued by the police, George returns to the bridge, praying for the restoration of his previous life.

George's prayer is answered, and, in the film's final scene, he returns home to a living room full of family, friends, and neighbors who had pooled their meager resources to replace the lost money. It is Christmas Eve, a sacred time in Bedford Falls, and the special significance of family, friendship, community, and mutual aid is expressed powerfully and experienced deeply. Bound together in common cause, in communion with one another, the people of Bedford Falls again learn that they can give one another what Potter's market cannot—compassion, generosity, sympathy, and goodwill. By keeping alive the spirit of the gift, they manage to sustain the sacred practices of society that "Pottersville" would have destroyed.

It's a Wonderful Life frames the story of George Bailey in terms of two central tensions (see Maland 1980:140–43), and draws on the related notions of gifts and sacredness to resolve them. The first tension, as noted above, is the one between the socially responsible George and the ruthlessly self-interested, market-oriented Potter. The problem is not that Potter is a capitalist, but that the unrestrained market he favors advances by undermining society, the fundamental basis of a wonderful life. As a banker and developer working in the market, George, too, is a capitalist, but one who believes there ought to be limits to the reach of the capitalist market. George knows that the things that matter most, solidarity and communality, for instance, cannot be bought and sold as commodities; they are available only as gifts people make to one another. Potter wants a market society, a society regulated by the logic of the market. George wants a market whose harsher tendencies are checked by the compassion and sense of common good nourished by the gift community.

The second tension is rooted in the conflict between George's sense of social obligation and his personal desire for adventure, career, and success in the modern world. At times, George experiences a lingering regret over the opportunities lost as a result of his sacrifices for others. This tension is resolved when, back on the bridge after his nightmarish tour of "Pottersville," George recognizes the gift-character of his sacrifices, the positive contributions they made to the lives of those with whom he shares family, friendship, and community, and, in turn, the positive contributions, the gifts, those people and their social contexts made to his life. In their absence, that is, in "Pottersville," George belonged nowhere and to no one. Alone amidst the profanities of Potter's unbridled market, greeted by friendless, suspicious, distrustful people, George could not give and there were no gifts for him to receive. Now, George yearns for the satisfactions given to those who meet their social obligations. Back home, back in Bedford Falls, back among those who relied on him as a gifted father, husband, son, friend, and member of the community, back in society, George embraces these satisfactions. He knows that society is a sacred gift people make to themselves.

The norm of reciprocity, social networks, and trust that make for sociability and cooperation for mutual benefit are alive and well in Bedford Falls, and they flow most powerfully from activities centered around the Bailey Building and Loan. The first building and loan in the United States, the Oxford Provident Building Association, was founded in 1831 outside Philadelphia by textile workers intent on creating a pool of money from which they could borrow to purchase homes (Day 1993:39). The Oxford Provident and the many building associations formed in its wake were modeled after the friendly societies English workers constructed in response to the volatility, insecurity, and harsh unpredictability brought by modernity's emergence in the first quarter of the nineteenth century. Locally organized, voluntary solidaristic associations, usually focused on the increasingly besieged family and community, friendly societies provided

> benefits to the aged and incapacitated members and those otherwise unable to work; aid to families of deceased members; compensation for industrial accidents; payments to unemployed members; monetary encouragement to members in search of jobs; funeral expenses; nursing and maternity care; and . . . educational opportunities for members and their families. (Putnam 1993a:139)

Unable to rely on the market economy and the liberal democratic state, both still in their early stages of development, the members of friendly societies relied on practices and rules that they created and sustained, and in the process became dependent on one another.

Building and loan associations grew rapidly in the United States, sparked in part by the steady arrival of new groups of immigrants quick to recognize the benefits of mutual assistance. By 1925, the over 12,000 business and loans were the country's primary source of home financing as the large commercial banks concentrated almost exclusively on commercial loans and short-term consumer loans (Day 1993:38). The stock market crash of 1929 and the ensuing Great Depression brought disaster to the building and loan industry: depositors lost over $200 million in savings and 1,700 associations failed (Pizzo, Fricker, and Muolo 1989:9). The federal government stepped in, not to assume the responsibilities of the building and loans but to shore up depositor faith in and allegiance to the small, locally operated, community-oriented savings associations. In effect, the government sought to preserve the building and loan, the sole port of entry into the housing market for most Americans, as an area conducive to the formation of resources of communality—an indication that national governments are able to promote as well as deplete such resources. To this end, in 1934 Congress created the Federal Savings and Loan Insurance Corporation which, drawing on funds contributed by member associations, insured deposits for up to $5,000. In exchange for this and other confidence-inspiring protections, savings and loans, as they now were called, were limited to providing home loans. "This was the pivotal idea behind the thrifts' social contract. Congress would give special breaks to a private industry so that it could promote home ownership for the masses" (Day 1993:48). The resulting arrangements assured that

> local insured deposits were loaned out to local home buyers, who then became solid members of the community, and new depositors—a business cycle that worked beautifully for 50 years. Savings and loans occupied a special place in America, making home ownership affordable for the emerging middle class primarily through 30-year, fixed-rate mortgages. . . . [In this setting] starting a small community-based savings and loan bordered on performing community service—local people pooling their resources to assure there would be a safe place for their savings and a source for home loans. (Pizzo, Fricker, and Muolo 1989:10, 25)

Ultimately, of course, the forces represented by Mr. Potter triumphed, leading in the 1980s to the "savings and loan debacle . . . the costliest scandal in the country's history. Bailing out the S. and L. industry will cost taxpayers at least $500 billion over the next few years and more than $1 trillion over the next several decades" (Day 1993:9). Early in the decade, Congress, with the encouragement of the Carter and Reagan administrations, eliminated restrictions that confined savings and loans to the provision of home mortgages in particular geographical areas. In addition, the limit at which individual deposits were insured was raised from $40,000, (the limit set in 1974) to $100,000. Overnight, savings and loans were transformed from local providers of home loans to their largely wage-earning depositors to repositories of blocks of federally insured $100,000 deposits made by wealthy investors and channeled into speculative, often shady if not illegal, land deals, real estate developments, automobile dealerships, junk bonds, and the like throughout the country. "The S. and L.'s acquired the deposits not from local savers but from rich investors, who shopped the nation for the highest interest rates. Brokers had no need to find well-run S. and L.'s as havens for their client's cash, since FSLIC guaranteed all deposits. . . . In fact, in most cases, depositors [were] better off choosing a bad Savings and Loan—since bad Savings and Loans, more desperate for funds, usually [paid] higher interest rates" (Glassman 1990:17; also see Sherrill 1990). Fed by the gift of mutual assistance, building and loans grew to a position of prominence in the United States, only to become in the 1980s still another financial mechanism through which high rollers pursued their initially risk-free search for quick and high returns on their investments. Before the decade was over, the savings and loan industry had collapsed. Unlike the first savings and loan bailout—when, from a sense of gratitude, his depositor neighbors and friends pooled their funds to give George Bailey the $8,000 stolen by Mr. Potter—the current bailout is undertaken in a place that closely resembles "Pottersville," a place where gifts, gratitude, and generosity, the very wellsprings of so-called social capital, have been displaced by extraordinarily powerful market forces.

GIFTS

Social relations and obligations are like those created in the giving of gifts. The easiest way to begin to understand this is to contrast gift relations with the contractual relations found in the marketplace.

Contractual relations have people focus on their individual self-interest. Individuals enter into and sustain such relations for personal advantage. The contractual relation is instrumental; it is a means individuals use to satisfy their self-interests and thus to benefit themselves. In contrast, in the gift relation people focus on the interests of the relation itself, and these interests have them act to benefit others. That is, the gift relation is an end in itself. The acts of giving that comprise it are valued for their own sake. The gift relation is not a means to some end outside itself, not a calculated device for pursuing external reward. In fact, the giving of gifts usually does get something in return, namely, the gratitude of the recipient. Gratitude is the reward that comes when there is no expectation of reward. As such, it is not found in the recipient of a bank loan who under contractual obligation to repay the loan with interest, knows the loan was made to benefit the lender. Hostility replaces gratitude when what ought to be given as a gift (e.g., a kidney to a seriously ill sibling, child, or parent) is offered in exchange for some stipulated reward. Gifts are gifts only when given in the absence of expectation of reward. The response they generate is gratitude, and, most usually, the giver strives to minimize the sense of obligation expressed by the gratitude, saying something like "Think nothing of it, it was the least I could do."

In this way, the giver expresses graciousness. If, as Thomas Murray argues, the gift obliges gratitude—grateful use, grateful conduct, and a desire to reciprocate—on the part of the recipient, it obliges graciousness, an effort to minimize the recipient's obligations, in the giver. Each of these obligations, Murray (1987) notes, stems "from the purpose of gift exchange—building moral relationships" by establishing "affirmations of interdependence" (p. 32). Ralph Waldo Emerson, in whose work the defenders of the liberal individual find a celebration of the strong, self-reliant individual standing outside and often against the town, criticized the gift for its imposition of obligations. "How dare you give them?," Emerson (1876) asked.

> We wish to be self-sustained. We do not quite forgive a giver. The hand that feeds us is in some danger of being bitten. . . . We are either glad or sorry at a gift, and both emotions are unbecoming. Some violence I think is done, some degradation borne, when I rejoice or grieve at a gift. I am sorry when my independence is invaded . . . and if the gift pleases me overmuch, then I should be ashamed that the donor should read my heart. . . . For the expectation of gratitude is mean, and is continually punished by the obliged person. It is a great happiness to get off without injury and heart-burning from one who has had the ill-luck to be served by you. It is a very onerous business, this of being served, and the debtor naturally wishes to give you a slap. (pp. 162–63)

Unlike the self-assumed, freely chosen obligations liberal individualism endorses, the obligations created by gifts, at least in Emerson's account, represent invasions of one's independence and cause injury, aggression, and perhaps even heart-burn to the individual seeking self-reliance. Here, there is no sense that the affirmations of interdependence nourished by the cycle of gift, gratitude, graciousness, and generosity are able to make the town (as they made Bedford Falls) a primary condition and not the enemy of the self-reliant moral individual.

The obligations incurred in gift relations are unlike those in contractual relations. Contractual obligations are stipulated in advance and precisely specified. The recipient of the bank loan knows clearly how much it will cost to repay the loan, at what intervals repayment must be made, and the penalties for nonpayment. Once the obligations set by the contract are met, the relation between the bank and the loan recipient is ended, a reflection of the temporary and expedient character of contractual relations. Obligations acquired in gift relations are de-emphasized, nonstipulated, and unspecified. Again, the gratitude the gift evokes is not a prior expectation, nor is the timing and form of its expression explicated. Further, unlike what we see in the contractual relation, fulfilling the obligation to show gratitude neither discharges it nor ends the gift relation of which it is a part. Rather, as James Carrier (1991) writes, "it recreates [the obligation] by reaffirming the relationship of which the obligation is a part. If one neighbor helps another move some stones, and if later the second loans the first a tool, this does not simply discharge the obligation. It also reaffirms the neighborly relationship, and so reaffirms the obligation to continue to give and receive in this way" (p. 124). Acting from a sense of gratitude, people return gifts with gifts, generosity with generosity, sustaining their obligations to one another in an ongoing gift relation. This, of course, is the lesson learned by George Bailey. His gratitude is a response to the gift given to him by his family, friends, and neighbors, a gift expressive of their gratitude for the gifts he had given them. Gratitude, graciousness, and generosity multiply, solidarity and mutuality increase, as long as the gift is passed along. And if the gift is to remain a gift, it must be kept in motion.

The importance of movement to gifts was well known to the original "Indian givers." As Lewis Hyde notes in his brilliant study *The Gift* (1979), the term was created by Puritans in colonial America to describe what was for them the curious and uncivilized habit of native Americans to ask for the return of their gifts. The gift, most often a stone pipe regularly circulated among the local tribes, had been a peace offering. Its Puritan recipient, a "white man keeper" in Hyde's account, added the gift to his property holdings, perhaps placing the pipe on the wall of his sparse cabin, or packaging it for future shipment to relatives or a museum in England, or trading or selling it for something more useful. Later, when the original givers or members of a different tribe requested the gift's return, the Puritan only could shake his head in dismay. Yet, as Hyde argues, the "Indian giver," unlike the "white man keeper," understood a cardinal property of the gift:

> whatever we have been given is supposed to be given away again, not kept. Or, if it is kept, something of similar value should be moved on in its stead, the way a billiard ball may stop when it sends another scurrying across the felt, its momentum transferred. . . . As it is passed along, the gift may be given back to the original donor, but this is not essential. In fact, it is better if the gift is not returned but is given instead to some new, third party. The only essential is this: *the gift must always move.* (1979:4)

When its movement is stopped, when it is kept as private property and used for personal pleasure and gain, the gift loses its socially constructive qualities. The obligation of those who receive gifts, the obligation of gratitude, is to pass the gifts along.

Only in motion does the gift—or, more specifically, the care, concern, and affection embodied in and symbolized by the gift—become abundant. The increase in social sentiments brought by the gift, in contrast to the profit earned by private property, joins people together in bonds of affection and cultivates the faithfulness and gratitude on which rest enduring social relations. The sense of communality that emerges from the movement of gifts, Hyde (1979) writes,

> nourishes those parts of our spirit that are not entirely personal. . . . [A]lthough these wider spirits are a part of us, they are not "ours"; they are endowments bestowed upon us. To feed them by giving away the increase they have brought us is to accept that our participation in them brings with it an obligation to preserve their vitality. When, on the other hand, we reverse the direction of this increase—when we profit on exchange or convert "one man's gift to another man's capital"—we nourish that part of our being . . . which is distinct and separate from others. (p. 38)

The difference between these two approaches appears, as we saw, in the contrasts between George Bailey and Mr. Potter, and between the gift community of Bedford Falls and the market society of Pottersville. An active participant in the gift community, George experiences his talents as gifts, and understands that in order to develop them, he must give them away, share them with others. George's altruism is a gift the community has bestowed on him. Potter, wrapped up in the market world of contractual relations, commodity exchanges, and profit, and using his talents and resources for private gain, separates himself from others in a world devoid of trust and gratitude.

Gift relations, then promote altruism and restrain selfishness. Disinterested, as opposed to self-interested, altruistic individuals conduct their lives as if the welfare of others matters a great deal. "What defines altruistic behavior is that the actor could have done better for himself had he chosen to ignore the effect of his choice on others" (Margolis, quoted in Piliavin and Chang 1990:28). By taking into account the probable consequences of his or her actions, the other-regarding altruistic individual often acts in a way that is inconsistent with his or her selfish interests. Motivated by a concern for the needs of others, performed without expectation of external reward, and usually undertaken with some cost to personal advantage, altruistic behavior is unlike the rationally calculative self-regarding behavior that prevails in both the liberal conception of human nature and the liberal market.

What distinguishes those who engage in altruistic acts from those who do not? Studies identify several important characteristics. In contrast to their counterparts, altruistic individuals have a more coherent and firmly developed set of internalized moral values from which emerges an explicit moral imperative and/or a strong desire to contribute to the well-being of others. In addition, they value more highly their communities and take seriously their personal responsibilities to these communities. Finally, they exhibit a much higher level of faith in people, proving to be more trusting and trustworthy, and as a consequence, are more willing to undertake the potential risks of altruistic acts (Piliavin and Chang 1990:32–33; Simmons 1991; Ruston 1980: chap. 2).

Whether or not altruism is an innate tendency, and there is some dispute about this, it is clear that individuals become altruistic only in a social context. Christopher Jencks (1990:54) identified empathy, community, and morality as the key social sources of altruism. Empathic altruism "derives from the fact that we 'identify' with people outside ourselves," showing sympathy for their misfortunes and seeking to understand their experiences as they understand them. Communitarian altruism "involves identification with a collectivity rather than with specific individuals," and sensitizes people to the interests of the collectivity be it a family, work group, community, or nation. Moralistic altruism involves the sense that people should take into account the welfare of others, and derives from both "the collective culture of the large group" and the concrete experience of taking responsibility for the fate of others in families, work groups, and communities. Empathy, community, the sense of personal responsibility for the welfare of others, the moral codes that reinforce and guide this sense, and the altruism they encourage arise from and sustain the social practices that enable people to rely on the gifts they provide one another.

Gifts and Markets

In his important book, *The Gift Relationship: From Blood to Social Policy*, Richard Titmuss (1970) develops a powerful argument against markets in blood and, by implication, markets in those goods and services necessary for the preservation or restoration of health. "There is a bond that links all men and women in the world so closely and intimately," Titmuss (1970:15) claims, "that every difference of color, religious belief and cultural heritage is insignificant beside it. The life stream of blood that runs in the veins of every member of the human race proves that the family of man is a reality." As a gift, blood nurtures the social bond; as a marketable commodity, it weakens that bond.

Titmuss's argument rests on a careful examination of two different approaches to blood acquisition for medical purposes, the nonmarket, voluntary British approach and the combined market, voluntary American approach, over the period from 1956 to 1968. In Britain, blood could be neither sold nor purchased. It was made available only as a gift, and the giver had no expectation of external reward—the giver acquired no privileges over nongivers if she needed blood in the future, nor since the recipient of her gift remained unknown to her, was she able to expect anything in return from those she helped. In this approach, blood was provided to those who needed it, without cost or obligation to replenish the supply used. The approach used in the United States combined a voluntary system of this kind with two others—a system that allowed people to give blood as a way of repaying supplies they have used in the past or as a way to amass credit for future use, and a market system for the buying and selling of blood.

Between 1956 and 1968 the demand for blood increased greatly in both Britain and the United States, largely as a consequence of the introduction of new surgical techniques. In Britain, the increase in need for blood was met by a corresponding rise in the donation of blood. In the United States, however, the number of voluntary donors declined, and the resulting shortages were overcome only by an increase in the number of sellers in the commercial blood banks. In the absence of any material incentive for blood, the number of gifts of blood increased sharply to satisfy the growing need. In the presence of a market for blood, the opportunity to make a gift of blood was taken by fewer and fewer people despite rising need. Why?

According to Titmuss, the existence of a market where some people are paid for their blood reduces the likelihood that others will make a gift of their blood. Market payment alters the altruistic attitude toward giving by diminishing what Peter Singer (1973) describes as the inspiring force behind such gifts, namely, the sense that "others are depending on one's generosity and concern, that one may oneself, in an emergency, need the assistance of a stranger, the feeling that there is still at least this vital area in which we must rely on the good will of others rather than the profit motive" (p. 318). With the commodification of blood, the link between the needs of some and the generosity and goodwill of others is made considerably less necessary. As people rely more on the market and less on their own practices of mutuality, the social sources of altruistic giving, empathy, community, and the moralizing experiences of group and associational life decline in strength.

Markets in blood not only minimize the obligation to help others, they also, Titmuss (1970) shows, are less efficient and safe than voluntary or gift systems. On four major measures, economic efficiency, administrative efficiency, price, and quality of blood obtained, the United States' commercial system was inferior to Britain's voluntary system.

In terms of economic efficiency it is highly wasteful of blood. . . . It is administratively inefficient . . . result[ing] in more bureaucratization, avalanches of paper and bills, and much greater administrative, accounting, and computer overheads. These wastes . . . are reflected in the cost per unit of blood [which is] five to fifteen times higher [in the United States]. And, finally, in terms of quality, commercial markets are much more likely to distribute contaminated blood. (p. 205)

On this last point, Titmuss found that blood supplied by the market carried a substantially higher risk of hepatitis. In 1968, accurate medical histories of the blood providers offered the only reliable means for screening for hepatitis. Givers of blood, acting out of altruistic concern for the welfare of others, had every reason to be truthful in their accounts. Many sellers of blood, motivated by personal gain, apparently had some reason to give dishonest reports.

The standard defense of the combined market-voluntary approach rests on two key claims, both of which are discredited by Titmuss's argument. The first claim is that the combined approach enlarges the freedoms available to people. Those who want to make gifts of their blood are free to do so, while others wishing to sell their blood are equally free to exercise their preference. As a consequence, and this is the second claim, the combined system has the capacity to generate larger supplies of and higher-quality blood. In addition to those who give altruistically, we also have those who are economically enticed into contributing to the blood supply. As the demand for higher-quality blood grows, and in turn, as the economic incentive for obtaining and supplying such blood becomes stronger, the market will respond efficiently to meet the demand. In fact, as mentioned above, the market system in the combined approach weakens the voluntary system by discouraging participation in it, and is a less efficient, more costly, and riskier method of acquiring blood. But what about the first claim, that the combined approach adds to people's freedom by affording the rights to buy and sell that are denied by the purely voluntary approach?

Titmuss's answer is that the freedom to buy and sell brought by the market detracts from the freedom to give. More specifically, as Singer (1977) develops this answer, market freedom in this area comes at the expense of the freedom to give in nonmaterial as well as material ways. "This means not merely the [freedom] to give money or some commodity that can be bought or sold for a certain amount of money, but the [freedom] to give something that cannot be bought, that has no cash value, and must be given freely if it is to be obtained at all" (p. 163). The freedom to make a gift to others of "something they cannot buy and without which they may die . . . relates strangers in the community in a manner that is not possible when blood is a commodity" (p. 161). This freedom is placed in peril by the market in blood. The gift system respects people's right to act altruistically, it does nothing to obstruct their freedom to exercise their capacities to help others in need, it promotes attitudes of concern for the welfare of others and provides abundant opportunities for developing the personal and social practices that facilitate giving, and it fosters solidarity and mutual assistance. For that which is most important to life, it has people rely less on the profit motive and more on the developed and socially sustained goodwill of each other.

Currently, the $2 billion market in whole blood in the United States is dominated by the Red Cross and two other nonprofit organizations. A pint of whole blood goes for about $100. Broken down into various components—plasma, albumin, Factor VIII, immune globulins—it will be worth up to $190 a pint. Commercial companies control the more lucrative components' markets, and now invest in research for new blood commodities and in expansion at a rate seven times higher than the Red Cross (Berry 1991). The commodifying spirit, aided by advances in medical technology, has spread to other areas as well. Infertile couples now can contract with healthy young women for "eggs that can be fertilized in the laboratory and implanted in the infertile woman's womb. . . . Even though it costs $10,000 for each attempt at a pregnancy with donor eggs," the *New York Times* (November 10, 1991, p. A1) reports brisk "consumer demand." In addition, there is growing pressure in the United States to establish markets in human tissue, corneas, kidneys, skin, and bones (Thorne 1990). Such markets turn gifts into commodities, givers into vendors, "generosity into trade, gratitude into compensation" and, writes Leon Kass (1992), bring us "perilously close to selling out our souls" (p. 83).

Titmuss's discussion focuses on the debilitation of altruism and community that results from the market's colonization of gift relations, but many of the same points can be made with reference to the state. Michael Walzer (1982) asks us to imagine "a tax on blood, a legal requirement that every citizen contribute so many pints each year. This would greatly improve the supply, since it would increase the number of donors and enable medical authorities to choose among them, collecting blood only from the healthiest citizens, much as we conscript only the able-bodied for military service" (p. 434). The coercive regulation of blood donations by the state, like the noncoercive market form of regulation, Walzer argues, would devalue the gift and all it creates. It too, would diminish people's sense of personal responsibility for the fate of others and lessen the need for them to rely on one another (by increasing the need for them to rely on the state). Conscripted blood, like commodified blood, would come without the generosity, care, and concern of altruistically given blood, the very qualities that make for the gratitude that keeps the gift spirit alive.

Gifts require a certain kind of equality. "The recipient of a gift should, sooner or later, be able to give it away again" Hyde (1979:137) notes. "If the gift does not really raise him to the level of the group, then it's just a decoy." Without a commitment to equality, what would otherwise be a gift becomes charity. The charity shown by the rich to the poor tends to encourage deference and humility, not gratitude, in the latter and a sense of arrogant self-importance in the former. The charity provided by the welfare state as a matter of right tends to foster dependence and passivity. In contrast, the gift of blood studied by Titmuss

> does not represent an exercise of power by men and women who happen to be rich in disease-free blood; nor does it make for deference and dependency among those in need. Donors act out of a desire to help [others], and they do help, and undoubtedly they feel some pride in having helped. But none of this generates any special self-importance, for the help is widely available. The great majority of citizens are capable of giving blood. (Walzer 1982:434)

Similarly, most people are capable of giving compassion, personal attention, and neighborliness. When they have the opportunity to express their gratitude in these ways, they become part of a community of equals, as George Bailey and the people of Bedford Falls discovered.

To recognize that the market and the state constrict the opportunity to give in a way that creates and sustains the personal and social predicates of altruism, belonging, and mutuality is not to argue for the elimination of market and state forms of provision. It makes far greater sense to rely on markets instead of gift communities for a vast multitude of goods and services—subway cars, refrigerators, milk, and television repair. The list is nearly endless—but it does have an end, and—as Titmuss shows with reference to blood, that end ought to be respected. Similarly, the effective provision of basic welfare services requires the taxation power and governing capacity of the state. Yet, at best, the welfare state only can create, Walzer (1982) writes, "well-lighted places—hospitals, day-care centers, old-age homes, and so on—intelligently managed, free from corruption and brutality. Anything more than that, men and women must provide for themselves and one another" (p. 434). Anything more than that—friendship, neighborliness, a helping hand, an attentive ear, and an affectionate story—can be neither mandated by the state nor purchased in the market. Anything more than that comes only from gifts, from the cycle of generosity and gratitude, from the practices of mutual assistance that constitute society.

Gifts, Gratitude, and Trust

A "society where people are disposed to be trusting, and where their trust is generally well placed," writes Philip Pettit (1995), "is almost certain to work more harmoniously and fruitfully than a society where trust fails to appear or spread" (p. 202). In the absence of trust, people become apprehensive of and estranged from others, withdrawing from a world they regard as unfriendly, if not dangerous. The vigilance and suspicion they bring to their contacts with others remind us of the lives lived outside society by those in "Pottersville" and in Hobbes's state of nature, the Ik, the Buffalo Creek survivors, and pathological narcissists, all of whom seek survival in places hostile to the giving and receiving of gifts.

Gifts, and the cycle of gratitude, graciousness, and generosity they initiate, activate the conditions of trust. Gratitude feeds trust while it makes people more interdependent with one another and more likely to satisfy the obligations they incur in those interdependencies (see Mauss 1967:10–12; Blau 1964:94–107). Gratitude creates bridges across which generosity can flow, Georg Simmel ([1908] 1950) observed, and this makes it "one of the most powerful means of social cohesion. . . . If every grateful action, which lingers on from good turns received in the past, were suddenly eliminated, society . . . would break apart" (pp. 388–89). Generating an "atmosphere of generalized obligation [supportive of] infinitely tough threads which tie one element of society to another, and thus eventually all of them together in a stable collective life" (p. 395), gratitude fortifies the ground of trust. The social orderliness essential to trust rests in large part on the willingness of people to meet their social obligations, a willingness made more robust by gratitude.

The acquisition of trustfulness and trustworthiness during the earliest years of life, Erik Erikson (1968) has shown, depends on the experience of orderliness, continuity, and mutuality, particularly as they are expressed in the relation between child and mother. "Mothers create a sense of trust in their children by that kind of administration which . . . combines sensitive care of the baby's individual needs and a firm sense of personal trustworthiness within the trusted framework of their community's life style" (p. 103). The trustworthiness of the mother, a gift of sorts from a trusted and trusting community, is the initial and, according to Erikson, the most significant source of the sense of basic trust.

The mothering relation has much in common with the gift relation. Traditionally female labor, the labor of caregiving—teaching, social work, volunteer work, child care, nursing, and, most especially, mothering—is far more animated by the spirit of gifts than is male labor, a consequence in no small part of the long-established discrimination that has kept women from full participation in the market and the state. The care and mutuality that encourage the trust that holds together social relationships distinguish women's labor and lie at the center of mothering, a practice, Virginia Held (1990) notes, that can be undertaken by males as well as females.

The relation between a mothering person and child, like the gift relation and unlike the contractual relation, is an end in itself, one that subordinates self-interest to an altruistic concern for others. "The emotional satisfaction of a mothering person," Held writes, "is a satisfaction in the well-being and happiness of another human being, and a satisfaction in the health of the relation between the two persons, not the gain that results from an egoistic bargain" (p. 298). Mothering exposes people to the vulnerabilities of others and obliges them to care about the needs of the helpless, the weak, and the powerless. Mothering sharpens and gives substance to the capacity to take responsibility for the fates of others and thus fosters the gift of care that nourishes trust.

The mothering relation works this way, as Erikson previously noted, only in the context of trusted communities and institutions. In their absence, as the Ik example showed, mothering is reduced to an often cavalier exercise in teaching survival techniques. The point to be emphasized, is that the trust available to larger social entities is that which is generated in smaller, more intimate social settings. It is here where people first receive gifts and express gratitude, where they cultivate the social sentiments of sympathy and empathy, and where they are taught the practices of mutual assistance. Trust not only sustains, it is sustained by, the gift community, and is generalized outward to the obligations we have to strangers with whom we share the market and the state.

The special power gifts have to generate and sustain enduring, trusting, and open-ended relations, Marcel Mauss (1967) observed, was recognized by the Romans, Trobrianders, Samoans, and others who distinguished the "ordinary articles of consumption" exchanged through buying and selling from *sacra*, "valuable family property—talismans, decorated copper, skin blankets and embroidered fabrics [which] constitute the magical legacy of the people. . . . Each of these precious objects "contains the quality of soul and the power of communion that give it sacred significance (1967:42). Only when made available as gifts is there any assurance that these objects will retain their sacred character. In matters sacred, the gift is the only appropriate form of provision.

SACREDNESS

The sacred is that which people love, respect, and revere more than anything else. It symbolizes what a community or a society most values. The sacred and its affinity with the gift is most often expressed in religious terms and contexts. Gifts are given on sacred occasions to mark and celebrate births, weddings, and holy days. It is Christmas Eve, recall, when George Bailey receives the gifts that confirm his wonderful life. It would be a mistake, however, to define the sacred exclusively in terms of the religious, as we shall see below. Cramped into the Bailey living room, George, his family, friends, and neighbors, filled with the generosity and gratitude that move the spirit of the gift, celebrate not so much the birth of Jesus as the trust, mutuality, and community they continue to give each other.

Durkheim on the Sacred

The best sociological treatment of the sacred is the one produced by Émile Durkheim as part of his effort to combat the anomic forces of modernity. Religious thought and practice, Durkheim argued, rest on the profoundly significant distinction between the sacred and the profane. In dignity and power and as a source of inspiration and identity, the sacred is superior to the profane. The profane world is the world of everyday life. The objects in it are dealt with matter-of-factly, and profane activities—working, shopping, getting from one point to another, running errands, and doing chores—are carried out expeditiously and efficiently. In contrast, people approach the sacred and undertake sacred activities carefully and respectfully, that is, ritualistically in accordance with rites that prescribe how people should comport themselves in the presence of that which matters most. To treat the sacred without the care and the respect it deserves, to treat it as we treat the profane—for example, to take the Lord's name in vain, to shout it in anger or to mutter it without the ritualistic bowing of the head—is to commit a profanity.

The division of the world into sacred and profane spheres results, according to Durkheim, from the human experience of society. It is unquestionable, he wrote, that "society has all that is necessary to arouse the sensation of the divine in minds, merely by the power that it has over them: for to its members it is what god is to his worshipers" (Durkheim [1912] 1965:236). God, Durkheim claimed, is a symbolic representation of society. It is society that is larger than and exerts moral authority over individuals. In worshiping God we in effect pay our respect to society; in experiencing God, we actually feel the sacred qualities and moral force of our communion with others. This experience is heightened during ritual observances, during which people's thoughts

> are centered upon their common beliefs, their common traditions, the memory of their ancestors, the collective idea of which they are the incarnation: in a word, upon social things. . . . The spark of social being which each bears within him necessarily participates in this collective renovation. (Durkheim [1912] 1965:348)

For Durkheim, the sacred is the social, indeed, it "is the social carried to its highest point" (Nisbet 1966:244). Sacred ideals symbolize what a group regards as most important to its identity, and rituals bring the individual members of the group together, concentrating their attention on what they have in common. In this way, community is strengthened and so, too, is the "individual soul . . . by being dipped again in the sources from which its life came" (p. 348). The soul, the sacred quality of the individual, represents the social part of the person, that part which, like society itself, lives on after the death of the body and its egoistic appetites and private desires. People "set apart sacred things from profane ones because they set apart meanings that give the group its life as a group from the ordinary things that sustain the lives of the group's individual members" (Swidler 1992:613).

The sacred realm is a kind of sanctuary where that which the group most values about itself—community, mutuality, and cooperation—is sustained against the profanities of everyday life. That which has been endowed with sacredness—a crucifix, a star of David, a mosque, or birth, marriage, parenting, or citizenship—has been taken out of the world of profane things where it would have been treated instrumentally and efficiently and with an eye toward self-interested gain. What makes things into "'sacred objects' is not any characteristic they objectively have in common, but the way that the group behaves toward them. Behavior toward the sacred is what constitutes ritual; it is action carried out by the group, which expresses respect" (Collins 1988:190). Ritual transports people from the profane world to the sacred, it enables them to regenerate and to celebrate that which is most valued about their life in common, and it assembles people in respectful observance of those acts—think again of the Christmas Eve reunion / communion at George Bailey's house, or wedding ceremonies or baby showers—that sustain the most significant elements of the group's identity. Set in this context, Durkheim argued, social obligations—the obligations of parenting, neighboring, or citizenship—are taken more seriously and attended to more carefully by individuals and enforced more strenuously by the group. What is important to recognize, he insisted, is that as an obligation becomes more sacred, its fulfillment is less motivated by self-interest and by fear of group coercion, and driven more by people's desire to contribute to the group's most special and valued ideals and practices (Durkheim 1974:59; Cladis 1992b:84–86). People fulfill the sacred duties of parenthood, marriage, and citizenship because they desire to be good parents, good spouses, and good citizens. We can be more trusting of people to meet those obligations regarded as sacred in their society.

The sacred consists of those places and activities in and through which the moral individual acquires his or her soul, those higher and deeper parts of the self that enable the person to initiate and maintain the connections generative of resources of communality. Soul, in Durkheim's view, is the expression and the experience of solidarity or group unity, and in the individual, the soul gains substance with the cultivation of the social sentiments that anchor solidarity and unity. The "belief in the immortality of the soul," Durkheim wrote,

> is the only way in which men were able to explain a fact which could not fail to attract their attention; the fact is the perpetuity of the life of the group. Individuals die, but the clan survives. So the forces which give it life must have the same perpetuity. Now these forces are the souls which animate individual bodies, for it is in them and through them that the group is realized. ([1912] 1965:304)

The qualities essential to effective social life and, as well, to efficient markets and responsive governments are fed by the soul. Mutuality, co-operation, and trust are rooted in the empathy, sympathy, sociability, compassion, and general moral sense developed in those contexts set apart and given sanctuary from the profane principles of market and state.

The weakening of the sacred, according to Durkheim, signifies the erosion of society, the desiccation of rich, ongoing, intimate and associational relationships and of the social sentiments that flow into and out of them. As the sacred fades so too does collective identity. People lose faith in once-valued social ideals, practices, institutions, and norms. That which once mattered most and was a source of social solidarity and individual soul, slips into the profane world. There, having lost its power to evoke love and reverence and no longer regarded as special and significant, its obligations are greeted less seriously, less carefully, and less respectfully. There, that which was once sacred comes to be treated profanely, with an instrumental, expedient, self-interested attitude. Desecrating the sacred, treating it as if it were profane, is a sign of the deterioration of people's commitment to social life. And it reflects itself, Durkheim said, in people's increasing tendency to apply the profane standards of modernity, particularly the market calculus of "What's in it for me," to the social relationships and the social obligations of institutions and communitarian interdependencies. As this continues, Durkheim warned, we risk creating a world where nothing is socially valued, where nothing really matters, where everything is profaned; a world without society. With the desecration of the sacred and its social bases, social obligations lose their hold on people, people lose their desire to uphold social ideals, social ideals lose their clarity, certainty, and significance, ritual assemblies lose their intensity and regularity, private propensities and personal satisfactions take precedence over collective values, and society comes to resemble "Pottersville" more than Bedford Falls.

"The great malady of the twentieth century, implicated in all of our troubles and affecting us individually and socially," Thomas Moore (1992:xi) writes, "is 'loss of soul.'" Undefinable but imaginable, the soul "is tied to life in all its particulars—good food, satisfying conversation, genuine friends, and experiences that stay in the memory and touch the heart" (p. xi). The loss of soul, Moore claims, is expressed in the primary "emotional complaints" of the age: "emptiness, meaninglessness, vague depression, disillusionment about marriage, family, and relationship, a loss of values, yearning for personal fulfillment, a hunger for spirituality." A Jungian psychotherapist and former Catholic priest, Moore appears to be well positioned to advise on "the care of the soul," the title of one of his three best-selling books, a collection aptly described by *Time* (June 24, 1996, p. 65) as "'owners guides' to late 20th century souls." Drawing from ancient psychologies and myths for "insight and guidance," the care of the soul Moore profitably pursues seeks to recover "a sense of the sacredness of each individual life . . . the unfathomable mystery that is the very seed and heart of each individual" (1992:19). In doing this, we refuse "to sidestep negative moods and emotion, bad life choices and unhealthy habits. [If] our purpose is first to observe the soul as it is, then we may have to discard the salvational wish and find deeper respect for what is actually there" (p. 9). The soul, like the inner child celebrated by Moore's therapeutic predecessors on the best-selling lists, requires not the hard work of salvation but the warm and comforting embrace of nonjudgmental acceptance. Moore is explicit in this regard: "Care of the soul is not a project of self-improvement nor a way of being released from the troubles and pains of human existence. It is not at all concerned with living properly or with emotional health. . . . We care for the soul solely by honoring its expressions, by giving it time and opportunity to reveal itself, and by living life in a way that fosters the depth, interiority, and quality in which it flourishes" (p. 304). In caring for the soul, "we ourselves"—not professional therapists, priests, nor even for that matter those with whom we share good food, satisfying conversations, and genuine friendship—"have both the task and the pleasure of organizing and shaping our lives for the good of the soul" (p. 4).

Neither self-improvement nor the construction of institutional and communal standards of the good with reference to improvement is defined and pursued, but the re-enchantment of life is Moore's prescription for the recovery and appreciation of the soul. "Enchantment is an ascendancy of the soul, a condition that allows us to connect, for the most part lovingly and intimately, with the world we inhabit and the people who make up our families and communities" (Moore 1996:xi). To what do soul-carers turn in search of re-enchantment? Moore suggests astrology, divination, magic, angels, medieval psychology, and sacred places: the road from Rome to Florence at sunset, the New England woods with

Henry David Thoreau as guide, castle ruins in England, an ancient seaside church in Ireland are high on Moore's list.

The re-enchantment of everyday life Moore advocates does not entail a rejection of the burdens of modernity. Just the reverse; it offers pockets of time and space in which modernity's individuals are able to secure the emotional comfort and spiritual meaning that anchor psychic satisfaction amidst the disillusioning forces of modernity. Moore urges his patients and readers to sample the wide variety of mythologies, spiritual practices, and re-enchantment techniques in order to create for themselves a package of sacredness appropriate to their personal needs and circumstances. In his hands, sacredness and soul no longer challenge; indeed, they are made to accommodate the complacent self-seeking egoism of the liberal individual. The soul Moore popularizes does not stand against the market, for many of its accouterments are supplied by the market, a point well recognized by Deepak Chopra, a fellow traveler of Moore's on the best-selling lists. Combining Indian mysticism, transcendental meditation, and Ayurvedic herbal cures, Chopra's books, tapes, lectures, and videotapes market with extraordinary success a spirituality that claims to reduce blood pressure, heart attacks, and stress, reverse illness, and retard aging (Van Biema 1996). Spirituality heals, the soul adds spice to food and conversation, and enchantment awaits the next trip to Italy or this weekend's hike through the woods in the backyard. No wonder consumer demand for the sacred is on the rise.

Yet as Durkheim knew, the yearning for soul that underlies the unease of modernity's individual cannot be answered by private vendors of customized spirituality. The sellers of instant soul betray their own loss of soul as they erect their Soul-Marts on once-sacred ground. The re-sanctification of this ground—the strengthening of institutions and communitarian interdependencies wherein social sentiments are nourished and practices of mutuality are cultivated—is the proper response to the loss of soul. Alas, it is not a response for which there is or even can be consumer demand.

Modernity and the Sacred

There is no inherent antagonism between the sacred and modernity. Indeed, Durkheim insisted, the central achievements of modernity—individual freedom, equality, democracy, justice, pluralist diversity, human rights, and dignity—require consecration for their continued sustenance. Only as part of society's sacred realm will they be accorded the respectful attention and given the personal commitment their continued existence requires. As sacred objects and ideals, they would be treated

with affection and reverence, and the obligations they impose on people—
the obligation to treat others fairly as individuals worthy of dignity, the
obligation to respect and tolerate different points of view, the obligation
of active and informed citizenship essential to democracy—would be
taken more seriously. As a sacred object, the individual stands more
securely and stronger than she does as a carrier of selfish interests or a
bearer of state-enforced rights. However, as Durkheim knew, as modernity develops social life comes to be regulated increasingly by the principles of the profane world of the market and the state.

Jacques Attali (1991) describes the tension between modernity and the
sacred in these terms:

> Having routed any historical alternative, the liberal ideals of democracy and
> the market now reign, from East to West. . . . Democracy and the market
> both intrinsically operate on the principle of "reversibility" within a short-
> term perspective. The essence of both . . . is choice: The capacity to change
> and reverse what is, be that ousting an incumbent political leader or replac-
> ing last year's car with the latest model. . . . Such is the temporary character
> of the culture of choice. . . . The ideology of reversibility, however, cannot
> be the basis of a civilization. . . . If there is no sanctuary from the regime of
> immediacy; if the very foundations of an enduring civilization are not
> placed off limits to the market and the politics of the moment, we will surely
> perish. (pp. 20–21)

The mentality of immediate reversibility focuses on individuals' ever-
changing desires and preferences, and is at odds with the long-term commitment and trust that maintain social relations and social obligations.
When brought to bear on what people care about most, be it family,
community, individual dignity, or justice, it leads to their devaluation.
The challenges to the liberal ideology of short-term reversible choice
made by religious fundamentalism and by various movements calling for
the restoration of traditional authority lead in the wrong direction, Attali
argues, and threaten the indisputable accomplishments of modernity. The
task is not to demolish the market and the democratic state. It is, rather, to
make sacred—to place off limits to the market and the state—those objects, ideals, social relations and social practices that matter most to a
civilized life and that require for their existence and growth the care,
respect, seriousness, affection, attention, and commitment discouraged by
the liberal market and the liberal state.

This is the point suggested by Elizabeth Anderson's objections to the
commodification of women's reproductive labor represented by commercial surrogacy. Anderson's argument, examined in Chapter 1, is not
that commodification is bad in itself. It is, rather, that certain *goods*—
childrearing, parenting, and family, among them—can exist and be valued properly only when beyond the reach of the market. Their preserva-

tion requires that they be treated with the care, respect, and reverence accorded sacred objects. Applying market principles to these goods profanes and corrupts them. As a consenting party to a commercial surrogacy contract, the mother is obliged to behave in ways appropriate to a seller of services and a legal subject. Thus, she is obliged to behave in ways that violate the social ideals and norms that define, make possible, and bestow significance on mothering. As a contracted supplier of a commodity, the mother is no longer a mother. Commodification is wrong, Anderson insists, when extended to those goods whose continued existence depends on social values and practices that run counter to the principles, attitudes, and behaviors advanced by the market.

Where Anderson focuses on the wrongness of commodification, Richard Titmuss, in his study of blood donations, concentrates on the rightness of noncommodification (Radin 1987:1910–14). Like Anderson, Titmuss argues that limits must be set on the market so that certain areas of social life can be given the special treatment they warrant. Only because they exist in noncommodified form, certain acts and practices, like the gift of blood, have the capacity to generate valued goods—altruism, trust, solidarity without deference, compassion without humility and passive dependency. Given the indispensability of such goods to a decent social life, Titmuss argues, it is important that their specialness, their sanctity, be upheld. When commodification detracts from people's ability to care seriously about the things that must matter if a tolerable, never mind civilized, human existence is to be maintained, it should be prohibited.

Noncommodification, Margaret Radin (1987) notes, "places some things outside the marketplace but not outside the realm of social intercourse" (p. 1853). The market is only one way of creating, distributing, and enjoying goods and services. The state offers a second way, but its administrative principles and tendency to juridify social relations share with market principles the capacity to degrade and diminish the sacred qualities of certain goods and services. Goods and services also can be made available socially in the form of gifts. Indeed, for some goods, as Radin (1987:1864) notes, the "preclusion of sales often coexists with encouragement of gifts." Thus, as Titmuss finds, gifts of blood increased to meet rising need in Britain's noncommodified system, but decreased, despite growing demand, in the mixed system of the United States. Moreover, the giving of sacred goods and services not only does not demean, it most often enhances their sacred qualities. Offered as a gift, given altruistically and with compassion, surrogate mothering would lose the power to degrade that it has in the commercial system and would have in a state-administered system. The gift of surrogate mothering does nothing to make either the child or the mother less worthy of respect and consideration, it does not diminish the social practice of pregnancy or require a rejection of the parental obligation to love the child, and like the gift of blood, it helps sustain the gratitude, generosity, and mutuality that make for trusted social settings.

If such social settings are to endure, their sanctity has to be respected, and this entails a reduced reliance on market and state forms of provision. Gifts are the appropriate form of provision for many goods and services that matter most to a society's conception of human flourishing. In the sacred realm, we get what we need as gifts. Indeed, much of what we need—the love of a parent, a friend's affection, a neighbor's empathy, the generosity of a community, the respect and consideration of a stranger— can come to us only in gift form. By having us rely on one another, gifts enlarge sociability and solidarity which, as Durkheim knew, give substance to the individual's soul. If modernity's individual is to be more than a possessor of selfish interests and a bearer of political rights, if he or she is to have a soul as well, it is necessary to recognize and protect the sacred character of society, and thus, to treat with seriousness, care, and respect our obligations to give as members of families, neighborhoods, and communities. The lessons learned and the capacities developed here are often carried outward to more general social commitments. To do otherwise, to set no limits to the market or the state, threatens both to degrade those social ideals and practices whose special significance resides in the fact that they are upheld by people without regard to self-interest or fear of external coercion and to sap the communality-giving power of the gift. To do otherwise is to risk doing to society what Mr. Potter intended to do to Bedford Falls.

In the absence of society, where we find Hobbesian man, the IK, the Buffalo Creek survivors, and the pathological narcissist, people do not come together to celebrate and to show their respect for that which they collectively most value. There is no common enterprise, nothing matters beyond individual survival, nothing is sacred, and there are no gifts. If modernity's individuals show some resemblance to those who dwell outside society, it is because they find themselves increasingly in a place where the sacred has been profaned and gifts have been commodified. The shrinkage of the sacred and the commercialization of the gift are registered as the loss of soul, and it is this that is captured, however vaguely, in the current accounts of the precipitous decline in America's so-called social capital.

THE LOSS OF SOCIAL CAPITAL AS THE LOSS OF SOUL

Over the past quarter-century, James Coleman (1990b) argues, the United States has experienced a precipitous decline in the social capital available for raising children, partly as a consequence of the spread of an "advanced individualism, in which cultivation of one's own well-being has replaced interest in others" (p. 336). Within families, parents devote increasingly less time and personal attention to their children and their activities. Within communities, "the erosion of social capital, in the form of effective norms of social control, adult-sponsored youth organizations, and informal relations between children and adults, has been even greater" (p. 336). Following Coleman's lead, Robert Putnam (1995a) documents a more extensive depreciation of America's social capital. Starting in the 1960s, trust and civic engagement, the two key aspects of social capital according to Putnam, entered into an accelerated pattern of decline that continues to this day. "The downtrends are uniform across the major categories of American society—among men and among women; in central cities, in suburbs, and in small towns; among the wealthy, the poor, and the middle class; among blacks, whites, and other ethnic groups; in the North, in the South, on both coasts and in the heartland" (p. 673).

Rates of civic participation have fallen steadily. Voter turnout is down as are attendance at public meetings and involvement in church-related groups and Parent-Teacher Associations. Civic and fraternal associations have weakened as fewer people claim membership in women's groups, like the League of Women Voters, or in men's service groups, like the Elks and the Shriners. Fewer volunteer their time to Boy Scouts and the Red Cross. Participation in bowling leagues, discussion groups, labor unions, and professional associations has plummeted as well (Putnam 1995a:666–67, and 1995c:68–70). This dilution of associational density and vitality has been accompanied by the deterioration of trust. Americans' willingness to trust government, people whose backgrounds are different from their own, and one another has followed the downward slide taken by civic engagement (Putnam 1995c:73). In a national survey commissioned by the *Washington Post* (January 31, 1996, A5), over "[s]ixty percent of the 1,514 adults interviewed . . . agreed with the statement that 'you can't be too careful in dealing with people,' while 35 percent agreed that 'most people can be trusted.' Half those surveyed believed 'most people would try to take advantage of you if they got a chance.'" Rising levels of distrust, the survey responses indicate, are connected to evermore virulent anti-government sentiments and growing support for right-wing policies which favor a larger and less regulated market presence (*Washington Post,* January 29, 1996, A1).

The market, many of its defenders insist, does not require trust, loyalty, compassion, or personal virtue for its efficient operation. Perhaps, a growing number of Americans are learning this lesson, and, finding no good reasons to trust either government or one another, accept the market precisely because, unlike government and civic associations, it works well amidst cynicism, indifference, heightened self-regard, and mistrust. Yet, as we learned in Chapter 3, not only does the market require little in the way of trust, it often promotes messages and attitudes that poison the ground from which rise good reasons to trust. Perhaps, the turn away from public projects and civic engagements and the turn toward the market currently taken by more Americans signify the triumph of these messages and attitudes as they have been relentlessly advanced by the meaner and increasingly more savage market economy whose development over the past two or three decades is as substantial as the drop in trust and civic associational life. Overexposed to this soul-denying market, Americans in larger numbers rush to it, not in search of salvation, which they probably suspect is found elsewhere, but on the lookout for individual survival in an unreliable world, a task whose burdens might be eased by the occasional herbal cure, re-enchanting tour, or some other form of market-supplied spirituality.

The political Right disputes the connection between the market economy and the decline of social capital, focusing instead on the growth of big government as the primary destroyer of trust and associational life. Indeed, the political Right has gravitated to the notion of social capital with its emphasis on mutual reliance and cooperation to justify its efforts to diminish the welfare and regulatory responsibilities of the state. According to Fukuyama (1995), "the expansion of the welfare state from the New Deal on, which tended to make federal, state, and local governments responsible for many social welfare functions that had previously been under the purview of civil society, accelerated the decline of those very communal institutions that it was designed to supplement" (p. 313). Compounding the problem, in Fukuyama's view, is "the vast expansion in the number and scope of rights to which Americans believe they are entitled, and the 'rights culture'" whose broadening interpretations of individual rights had the effect of making

> the state . . . an enemy of many communal institutions. Virtually all communities saw their authority weakened: towns were less able to control the spread of pornography; public housing authorities were forbidden from denying housing to tenants with criminal or drug abuse records; police departments were enjoined from even such innocuous activities as setting up sobriety checkpoints. (1995:314–15)

Big government in its various manifestations, Fukuyama claims, shuts down opportunities for spontaneous sociability while supplying disincentives for mutual reliance.

Putnam concedes that "some government policies have almost certainly had the effect of destroying social capital" (1995a:671). Yet, he cautions against the right-wing attack on big government and the welfare state in the name of social capital, noting first, that differences in social capital among states in the United States "appear essentially uncorrelated with various measures of welfare spending or government size," and, second, that "indicators of social capital" taken from nineteen developed countries "are, if anything, *positively* correlated with the size of the state" (1995a:671). It may be the case that under proper circumstances, the state is able to shore up the conditions of trust and civic engagement, or, at least afford them some protection against otherwise unbridled market forces.

The loss of social capital is attributed most commonly to a combination of related developments. One takes the form of an increasingly tighter squeeze on time and money. On the one hand, more Americans are working longer hours and more parents with children at home are working full-time than was the case twenty or thirty years ago. They have less time to devote to associational life. On the other hand, more Americans are unemployed and underemployed, their participation in the much celebrated "just-in-time," or contingent work force producing the economic insecurity that discourages trust and engagement. Relatively high levels of geographic mobility suggest that many Americans are frequently uprooted and, in the absence of a stable residence are unable to nurture the habits and practices of neighborliness. Women's greater participation in the labor market is said to come at the expense of their involvement in community activities. The rise in single-parent families, related to higher rates of divorce, adds to the squeeze on time and money that discourages trust-enhancing civic participation (Putnam 1995a:668–71).

More important than any of these factors, Putnam argues, has been the impact of television. Television has become a primary activity in the United States, absorbing "[f]orty percent of the average American's free time, an increase of about one-third since 1965" (pp. 677–78). Assessing research on the connection between television watching and social participation, Putnam concludes that "each hour spent viewing television is associated with less social trust and less group membership. . . . An increase in television viewing of the magnitude that the United States has experienced in the last four decades might directly account for as much as one-quarter to one-half of the total drop in social capital" (p. 678). By keeping viewers away from social gatherings, community projects, and informal conversations outside the home and by fostering skepticism about the motives of others, a generally pessimistic understanding of human nature, and a passive orientation to the world, television, in Putnam's account, sponsors a process of privatization harmful to trust and civic association.

Advanced by television, divorce, government policies, time and money pressures, mobility, or some combination of these factors, privatization, according to Putnam and most other observers, is the bane of social capital, driving people from the collective pursuits of associational life into the narrower confines of private life. The problem with this argument is that increasingly there is no private life into which people can be driven. As it was conventionally understood prior to the past thirty years or so, private life consisted of marriage and family, friendships, neighborly relations, community involvements, and other collective pursuits. Private life, in short, was centered on trust and engagement. Thus, the problem is not the withdrawal to private life but the deterioration of private life as a place set apart from the social capital–destroying forces of modernity. The differences between this older conception of private life and the current liberal individualistic understanding are important.

PRIVATIZATION AS INDIVIDUALIZATION VERSUS PRIVATIZATION AS SACRALIZATION

Shaped by liberal individualism, the current conception of privatization equates privatization with individualization, a process favored by both the rights rhetoric used by defenders of the welfare state and the market rhetoric employed by supporters of the market economy. For the former, the extension of rights enlarges the domain of privacy within which individuals are able to choose their lifestyles free from the impositions of others. For the latter, privatization as public policy scales back government and expands the market as that arena where individuals freely choose to act or not in accordance with their personal preferences. In both cases, privatization is defended for its contributions to individual freedom. Putnam's opposition to privatization—his argument that the retreat to the private concerns of personal life taken by rights-holding, preference-seeking television viewers depletes the stock of social capital— accepts the characterization of privatization as individualization given by the shared assumptions of rights and market rhetoric. This liberal individualist understanding of privatization rose to prominence over the past three decades. The individualization of private life it describes reflects the erosion of trust and engagement. Thus, it is not a coincidence that its increasing incorporation into popular consciousness, legal thought, and political policy closely parallels the decline of social capital. In each case, the process begins in the 1960s and accelerates from that point on.

The older understanding of privatization offered a defense of privacy that endorsed the autonomy of small-scale social settings, the family especially, in opposition to the autonomy of the isolated and, by implication, unaccountable and irresponsible individual. This view, as Milton Regan (1993) shows, received its first explicit expression in England in the last half of the nineteenth century as part of a largely middle-class effort to resist the atomizing, fragmenting, and disintegrating forces of modernity. To place limits on what they perceived to be an ascendant, often callously selfish individualism, the English middle class constructed and successfully sought legal sanction for a private sphere, "a sanctuary of emotional comfort and intimate companionship," which would foster bonds of altruism, a relational sense of self, and the personal character and ethic of duty that would restrain the push of market egoism. Comprised of relations that "reflected a network of complementary obligations rather than purely voluntary commitment of individuals to each other," the private sphere provided "a model of how a sense of community might be preserved" amidst the evermore powerful isolating and egoistic tendencies of the still emerging modern world (Regan 1993:33).

Throughout most of its history, American constitutional law devoted little systematic attention to privacy. When it did, as Michael Sandel (1989) notes, it defended privacy not in the name of the freely choosing individual but with reference to "the intrinsic value or social importance of the practice it protects" (p. 524). In its 1965 decision striking down the Connecticut law against contraceptives, *Griswold v. Connecticut,* the Supreme Court for the first time clearly explicated a constitutional right of privacy, relying on the older, then still dominant, view of private life.

> Would we allow the police to search the *sacred* precincts of marital bedrooms for telltale signs of the use of contraceptives? The very idea is repulsive to notions of privacy surrounding the marriage relationship. . . . Marriage is a coming together for better or worse, hopefully enduring, and intimate to the degree of being *sacred.* It is an association that promotes . . . a harmony in living . . . a bilateral loyalty. . . . It is an association for as noble a purpose as any involved in our prior decisions. (cited in Sandel 1989:526–27, emphasis added)

Like the Victorian understanding of private life, this one gives expressed recognition to the sacred character of the practice or institution whose privacy (or sanctity) it protects.

In its 1972 decision, *Eisenstadt v. Baird,* the Supreme Court struck down a law limiting the distribution but not the use of contraceptives on the grounds that it violated the right of privacy, such right now understood as inhering in people as individuals and not as participants in intimate associations or members of social institutions. *Eisenstadt* accords privacy to the individual separated from and, perhaps, in need of protection against, associational and institutional attachments.

> The marital couple is not an independent entity with a mind and heart of its own, but an association of two individuals each with a separate intellectual

and emotional make-up. If the right of privacy means anything, it is the right of the *individual*, married or single, to be free from unwarranted governmental intrusion into matters so fundamentally affecting a person as the decision whether to bear or beget a child. (cited in Regan 1993:40)

This view of the right of privacy as a right of the individual to choose a course of life independent of state interference was extended to include a woman's decision to continue or not her pregnancy in the landmark 1973 *Roe v. Wade* decision, and broadened still further three years later to make that choice also "free of interference by husbands or parents. In *Planned Parenthood of Missouri v. Danforth*, the court struck down a law requiring a husband's consent, or parental consent in the case of unmarried minors, as a condition for an abortion" (Sandel 1989:528). By this time, the older conception of privacy, with its view of private life as a sanctuary protective of the intimate associations and social institutions that sustain the "nobler purposes" of human existence, had effectively been laid to rest. The new conception of privacy as a right held by individuals abstracted from the world of trust and engagement rose to reflect and promote the liberal individualization and desecration of private life, leading to its transformation into an arena of detached individuals governed by the profane principles of market and state.

Privatization as individualization has replaced privatization as sacralization—the effort to preserve within modernity the sacred contexts and practices in which the individual develops the social sentiments and moral sense that constitute the soul. Privatization as liberal individualization profanes the sacred, buries the gift-spirit under an avalanche of commodities, and floods the space vacated by the soul with more keenly delineated personal preferences and individual rights. The consequence is the loss of those resources of communality that Putnam and others call "social capital."

CONCLUSION

In his analysis of the civic and uncivic regions of Italy, Putnam (1993a) concludes that the prosperity of the former, measured in terms of social capital, economic development, and government responsiveness, "rests on the expectation that others will probably follow the rules. Knowing that others will, *you* are more likely to go along, too, thus fulfilling *their* expectations" (p. 111). Behind this important claim, Margaret Levi (1996) writes, are a couple of yet to be clearly answered questions: "What are the origins of such an expectation? What are the mechanisms that maintain such an expectation?" (p. 45). I have argued that the answer to each question is found initially in the sacred act of gift-giving. Gifts initiate and sustain the expectation of reciprocity in a particularly powerful way by rooting it in a cycle of gratitude, graciousness, and generosity capable of generating cooperative interdependencies and ongoing practices of mutual benefit in the context of which people cultivate the compassion, goodwill, and trustworthiness that energize spontaneous sociability and feed the resources of communality. Expectations grounded in gratitude and regarded as sacred, that is, valued as important to the preservation of the places and activities that nourish a higher sense of self, are taken quite seriously. If this is correct, then privatization properly understood as sacralization, as the effort to reconstruct a sacred sphere of intimate and civic associations and social institutions alive with the spirit of the gift, and, thus, a sphere resistant to the quantitatively precise measurements demanded by economists and other counters of capital, is an important part of any attempt to reverse the decline of the resources of communality.

CHAPTER

6

The Politics of Social Breakdown: Revitalizing Civil Society

Twenty years ago, Christopher Lasch (1978) used the psychoanalytic term *narcissism* to illuminate his insightful and widely influential critique of American society. Displaying in muted form many of the traits of patholog-ical narcissism, America's liberal individuals as normal narcissists increas-ingly found themselves psychologically incapable of meeting even the most elementary social commitments. Placed within an expanding culture of narcissism, Lasch argued, this psychological incapacity was refashioned to appear as a liberating impulse animating revolt against the oppressive restraint of institutional obligations and communal expectations.

The narcissism metaphor already has lost much of its power to capture the spirit, or, better, the spiritlessness, of America's liberal individuals at the end of the twentieth century. Partly as a consequence of the successful revolt against society celebrated by the culture of narcissism, the institu-tional ideals and obligations and communal expectations that society comprises have become so diluted that few experience them as oppres-sive restraint. The culture of narcissism is being replaced by a culture of inattentiveness, in the context of which damaged institutional and asso-ciational life are experienced as boring, not oppressive. Attention-deficit disorder supersedes narcissism as the diagnosis of choice, a further sign of the collapse of the social places wherein people cultivate the psycho-logical resources and social practices of attention.

THE INABILITY TO ATTEND

Attention-deficit disorder (ADD) is a neurobiological malfunctioning of the brain and central nervous system that causes extraordinary impul-siveness, distractibility, lack of concentration, and, in some cases, hyper-activity. It is treated most commonly with stimulants such as Ritalin.

Currently, ADD is "the most common behavioral disorder in American children [and] one of the fastest growing diagnostic categories for adults" (Wallis 1994:43–44). In the United States, prescriptions for Ritalin rose by nearly 400 percent between 1990 and 1994, while its production increased by 500 percent between 1990 and 1995 (Diller 1996:12). The recent epidemic in ADD appears confined to the United States. In other countries, where the disorder is rarely found in adults, the incidence of ADD has remained steady, and the number of cases is typically 10 percent of the current total in the United States (Wallis 1994:45). In the absence of evidence of spreading neurobiological deterioration among American children and adults, it makes sense to understand the ADD epidemic as a reflection of a social and cultural deterioration that produces in people many of the traits associated with attention-deficit disorder.

Among the criteria used to clinically diagnose ADD are the following: difficulty getting organized, focusing attention, getting started and following through, chronic procrastination, low tolerance for boredom and frustration, impatience, easy distractibility, impulsiveness and restlessness, a strong sense of insecurity and underachievement, low self-esteem, and a strong need for high stimulation expressed behaviorally as a frequent search for the novel and the exciting (Hallowell and Ratey 1994:73–76). To be eligible for the ADD diagnosis, children and adults must display an inability to plan and lead a coherent life, and show a marked tendency to experience as boring and frustrating routine activities and tasks demanding attentive care, patience, disciplined concentration, and perseverance. In short, they must evince a predisposition to both boredom and a reliance on external sources of stimulation.

In the absence of neurological malfunctioning, what accounts for these traits? Douglas Heath argues that the tendencies to be bored by the routine, the complex, and the long-term and to pursue constantly novelty and excitement reflect the impoverished status of resources that help make up character: An underdeveloped willpower weakens the ability to control impulses and to resist distraction and frustration in the face of complexity and tediousness; inadequately realized coping skills undercut persistence, dedication to task, adherence to plan, and devotion to the completion of projects; diminished capacities of empathy and collaboration discourage the effort to know the views of others, an effort that gives rise to habits of reflection and cooperation which provide direction and meaning to difficult tasks (1994:8–21). According to this view, inattentiveness caused by deficit of character, not by some chemical misfiring between the brain and the central nervous system, is the primary force behind the ADD epidemic in the United States.

Showing in less extreme form many of the characteristics of ADD, culturally endorsed inattentiveness finds a wide variety of expressions. It has a prominent role in the consumerist culture that supplies in the form of amusement and entertainment an endless proliferation of distractions that extend the operating principles of MTV and national tabloids—that is, short attention span plus stimulation by images that shock and titillate, equals more buyers—to news broadcasts and magazines, to political campaigns and senate hearings, to television and radio talk shows and murder trials. Inattentiveness born of meager inner resources appears in America's schoolrooms as well, in the form of students less educable than in the past. Students at all levels, compared to their counterparts twenty years ago, Heath (1994) finds, are less able to stay with tasks for an extended period; they experience greater difficulty in formulating and implementing plans and carrying out cooperative tasks; they are more easily bored, less likely to work on projects for which they have no interest, and in greater need of entertainment; they are less intrinsically motivated and able to manage time; they lack the self-discipline, persistence, and the ability to concentrate for long periods as did their predecessors; and they display lower levels of confidence in their abilities alongside higher degrees of self-doubt (Heath 1994:3–6, chap. 3).

To attract the interest of their students, schools may wish to follow the lead of megachurches, whose recent and rapid development puts them among the most influential forces in American Protestantism. Amidst the stagnant or declining rates of membership affecting most churches, megachurches have grown substantially in size by employing "a well-developed array of methods rooted not only in scripture, but also in commercial marketing" (Spiegler 1996:42), to appeal specifically to people who find church irrelevant and boring (Niebuhr 1995a:14). In place of long, ritualized services and detailed creeds and catechisms, Willow Creek Community Church, outside Chicago, offers its 27,000 members shorter, more casual services that supply practical advice in a setting modeled after late-night television talk shows as well as "aerobics classes, bowling alleys, counseling centers, and multimedia Bible classes where the presentation rivals that of MTV" (Niebuhr 1995a). In Houston, the Second Baptist Church, with over 20,000 members and a staff of 500, has with equal success used its "vigorous entertainment schedule [drawn from] expertise the church gained through consulting with Walt Disney World" both to justify its image as "The Fellowship of Excitement" and to provide spiritual stimulation to the religiously inattentive (Spiegler 1996:48; Niebuhr 1995b). If the sprawling structures that house the megachurches "evoke any sense of wonder," Paul Goldberger writes,

it is over the notion that they are churches at all. . . . Willow Creek Community Church has no religious symbols, not even a cross on its facade. . . . After the 4,500 seat auditorium in which services are held—that's theater seats, not pews—its largest rooms are two huge gymnasiums and a two-story atrium with tables in the middle and fast-food counters along the side. Add a McDonald's arch and it could be the food court in a nearby shopping mall. (1995:C1)

Like the shopping mall—and MTV, Walt Disney World, the purchasers of market research, and the suppliers of Ritalin—the megachurch draws its customers from a place that discourages focus and inhibits the cultivation of inner resources. The megachurches, in Goldberg's eyes, are built for "public entertainment," not for "private soul-searching" (1995:C6). But, of course. The prevailing inattentiveness signifies the impoverishment of the inner resources and social sentiments that give life to the soul. For those without a soul, hell is boredom, and salvation is something delivered by a "vigorous entertainment schedule."

Attention, Mikaly Csikszentmihayli and Eugene Rochberg-Halton write, "is the medium through which intentional acts can be accomplished. . . . When attending to something, we do so in order to realize some intention" (1981:4). Attentive people "are not only aware of their own existence but can assume control of that existence, directing it toward certain purposes" (p. 2). Consciousness, self-control, and the cultivation of purpose and habits of reflection mark the capacity to attend, a capacity that underlies the sense of responsibility for others and, more generally, an ethical life. Attention involves a "mental devotedness to something other than the self," and so promotes "a decrease in egoism through an increased sense of the reality of, primarily of course other people, but also other things" (Lipson and Lipson 1996:18). Attending to other people and other things means caring about and for them, often in selfless ways that have us focus on the requirements of the caring performance and the needs of others it is intended to meet. Hence, the resources of attentiveness—the self-control or willpower that sustains dedicated concentration and resists distraction; the coping skills that enable persistence in the face of frustration caused by complexity or tedium; the abilities to empathize and collaborate that propel a mental devotedness to the needs of others—these resources are easily enough put in the service of moral responsiveness.

Like trust, these resources, and the capacity to attend which they support, are developed in the social institutions and communitarian interdependencies that make up society. Viable institutions focus the awareness and energy of their members, imposing on them responsibilities and accountability, and challenging them to acquire the virtues that will enable them to achieve institutional goods and maintain a relational sense of self. Communitarian interdependencies, particularly those that make up the associational networks that generate resources of communality, have the same effect. "Associational life," Peter Berkowitz (1996) writes, "shifts the gaze of individuals away from themselves toward others; it generates in each an awareness of the needs and the limitations of others; it enlarges self-interest narrowly conceived by making vivid the private advantage that flows from cooperation for the public good; and it teaches the habits of cooperation and self-restraint by giving individuals regular opportunities to practice them" (p. 46). In short, attentive people—attentive children, parents, neighbors, community members, citizens, students and teachers, worshipers and clergy—come from attentive social institutions and communitarian interdependencies. The devastation of these social contexts is most responsible for both the growth of a culture of inattentiveness that makes distraction a way of life and the surge in the production of drugs designed to provide temporary relief from the emptiness and exhaustion that accompany the inability to attend to anything for an extended period of time.

The acquisition of attentiveness is facilitated by warm, supportive families where parents bring a caring and patient involvement to the concerns and activities of their children (Csikszentmihayli and Rochberg-Halton 1981:chap. 8). Attentive families are linked to the world outside the home by their members' engagement in civic, neighborhood, and community groups. In contrast to members of "cool families," members of "warm families [tend] to participate in voluntary groups. . . . The capacity to sustain attention [is] generalized beyond the family" (Bellah et al. 1991:257). In this way, warm families contribute to the neighborhood and community resources that reinforce the value and ease some of the burdens of attentive parenting. The evidence, some of it presented in Chapter 1, shows that the number of attentive families in the United States has declined significantly over the past several decades, a consequence of time and resource deficits caused by divorce, the entrance of more parents into the work force, and an ethos that encourages personal freedom as either self-fulfillment or individual survival.

The significant rise in the number of Americans diagnosed with attention-deficit disorder and in the production of and prescription for Ritalin, Lawrence Diller (1996) observes, "may reflect how the demands on children and families have increased as the social network supporting them has declined" (p. 17). As parents and other adults in the community have become less attentive to the needs and activities of children, "the pressure on the children to perform has increased while support needed to maximize performance has declined" (p. 13). As parents and other adults become less competent, children are expected to become more competent. With seeming irony, the culture of inattentiveness promotes the perception of and the movement for competent children (recall Hillary Clinton's and Penelope Leach's defense of children's rights, examined in Chapter 1). The irony disappears, of course, upon the recognition that inattentive families, neighborhoods, and societies have a powerful need for children who are sufficiently competent so as not to require attentive adults and social settings. In these circumstances, children at ever young-er ages are pressured to perform competently at ever-higher levels as life responsibilities and school tasks are pushed downward. The stress such pressure produces creates in many the inability to concentrate and the distractibility that mimic attention-deficit disorder. At the same time, par-ents and teachers are attracted more easily to Ritalin and other medicines that promise to enhance performance and competence by concentrating attention.

As recently as two or three decades ago, David Elkind (1995) observes, the family coalesced around the value of togetherness which held that "the family must be placed ahead of self and that doing things for and with the family must take precedence over doing things for oneself and with friends" (p. 11). Complementing the value of family togetherness, schools were designed to promote the personal adjustment of innocent children and immature adolescents to the expectations and rigors of the larger order. Currently, Elkind notes, the reigning value is autonomy, "whereby each family member pursues his or her own interests and puts these interests before those of family" (p. 13). With the shift from together-ness to autonomy, schools rejected personal adjustment as their primary task in favor of the cultivation of a self-esteem, which has as its core the perceived competence of self that is said to be essential for individual achievement in a highly competitive world. Self-esteem, Elkind writes, "reflects the permeable family value of autonomy and the need of each individual to be able to go at it alone if necessary. . . . Yet self-esteem, unlike adjustment, is regarded as largely the child's problem, not the joint responsibility of parents and schools" (1995:14). The view of self-esteemed and competent children allows incompetent adults to rest more easily. Children able to recite the alphabet at three, master decimal frac-tions by the fourth grade, and speak knowledgeably about sexually trans-mitted diseases by the time they reach puberty, may be children capable of succeeding despite family instability, neighborhood disorder, and the reduced time they spend with parents and in community-sponsored, adult-organized activities.

The culture of inattentiveness makes it difficult for parents to arrange their lives to support warm, attentive family settings. Yet, it does offer to inattentive parents two other ways to enhance their children's capacity to attend and improve their self-esteem or perceived competence and their performance. First, by fostering a cosmetic psychopharmacology that makes the use of prescribed mood-, focus-, and performance-enhancing drugs a matter of personal choice, it makes it easier for parents to obtain for their children the diagnosis of attention-deficit disorder and the prescription for Ritalin. Second, through the Individuals with Disabilities Education Act of 1990, it extends to those suffering from ADD and other impairments the right to special benefits and allowances (Zuriff 1996). Thus, the ADD diagnosis comes not only with a Ritalin prescription but with an entitlement to additional help, extra time, and customized measures of evaluation as well. In addition, the ADD diagnosis relieves parents of responsibility for the inattentiveness of their children and so conceals from them the real problem.

The real problem, once again, is the deterioration of the social settings within which people learn responsibility, cultivate trust, and develop willpower, coping skills, the capacity for empathy, and other character traits. In the United States, the ground ceded by these shrinking social settings has been taken over primarily by the market. Unable to reliably count on those inattentive others with whom they share family, neighborhood, and society, Americans more intensely look to the market for essential goods and services and for external stimulation (Bellah et al. 1991:261–62). Survival, security, and novel forms of excitement are available in the market in commodity form. Accompanying this increased reliance on the market has been a surging cynicism about the role of government. A *Washington Post* (January 31, 1996, A6) study released in early 1996 found that Americans had become "highly receptive to conservative, anti-government messages, and inclined to be hostile to liberal, pro-government themes," and related this development to an increasingly inattentive citizenry. Noting that anti-government animus exists most powerfully and most rigidly among less politically knowledgeable citizens, the survey reported that "two-thirds of those interviewed could not name the person who serves in the . . . House of Representatives from their congressional district. . . . Four in ten . . . did not know" who is the Vice President; two out of three could not name the majority leader of the U.S. Senate . . . three out of four were unaware that the U.S. senators are elected to serve six-year terms . . . nearly six in ten incorrectly believed that the government spends more on foreign aid than on Medicare" (January 29, 1996, p. A6).

The political Right has been the primary beneficiary of spreading inattentiveness. Its opposition to government and call for cutting taxes, spending, and regulations resonates well among inattentive citizens possessed of a confused, mistaken, and antagonistic understanding of government. Similarly, the Right's glorification of the market makes sense to those who depend on the market for the resources once supplied by attentive families and communities and for the stimulation once granted by the personal character developed in attentive social contexts. The politics of the Right—"the end of the era of big government," as the once left-wing leaning President Clinton favorably commented in his 1996 State of the Union Address—comes to fruition in the culture of inattentiveness, and it does so promising to restore the attentive social contexts whose demise contributed to its victory.

INATTENTIVE PARENTS AND THE POLITICAL RIGHT

Parental inattentiveness that makes parents bad by diminishing their capacity to meet their obligations to their children has strongly captured the interest of the political Right. Right-wing Republicans, reborn Christians, radio talk show hosts, and political strategists have ridden the issue of the declining fortunes of social obligation, especially in its parental form, to higher poll ratings, larger mailing lists and listening audiences, and increased contributions and book sales. According to their well-received view, the failure of personal responsibility and attentiveness that underlies the erosion of the sense of social obligation is attributable to two developments endorsed by various constituencies of the Democratic party: The 1960s–1970s counterculture which sapped the power of moral and religious stigma to enforce conventional expectations, and the welfare state that encouraged and enabled many to evade their responsibilities to their children and spouses.

To combat the consequences of countercultural decadence, the right-wing coalition offers prayer for the young, shame for the wicked, and Christian values for all. Yet, as Charles Murray (1994b) writes, the force of "non-economic social stigma . . . and religious belief" is largely "underwritten by economics" (p. 31). In the last analysis, people assume responsibility for their obligations and pressure others to do the same when they know that the failure to do so will hurt them economically. Thus, the centerpiece of right-wing Republican policy is the dismantling of the welfare state and its economic disincentives to personal responsibility. Disciplined by the market and shamed and stigmatized by re-moralized friends and neighbors, people will do what is right, not because it is right but because it is the most economically advantageous and least humiliating course of action. Self-interest and fear of reprisal focus people's attention and, just as Hobbes said, secure the fulfillment of social obligation.

Like the Hobbesian solution to the problem of social disorder, the right-wing response to personal irresponsibility and inattentiveness and the decay of social obligation is rooted in the principle of contract. The Personal Responsibility Act of 1995, which slashes nearly $81.5 billion over the next seven years from means-tested programs and limits the duration of welfare eligibility, is a featured provision of the Republicans' Contract with America. However, as we already have seen, approaching the problem of social obligation from assumptions appropriate to contractual obligation jeopardizes the already weakened contexts and diminished resources that enable people to attend to, that is, to recognize, take seriously, and carry out their social obligations.

As examined in previous chapters, a strong sense of social obligation has three primary roots: the understanding that arises from close interdependencies that others, given their special reliance on us, are particularly vulnerable to the choices we make and the actions we take; institutional identities that dispose us to seek the achievement of institutional goods and the satisfaction of role expectations as a way of affirming who we are; and a way of life whose appreciation for the importance of obligation is expressed concretely in the assistance provided by friends, neighbors, kin, and community associations and in a collective commitment to provide when necessary the minimal resources required for satisfying the obligation. Responsible and attentive parents require not economic incentives and threats of external sanction but close interdependencies, vital institutions, and a supportive social order.

Most people most of the time have little difficulty recognizing the responsibilities given them by the reliance and vulnerability of others with whom they share close interdependencies. Parents especially, are usually quick to acknowledge their obligation to their children. Certain circumstances, however, work against this. Conditions that place a premium on individual survival—conditions that accompany severe, prolonged food shortages and death camps, to take two well-documented examples—dispose people to regard others, including those closest to them, as potential threats to self-preservation. Environmental deprivation and extreme adversity teach people that the world is a hostile, dangerously unpredictable place and that indifference toward the needs and sufferings of others is a prerequisite for individual survival. The elimination of billions of dollars from nutrition, medical, and housing assistance programs and the limitation of welfare eligibility proposed by right-wing Republicans promise to push many of the desperately poor into the land of extreme adversity where the sense of social obligation is turned into a liability. More generally, the message conveyed by right-wing policy, namely, personal responsibility means you're on your own, powerfully reinforces as it reflects the survivalist mentality that has become more pervasive and deeply rooted with the steady decline of security in the lives of most Americans. Within the growing culture of individual survivalism, confidence in the trustworthiness of others and in the efficacy of collective cooperative solutions wanes, the range of mutual reliance sharply contracts, the call of vulnerability is muted, and the right-wing Republican message resonates well.

The political Right also threatens the already fragile institutional foundations of social obligation. In her influential article "Dan Quayle Was Right," Barbara Dafoe Whitehead attributes the deinstitutionalization of marriage and family in the United States in part to the political Left's popularization of rights rhetoric over the past quarter-century. Increasingly under the influence of political principles of individual rights, she writes, "[f]amily relationships are viewed not as permanent or binding but as voluntary and easily terminable [and] the family loses its central importance as an institution in civil society, accomplishing certain goals such as raising children and caring for its members, and becomes a means to achieving greater individual happiness—a lifestyle choice" (Whitehead 1993:84). Whitehead's point is a good one—when the quasi-legal language of individual rights displaces the institutional language of social virtue in the way people seek self-understanding, institutional authority and the social approval it confers are dissolved. But the point (and the former Vice President in whose name it is made) is, at best, only half right. The diminution of the institutions of marriage and family has been fueled as much by the market rhetoric championed by the right-wing as by the rights rhetoric promoted by left-wing Democrats.

Market rhetoric constrains its users to regard themselves and others as maximizers of self-interest whose wants and needs are satisfied most efficiently by commodities provided by the market. Market principles of ease of entrance, quick turnover, ease of exit, and cost-benefit calculation that guide the pursuit of the best deal are as corrosive of institutional obligations and identities as are the political principles of individual rights. Right-wing Republicans and their business and religious sponsors have used the media effectively to make market rhetoric more accessible and to legitimate its application to political, social, and moral problems.

The Right does more than disseminate and sanctify market rhetoric. Its policies empower, by deregulating, the market and leave people with fewer protections against the harsher consequences of a less restrained and thus meaner market. These consequences are particularly destructive of the familial institution. Market deregulation carried out by Republicans in the 1980s, an exercise current Republicans pursue with considerably more vigor, has been a primary contributor to the extraordinary increase in the inequality of wealth and income, the drop in real wages, the rise in the number of poor families, and the dramatic decline in the measure of economic security once provided by unions, government, and the employers they constrained. Family instability prospers in the resulting environment. Worn down by overwork or beset by the tensions and self-doubts produced by the reality or threat of unemployment and by downward mobility, parents devote increasingly less time to familial responsibilities and rituals and to interaction with their children.

The third basis of social obligation, a way of life concretized in stable neighborhoods, informal social networks, and community associations whose practices of mutual assistance ease some of the burdens of social obligation, has been diminished by the same forces responsible for the deterioration of close interdependencies and institutions. Preoccupied with the tasks of individual survival, applying the logic of market exchange to social responsibilities, struggling with the demands of overwork or with the demoralization of unemployment and downward mobility, American adults have decreased substantially their participation in neighborhood, community, and civic life. Hard pressed to give time and care to their own children, parents, unsurprisingly, have even less to offer the children of others. Tax cuts and runaway and downsizing corporations, more of which are promised by current right-wing policy, have sapped the ability of local governments to maintain programs and places capable of supplying temporary sustenance to overwhelmed parents and unattended children.

Right-wing Republicans formalized their contempt for the way of life appropriate to social obligation in their April 1995 vote to gut the Community Redevelopment Act (CRA) and to eliminate funding for the Community Development Financial Institution (CDFI) program (*U.S. News and World Report,* April 17, 1995, pp. 51–59). The CRA required banks to provide credit services, especially home mortgages, to all segments of the communities in which they operated, and thus protected poor, largely black and Latino neighborhoods against redlining. CDFI's nonprofit community development banks were designed to provide low-cost loans and practical assistance to credit-worthy members of declining neighborhoods for housing, rehabilitation, and small business creation. Like the CRA, the CDFI program was intended to give stability and continuity to threatened neighborhoods, and both were crafted to encourage members of such neighborhoods to involve themselves in the kinds of common projects that teach the skills and feed the spirit of mutuality. In their absence, the fragile obligation-enhancing qualities of neighborhoods on the edge surely will give way to the physical decay, incivility, and disorder that mark bad neighborhoods.

In short, with the active support of the business community and Christian fundamentalist groups, right-wing Republicans take aim at the essential underpinnings of social obligation. By advancing the conditions and attitudes that place a premium on individual survival, they help to cultivate indifference toward the vulnerabilities of others. In the market rhetoric they promote, institutional goods and the virtues that enable their achievement, both increasingly devalued by reinvigorated market forces, receive no expression. Their gleefully enacted tax and budget cuts deplete the resources used to support the informal and formal networks of assistance through which communities honor their collective commitment to important and difficult social obligations, like those involved in childrearing.

Clearly, the political Right is on to something. They have enhanced the popular appeal of their policies by presenting them as weapons in the war against the conditions that enfeeble social obligation and personal responsibility and destroy attentive social contexts. Moreover, there is more than an element of truth in their claim that personal responsibility and attentiveness find few friends among the long-term dependent clients of the welfare state and the more ardent practitioners of the culture of lifestyle freedom. In the final analysis, however, by adding muscle to already enormously powerful market forces, the policies of the Right make it even more difficult for people to attend to their social obligations.

So far, the Right has been the clear victor in the politics of social breakdown, in part because it not only was the first on the scene, it also helped define the scene, and in part because the consequences of social breakdown—spreading inattentiveness, especially—incline people to its antigovernment, promarket message. Lately, the political Left has joined the battle, arguing that its policies are more appropriate to the reversal of institutional, neighborhood, and community decline. The key notion in the politics of social breakdown is civil society. As 1995 drew to a close, Newt Gingrich defended the Republican party budget cuts in welfare and cultural programs as indispensable to the restoration of America's damaged civil society. A week and a half earlier, President Clinton promised to veto several Republican-proposed budget reductions, convinced they would impair an already sorely weakened civil society. One week after the Gingrich pronouncement, Senator Bill Bradley announced he would not seek re-election, using the occasion to criticize both Republicans and Democrats for doing little to stop and much to promote the deterioration of civil society. It comes as no surprise, then, that Faveed Zakaria (1995) reports that "civil society is hot. It is almost impossible to read an article on foreign or domestic politics without coming across some mention of the concept. And 'civil society' has bipartisan appeal; from Hillary Rodham Clinton to Pat Buchanan, politicians of all stripes routinely sing its praises" (p. 1). While the various defenders of civil society disagree over exactly what they are defending, each uses the term in order to examine and propose solutions to the dry rot eating away at the country's social infrastructure—family, community, social obligation, personal responsibility and attentiveness. Unfortunately, each also uses the term largely as it was originally formulated in the late eighteenth and nineteenth centuries by the defenders and mappers of liberal modernity. Civil society can be an effective guide to the reconstruction of America's social infrastructure only when understood in sociological terms.

CIVIL SOCIETY

Liberal modernity and the languages of individualism it sponsors develop at the expense of a language of solidarity whose words combine to enable people to speak of belonging and mutuality, of social virtue and common good. More to the point, as I have argued throughout, liberal modernity, on the back of the liberal capitalist market and the liberal democratic state, develops at the expense of the social settings of solidarity. The topographical map of liberal modernity, constructed by its defenders with increasing specificity throughout the nineteenth century, identifies two major settings of solidarity. One we may call society, and it consists of family, community, and the groups, associations, and relations that center around family and community. The second setting is made up of "publics," places where individuals meet to discuss matters of common concern and public interest. On the map of liberal modernity, society is counterpoised to publics. Society is particularistic, home to the narrow and exclusive solidarities of different groups and communities; publics are universalistic, requiring their participants to subordinate the limited concerns of their particular families and communities to the public good, the higher, more inclusive solidarity. On the map of liberal modernity, the market and the state are arranged to make it appear that they ease the tension between society and publics without seriously damaging the integrity of either.

In the real world of liberal modernity, as we have seen, the market and state have expanded in ways that have detracted significantly from the social settings of solidarity. Indeed, their expansion has seemed to extinguish the voices of solidarity that might counterbalance the estranging power of liberalism's market and rights rhetorics. This story is told best from a sociological perspective. Almost from the beginning, the sociological understanding of liberal modernity focused on the spheres of solidarity and the threats to them posed by constantly expanding markets and states. As the discipline of economics chose the modern liberal market as its field of study and political science set itself to examine the modern liberal state, sociology, at least for a while, devoted itself to the study and the defense of the solidarity-producing spheres of society and publics. The current low standing of sociology relative to economics and political science in academia, in policy-making circles, and in the popular imagination is just one sign of the emaciated condition of its object of study. Nevertheless, a sociological perspective is indispensable to both an account of the forces driving the starvation of solidarity and an effort to contain those forces before they completely destroy the social contexts that nourish the strong individuals liberal modernity claims to defend.

In what follows, I undertake two tasks. The first is to present the contours of liberal modernity by examining in greater detail the above-mentioned map, at the center of which is the liberal notion of civil society so influential to the contemporary politics of social breakdown. The second is to examine the sociological critique of liberal modernity and its alternative conception of civil society as a place where modernity's individuals learn to attend to the obligations they have to loved ones and strangers alike.

The Contours of Liberal Modernity

The map of liberal modernity rests on a couple of fairly simple yet enormously important distinctions. The first distinguishes the modern world from the premodern world. The second divides the modern world into private and public spheres.

Modern–Premodern Distinction. The last half of the nineteenth century witnessed numerous efforts to capture the fundamental differences between premodern and modern social life. Among the most influential is the contrast between gemeinschaft and gesellschaft drawn by the German sociologist Ferdinand Tonnies ([1888] 1957). On one level, the gemeinschaft–gesellschaft distinction represents two different types of social relations; on another, two different ways of thinking and feeling.

Unity is the defining condition of gemeinschaft—organic, communal, and moral unity, resting on a like-mindedness sustained by small-scale, close-knit, locally organized groups firmly rooted in common place and shared tradition. Bound to one another by ties of blood, kinship, and place, their lives regulated by time-honored customs and institutions they neither chose nor created, premodern people engage each other as whole persons in highly personal, face-to-face relations. While a primary source of mutual benefit, these relations and the obligations they impose are experienced as intrinsically worthwhile, and thus valued for their own sake. In contrast, the relations, associations, and institutions that define the modern world of gesellschaft are artificial, impersonal, and instrumental. They separate, fragment, compartmentalize, and so set asunder the bases of moral unity. Contractual relations, freely chosen and rationally designed by individuals seeking to achieve some limited and specific goals, reside at the center of gesellschaft. Bringing people together in a loosely connected, superficial, and usually temporary arrangement that permits the expression of only those traits pertinent to the specific purpose at hand, contractual relations and the rationally constructed rules and institutions that regulate them are valued not for their own sake but only to the extent they enable the efficient pursuit of limited ends.

The tradition-based, person-centered, organic ties of gemeinschaft, in Tonnies's account, are motivated by a natural will, impulsive, spontaneous, vital, and sociable in character. The ties that bind in gesellschaft, and they do so weakly, are the artificial creations of a rational will attuned to the calculation of advantage. In premodern gemeinschaft, ends are given by tradition, purposes by communal moral codes and institutional ideals, and choices are a reflection of character, of who one is, and thus are restricted in scope. In modern gesellschaft where the rational will prevails, "ends are forever posited anew, in response to changing circumstances and desires, by independent and rational actors. [Here] the choice of ends is arbitrary, but their pursuit is governed by rational calculation" (Selznick 1992:366). Reflecting the rational wills that consciously establish them, the beliefs and structures of gesellschaft isolate and uproot modern people, estranging them not only from one another but from their natural disposition toward solidarity as well.

Tonnies's antimodernism is transparent in his characterization of gemeinschaft and gesellschaft. Modernity is a cold, impersonal, often heartless place whose tenuous unity is supplied by calculated arrangements that appeal to personal interest. In contrast, gemeinschaft, in Philip Selznick's words, "brings to mind a society warmed by intimacy and united by brotherhood" (p. 366). A somewhat different account of the key differences between premodern and modern society, one that examines the dark side of the former and the positive achievements of the latter, is found in the work of the contemporary sociologist James Coleman (1991, 1993).

Coleman's distinction between primordial and purposively constructed social organization parallels the gemeinschaft–gesellschaft distinction in several important respects. As it existed prior to the great transformations initiated by the French Revolution and the Industrial Revolution, the premodern world, in Coleman's account, revolved around primordial social organizations rooted in

> birth and the social relations of blood ties. The elementary social unit [was] the family, and in nearly every society . . . the social structure grew outward from this elementary unit, and economic production took place in and around it. . . . The clan and the tribe, the manor of the Middle Ages, and the feudal structure [were] in some way derivative of the family. [S]ociety took the family and kinship relations as the basis for larger social structures. (1993:2)

Emergent from the family, rather than designed, primordial social organizations served multiple purposes and brought their members together in dense, personal, close (and usually closed) social relations.

In contrast, the purposively constructed organizations that make possible and drive the modern world are rationally designed for some specific purpose, the achievement of a particular goal or the resolution of a particular problem. Purposively constructed organizations like the bureaucratic state and the modern business corporation are highly impersonal, comprised as they are of relations between formally defined positions or offices to which people are temporarily assigned and in which they become, like the positions themselves, a means for the achievement of the organization's purpose. In addition, purposively constructed organizations use "rules, laws, supervision, formal incentives, and sanctions by designated agents [and are] in a position to provide positive incentives for performance" (Coleman 1993:9). In Coleman's assessment it is this reliance on positive incentives and rewards to elicit desired behavior that makes the modern world of rationally designed social arrangements potentially superior to the primordially organized premodern world.

The social order achieved by primordial social organizations was supported by control measures based on "coercion, constraint, and negative sanctions, under the oppressive blanket of closed communities" (Coleman 1993:14). The essence of gemeinschaft, Coleman suggests, is captured best not by "warm intimacy" but by a harsh and repressive tyranny of the group that promoted inequality and discrimination, stifled hope, aspiration, and individuality, and blocked innovation and creativity. Purposively constructed social orders, to the extent that they employ positive incentives and rewards to motivate performance of valued tasks, substantially minimize the hostility toward equality, justice, innovation, and individuality found in the premodern world.

Drawing from Tonnies's and Coleman's characterizations, we are able to sketch the premodern–modern distinction as it was generally regarded in the nineteenth century. Premodern society is traditional, communal, and largely centered on locally organized particularistic groups, most especially family, kinship, and community groups. The dominant relations are personal in character, relations between and among particular, more or less familiar persons, and they are regulated by nonrational customs and institutions, that is, customs and institutions that arose over long periods of time spontaneously (Coleman) or as a consequence of the exercise of natural will (Tonnies). The small-scale, tightly knit exclusive units of premodern society give rise to a powerful value consensus and employ negative sanctions, ranging from gossip to physical beatings, to enforce adherence to rigidly defined expectations. While actively nourishing solidarity, the premodern world mobilizes its resources against the growth of individualism. In contrast, the modern world is individualistic and rational. Social relations are impersonal, structured either by contract or by bureaucracy, and are regulated by rationally designed rules and associations. Marked by a high degree of value diversity and a curiosity about and tolerance for the differences that make possible the development of the individual, the arrangements of the modern world display an abiding respect for the rights of the individual and are constructed in an effort to assure that most individuals most of the time will find it in their personal interest to freely choose to abide by the minimal rules that underlie orderly existence.

Public–Private Distinction. On the map of liberal modernity, the modern world is divided into a public sphere and a private sphere. As liberal modernity developed, the public sphere came to be equated with the liberal democratic state, the private sphere with the market-driven capitalist economy. The liberal state and the liberal market alike are justified in terms of their contribution to individual freedom. Yet, the map also identifies two primary sources of solidarity within liberal modernity. The first shares the private sphere with market relations and consists of the intimate, premodernlike settings formed by family and communal groups, what we previously referred to as society, from which emerge particularistic solidarities rooted in blood, common place, and sentiment. The second, located in the public sphere alongside the liberal democratic state, are those public spaces where individuals meet to discuss matters of common concern in an effort to rationally construct an inclusive, universalistic solidarity of common citizenship.

The liberal democratic state, like any other state, is an agent of coercion, yet its exercise of coercive power is limited by its liberal democratic character. As a liberal state, it is designed to preserve the conditions of individual freedom. As a democratic state, it is obliged to be accountable and responsive to the democratically expressed will of its citizens (within the limits allowed by its uncompromisable commitment to individual freedom). On the map of liberal modernity, the state appears largely as an administrative agency (though given its concentration of power, a potentially dangerous one), primarily responsible for defending and developing the ground of individual freedom. In part, this requires the state to support those political freedoms of speech, thought, assembly, and press that enable individuals to constitute themselves as critical publics.

In publics, individuals "confer in an unrestricted fashion, with the guarantee of freedom of assembly and association and the freedom to express and publish their opinions—about matters of general interest" (Habermas 1974:49). Publics are autonomous and protected arenas for rational public discourse. Such discourse is carried on by individuals without fear of reprisal, takes place in accordance with the standards of reason, not those of emotion or established authority, and is critical in the sense that views are challenged, debated, contradicted, and if necessary, rejected. The result is public opinion—normative judgments about the general interest or the common good from which derive the standards of legitimacy to which the state is held accountable.

In this context, publics are seen as constituting an independent base from which the state's public authority and exercises of power are debated and critically assessed by private persons assembled into a public body for the purpose of public discourse. Uniting in this fashion, rational individuals as citizens are able to construct for themselves in the form of public opinion a solidarity before which the state is compelled to justify—and thus make public—its decisions and actions.

The private sphere of liberal modernity consists of those activities into which the state cannot legitimately intrude and over which democratic politics, majority will, and public opinion cannot reach. Defined in this way, the private sphere includes the intimate realm of family, kinship, friendship, and community relations. In other words, it incorporates what remains of gemeinschaft after the French and the Industrial revolutions are through with it. Though far weaker than they once were, primordial social ties and arrangements continue to generate particularistic solidarities rooted in exclusive ethnic, religious, and communal relations that often are antagonistic toward the critical discourse from which rises the universalistic solidarity of public opinion. Nevertheless, what people choose to do in the privacy of their families, churches, and other intimate associations is generally neither a matter of public deliberation nor subject to state intervention.

The intimate realm of nonrational sentiments and loyalties—gemeinschaft reduced and modified by the force of modernity—occupies a small spot in the large private sphere fortified against the illegitimate incursions of the state and the pressure of public opinion. Most of this region is taken up by the free or capitalist market economy, which resting on the right to private property, is the primary home to the self-sufficient, self-assertive, and self-interested individuals produced by the transition to modernity. Here, free and equal individuals meet as property owners. Seeking not solidarity but the satisfaction of their personal needs and desires, individual property owners engage one another in ways calculated to facilitate their pursuit of private interests. The contractual obligations they incur along the way are freely chosen with a calculated eye toward personal gain. Unlike the intimate relations of society with which they share the private sphere, market relations are impersonal, anonymous, instrumental, or purposively constructed, and based exclusively on voluntary consent. Therein, individuals are freed from the dictates of the state, the demands of public opinion, and the imperative expectations of primordial arrangements to pursue the satisfaction of what they take to be in their best interests—a most private matter, indeed, according to the map of liberal modernity.

Liberal Civil Society. Developed amidst the recurring and increasingly more serious problems of social disorder that accompanied the transition to liberal modernity between the mid-eighteenth and mid-nineteenth centuries, the modern liberal notion of civil society addressed the question of how autonomous, largely self-seeking individuals might achieve the minimum level of harmonious cohesion required for a civil and orderly social existence. Civil society has the most prominent place on the map of liberal modernity. In recent years, its influence has risen considerably as many of the former Soviet-dominated countries of Eastern Europe and many Third World countries as well, chart their course to the modern world in terms of its stars. For some, this already widespread and still growing commitment to civil society represents the culmination of history—liberal modernity as the best of all possible worlds (Fukuyama 1992).

"Civil society," Edward Shils (1991) notes, "lies beyond the boundaries of the family and the clan and beyond the locality; it lies short of the state" (p. 3). Thus, the space of civil society is constituted by the private sector of market relations on the one hand, and by the public settings established by private individuals for the purpose of public discourse on the other hand. Civil society brings together the particularity—the particular interests—of market individuals freely expressing and seeking satisfaction of their personal needs and private wants, and the generality—the general interest—freely discussed and evaluated by the same individuals as participants in the life of publics. As civil society, market relations and publics form an autonomous realm of private individuals engaged in various acts of self-determination safeguarded against the arbitrary and oppressive pressures of both the state and organic primordial community.

The market economy, where private owners freely associate on the basis of interest and preference, is the foundation of civil society. Next to it, publics constitute an "organ for the self-articulation of civil society" (Habermas 1989b:74) to state authority, an arena in which private individuals assemble in an effort to reach common judgments and exert concerted influence on the affairs of the state. To sustain their independence from the state, the market and public life depend on a range of institutions, and these, too, are part of civil society. Among the most important of these supporting institutions, according to Shils, are: "a system of competing political parties" seeking the backing of a universally enfranchised citizenry; "an independent judiciary which upholds the rule of law and protects the liberty of individuals"; a free press and other "institutions for making known the activities of government"; "voluntary associations and their exercise of the freedoms of association, assembly, and representation"; and the institutions that nourish the freedoms of "religious belief and worship" and academic teaching, study, research, and publication (1991:10).

Broadly conceived as the free interplay of self-assertive, self-determining individuals and their consciously organized, purposively constructed business enterprises, contractual relations, voluntary associations, political parties, and public debates, civil society is a source of constant diversity, cultivating a pluralism of different religions, ideologies, lifestyles, and interest groups. According to the mappers of liberal modernity, what holds these potentially disintegrating differences together is civility. The civility of civil society appears in two related ways: as good manners that hold "anger and resentment in check . . . and have a calming, pacifying effect on sentiments" (Shils 1991:13); and as a commitment to the common interest in maintaining the autonomy of civil society, the very context of the personal autonomy that enables individuals to define for themselves, away from the restraints of state and intimate community, how and with whom they wish to live their lives.

On the map of liberal modernity, civil society is explicitly defined in opposition to the state. While regularly seeking to shape state decisions and reliant on the state's enforcement of contractual obligations, and its protection of the right to private property and other essential liberties, civil society is structured to be relentlessly vigilant against the expansive inclinations of state power. Much less explicitly, but more significantly, civil society also is defined in opposition to society as the intimate realm of primordial social attachments within the private sphere. If market relations, publics, and their supporting institutions make up civil society—a society of good manners and civilized behavior tolerant of differences and the strangers who bear them—then the intimate realm composed of gemeinschaft leftovers is a society of bad manners and uncivilized behavior where differences are scorned and strangers greeted with intolerance and hostility. Society, as distinct from civil society, is no friend of pluralist diversity. It harbors suspicion and distrust of all that resides outside its closed borders. Here we find a particularism of communal interests which is commonly at odds with the particularism of self-determining individuals that characterizes the market economy. Nevertheless, as is clearly shown on the map of liberal modernity, the families, kinship networks, and ethnic communities of uncivil society do take care of their own, providing the comfort, the care, the affection, the sympathy, and the personal attention that can be neither purchased in the market nor commanded by the state. The primordial elements that make up society often present themselves as warm havens in an otherwise cold and impersonal world, but to spend one's entire life within them is to sacrifice the chance for individual freedom.

The sovereignty of the individual, John Stuart Mill ([1859] 1975) observed, is central to civil society. However, the requirement that it be respected, Mill argued, applies not to all human beings but only to those

> in the maturity of their faculties. We are not speaking of children. . . . Those who are still in a state to require being taken care of by others, must be protected against their own actions as well as against external injury. For the same reason we may leave out of consideration those backward states of society in which the race itself may be considered as in its nonage. . . . Despotism is a legitimate mode of government in dealing with barbarians, provided the end be their improvement. (p. 11)

Suggested here, as Samuel Bowles and Herbert Gintis (1986) note, is a distinction between choosers and learners. Choosers, participants in civil society, are rational agents whose intentions and free choices move the market economy and publics and influence state action. Incapable of rational action and the exercise of free choice and thus deserving of enlightened despotism, learners include "children, prisoners, the 'insane', and the 'uncivilized'" (p. 124). More generally, learners, as those who are precluded from civil society, dwell in the societal realm of premodern sociability. In this context, as a growing body of feminist scholarship demonstrates, women make up the most significant body of learners.

The contrast between civil society and society that appears on the map of liberal modernity is a contrast between the world of men as free individuals emancipated from the oppressive shackles of the old order, and the world of women still firmly bound by the restraints of gemeinschaft. Civil society, in Carole Pateman's description, "the universal sphere of freedom, equality, individualism, reason, contract and impartial law—the realm of men or 'individuals'" is contrasted to "the private world of particularity, natural subjection, ties of blood, emotion, love and sexual passion—the world of women, in which men also rule" (1989:43). If civil society is a world of consent, of freely chosen contracts, associations, and obligations, then society is a world of duty, of deep, ongoing social bonds rooted in given, nonvoluntary obligations, most especially the obligations of caretaking—of providing nurturance, affection, attention, and involvement to children, the elderly, the sick and otherwise vulnerable, obligations that demand the sacrifice of the rationally calculated self-interest at the center of civil society. Civil society as a realm of entirely voluntary relations and obligations, Nancy Hirschmann (1992) writes, "is possible only because of the existence of a class of people who take care of the nonconsensual obligations that characterize human life" (p. 183). In the mapping of liberal modernity, nonvoluntary or noncontractual obligations, essentially relics of organic and primordial ties, become the responsibility of women in the intimate areas of society. Men, thus, are freed to do the more important work of civil society.

Summary. Liberal modernity, according to the map at hand, consists of two spheres of two regions each. The public sphere consists of the liberal democratic state impersonally exercising its coercive authority to defend individual liberty, and the region of publics cultivated by free individuals intent on constructing a general, inclusive solidarity in the form of public opinion. The private sphere includes the impersonal market economy wherein individuals freely pursue the satisfaction of their particular preferences, and the intimate realm, or society, home to the particularistic ties and noncontractual relations of family and organic community. Standing at the center of liberal modernity is civil society, which comprises market relations, publics, and their supporting institutions. While civil society presupposes both the state (to ensure that contracts are enforced) and society (to assure that children and others needing care receive it), it regards each as a potential source of restraint on the freedom of individual choice which makes liberal modernity both liberal and modern. At all costs then, the autonomy of civil society from state and society must be secured.

This map clearly reflects the bourgeois and male background of its makers. The notion of civil society as an autonomous realm where free male individuals spend most of their time trying to maximize their property holdings and the rest engaged in public activities designed to limit the capacity of the state to intrude on their lives suits well the interests of propertied, educated white males. When we look at those countries whose journey to the modern world was guided by this map, we discover that while these biases remain, they have been weakened by nearly a century's worth of resistance on the part of the excluded. Movements of women, poor people, workers, and people of color have drawn from the language of liberal modernity to press their resistance in the name of individual freedom, equality, and democracy. This is all to the good. When we look at these contemporary, liberal, modern countries we also discover that two of the map's regions, where we find the settings of solidarity, publics, and society, are in danger of becoming ghost towns of sorts, a consequence of the steady expansion of the market and the state. This development, which is all to the bad, has been at the forefront of the sociological critique of liberal modernity from the beginning.

Sociology and Civil Society

Sociology developed as a critique of liberal modernity. Carefully observing liberal modernity as it assumed decisive shape in England between 1840 and 1880, and in France, Germany, and the United States during the period between the final years of the nineteenth century and the first twenty-five years of the twentieth, Karl Marx, Émile Durkheim, Max Weber, and George Herbert Mead, respectively, made important contributions to the themes and assumptions of the then-emerging socio-logical perspective. This perspective clearly recognized and was duly laudatory of liberal modernity's achievements and potential. At the same time, it constantly was alert to liberal modernity's dark side, especially its burgeoning power to create alienated, anomic, disenchanted, narrow, and amoral lives. This paradox of liberal modernity, Alan Wolfe (1989) shows, generated a dilemma for the founders of modern sociology:

> [B]oth morality and modernity were important, yet each seemed to work at cross purposes to the other. To be modern was to be free from ties of community and tradition and to live instead with forms of regulation that were formal, specified, and impersonal, whereas to be moral was to live with common cultural values and strongly inscribed traditions that effec-tively denied democracy, individual self-development, and equality. (pp. 191–92)

Tonnies, as we saw above, resolved this dilemma in favor of the moral codes of gemeinschaft. Marx and Weber, with occasional, usually fleeting signs of reluctance, sided with modernity. Durkheim and Mead regarded the dilemma as false and dangerously misleading. We need not choose between a traditionally moral social order antagonistic toward individual freedom, equality, and democracy and an impersonal, amoral, purpos-ively constructed social order supportive of individual rights. Rather the task, and for Durkheim and Mead it was a particularly urgent task, is to defend and strengthen the conditions that nurture the growth of a morali-ty appropriate to modernity, a morality that not only honors but also sustains the individual freedom, equality, and democracy promoted by liberal modernity.

Where it was influenced by Durkheim and Mead, the emerging socio-logical perspective took as its primary object of study that which liberal modernity most seriously threatened, namely, those social settings that sustained the solidaristic principles and practices of mutuality that give life to a moral order capable of holding its own against the demoralizing tendencies of the modern market and the modern state. According to this view, the presence of a strong, vibrant civil society, one defined differ-ently than it is on the map of liberal modernity, diminishes the possibility of both state coercion and the human misery brought by a market driven only by rational self-interest.

The Sociological View of Civil Society. For Durkheim and Mead, the key distinction in the liberal modern world is not the distinction between the public and the private spheres but the one between the impersonal and the interpersonal spheres. Comprising the market economy and the liberal democratic state, each of which is structured to promote individual freedom, the impersonal sphere is where people exist as followers of the impersonal rules of the market and the state. In the interpersonal sphere, a realm of solidarity and morality, people abide by rules they make and sustain as parents, friends, neighbors, and co-workers in society and as active participants in publics. From Durkheim's and Mead's sociological perspective, civil society as an autonomous, self-regulating sphere essential to individual freedom and democracy consists of society and publics and the relations between the two.

Durkheim insisted that the achievement of liberal modernity's highest ideals required "a coherent and animated society" where "there is from all to each and from each to all a continual . . . mutual moral support which makes the individual, instead of being reduced to his own forces alone, participate in the collective energy and rejuvenate his life when it is exhausted" ([1897] 1951:210). What gives a society coherence, animation, and revitalizing power are centers of dense social interaction which locate people in interdependencies that nourish trust and morality. Families, religious groups, and professional and political associations are settings of moral density, as are, most importantly according to Durkheim, occupational groups whose members regularly assemble to work on job-related issues, to carry out projects of mutual assistance, and to socialize with one another and their families ([1893] 1947). No doubt, Durkheim's image of occupational groups was influenced by the "great surge in popular sociability" (Agulhon 1982:126) that accompanied the development of modernity throughout the nineteenth century. In response to the volatility, insecurity, and unpredictability modernity's emergence brought to social life, there arose a number of locally organized yet voluntary solidarity groups—drinking clubs, religious fraternities, friendly societies, choral groups, and mutual aid societies—in the context of which members sought out one another for assistance and, often, protection against the still developing market economy and liberal state.

Like Durkheim, Mead understood society as those forms of human association that rest on and promote morally nourishing cooperative processes. Of particular importance are local associations established to further the needs of families, communities, and their members. Amidst the close personal relations supported by these social settings, the individual defines herself in part with reference to those significant and generalized others with whom she interacts so that her self-interest is generally compatible with the interests of others. In these contexts, Mead (1964:249–82) argued, people are able to cultivate their sympathetic and charitable impulses, to perfect their cooperative skills, and to develop their capacity to arrive at a set of common purposes and ideals which set the terms by which they regulate their lives.

Like the mappers of liberal modernity, the sociological perspective shaped by Durkheim and Mead includes the primordial ties of family and organic community in society. It includes as well voluntaristic mutual aid activities, local associations, and occupational groups created by people to bolster their primordial and communal arrangements. The familial and communal forms defended by the sociological perspective were not those that sat at the center of premodern society. Rather, they were new forms that embodied the elementary principles of sociability in ways that reflected the impact of the impersonal forces of modernity on the one hand and the associations of mutual aid on the other. The communities, local associations, and occupational groups described by Mead and Durkheim were not the closed, restrictive, traditionally hierarchical arrangements of the premodern world. They were more horizontally organized, less vertically structured, and more open to the active participation of their members. Increasingly dependent on these broader arrangements, the family too, had changed, shedding the "amoral familialism" (Banfield 1958), which encouraged a unrelenting distrust of all outside the ties of blood and marriage. The morality engendered in the society sphere of liberal modernity is unlike the harsh and repressive morality found in premodern gemeinschaft. Drawing on the work of the child psychologist Jean Piaget (1965), the former may be characterized as a morality of cooperation, the latter as a morality of constraint. Incorporating Durkheim's distinction between premodern simple societies and modern complex societies and generally consistent with Mead's analysis of the development of the self, Piaget's study of the moral growth of children identifies two key stages. The first

> is characterized by submission to authority and externality of rules. It is a stage of "strict law," in which the bare fact of infraction, regardless of context or intent, warrants corrective punishment. In the second stage . . . there is greater awareness of reciprocity, equal treatment, and mutual respect among peers, as well as an increased capacity to distinguish a just rule from one that is merely authoritative. (Selznick 1992:165)

The morality of constraint demands obedience to an established, external, coercive rule. In contrast, the morality of cooperation depends on "a sense of fairness, mutuality, and respect for the ends the rule is meant to serve" (Selznick 1992:165), and these, Piaget claimed, are cultivated by the active participation of peers in close, face-to-face relations of interdependency. Similarly, Durkheim and Mead observed signs of a moral sensibility and moral ideals appropriate to modernity emerging from the cooperative processes and practices of mutual aid found in horizontally organized communities, local associations, and occupational groups. In these contexts, they argued, people help create the rules and they abide by them not simply from a sense of duty but because they also desire to do the right thing.

The primordial organizations of premodern society rested on oppressive, stultifying, highly coercive measures of social control. In contrast, the morally dense associations, primary groups, and communities Durkheim and Mead saw struggling to take root sought to regulate themselves in accordance with a morality of cooperation both authoritative enough to counter unbridled self-interest and modern enough to respect the dignity of the individual. Social control guided by the morality of cooperation involved not "coercion or the repression of the individual [but] the obverse of coercive control" (Janowitz 1978:3). According to this view, neighborhoods, communities, and associations could avoid the coercive presence of the government in their lives to the extent that they were capable of regulating themselves, in part by instilling in their members the personal controls of conscience. Individuals and groups incapable of controlling themselves invite the imposition of external, usually governmental, forms of control which detract from both the freedom of individuals and the autonomy of groups. Social control exercised in accordance with the morality of cooperation, Mead (1962) insisted,

> so far from tending to crush out the human individual or obliterate his self-conscious individuality is, on the contrary, actually constitutive of and inextricably associated with that individuality; for the individual is what he is, as a conscious and individual personality, just in so far as he is a member of society, involved in the social process of experience and activity, and thereby socially controlled in his conduct. (p. 255)

Mead's point, one made regularly by Durkheim as well, is that there is no necessary tension between society—comprising primordial and organic ties and the local, communal, mutual, voluntaristic groups that develop around them—and the equality, justice, and individualism promised by a modernity driven by purposively constructed market and state organizations. Indeed, for them, these promises required for their redemption the kinds of sentiments, capacities, and practices that are developed only in the relatively small scale, closely interpersonal social settings that regulate themselves in ways consistent with the respect for freedom and equality demanded by increasingly more modern conditions of existence.

Durkheim and Mead recognized that modernity undermines what it needs, namely, centers of vigorous group life that nourish the trust, responsibility, mutuality, and cooperation that make for fair and efficient markets and legitimate and effective democratic states. Accordingly, they defined the task of sociology as the moral reconstruction of society, the goal of which is to reconstruct, and not simply recapture, the bases of elementary sociability, making them appropriate to the conditions and ideals of the modern world. Modernity requires neither the loose individuals of the market economy nor the passive individuals dependent on the protection of the liberal democratic state. Rather, it requires moral individuals actively interdependent with one another in the self-regulating segments of society.

Society is home to many different communities, primary groups, and local and work-related associations. It is important that they be strong enough to restrain both the self-interested, egocentric impulses unleashed and encouraged by liberal modernity and the expansive tendencies of the modern state, but not so strong that they "swallow up their members" (Durkheim [1950] 1958:62) and confine them to their particular moral codes. Durkheim and Mead agreed that a vibrant public life, the second component of the sociological view of civil society, is needed to check the excessive particularism of the various small-scale social settings and to provide the opportunities and experiences that lead to public spiritedness, civic morality, and a commitment to the shared traditions and common good that underlie and, indeed, make possible the peaceful coexistence of the different societal groups and communities. Publics, according to Durkheim, constitute an inclusive political community wherein the members of particularistic groups gain consciousness of the shared aims and moral ideals in whose terms they examine the great issues of the day. Similarly, for Mead the public "is distinguished by members' willingness to consider the interests of all groups and individuals from the standpoint of what is good for the community as a whole" (Shalin 1988:933). Public interaction, the two argued, generalizes the moral sensibilities cultivated in society by enlarging the circle of people with whom communication and interdependence take place. It also promotes public opinion and active citizen participation that assure the democratic character of the modern state. Publics, like the groups and communities that make up society, are solidarity producing. Public opinion as a mode of regulation, like social control, is interpersonal. The guiding ideals and governing rules it espouses are constructed and upheld by the active participants of publics. In publics, as in society, people learn to take responsibility for the consequences of their actions and for the fates of others. In publics, these others are strangers for the most part, and the public opinion they struggle to construct reflects a solidarity more general and less intense than the solidarities rooted in the more intimate realms of society. It is the solidarity of strangers who, recognizing that the modern world has brought them into regular contact with one another, have decided that they will decide how these contacts are to be regulated. The solidarity of strangers draws sustenance from the solidarity of intimates—

John Dewey (1988), whose work influenced and was influenced by Mead, noted that the "heart and final guarantee" of democratic publics "is in free gatherings of neighbors on the street corner . . . and in gatherings of friends in [their] living rooms" (p. 227).

Durkheim and Mead were very much aware of the damage done and the continuously severe threats posed to civil society by liberal modernity's market economy and state. Both, however, saw the state, one whose democratic character is constantly reinforced by active publics and a thriving group life, playing an indispensable role in revitalizing civil society in opposition to market forces. From the perspectives of Marx and Weber, Durkheim and Mead seriously underestimated the damage to civil society already inflicted by the market and the state, and to the same degree overestimated the feasibility of reinvigorating civil society within the framework of liberal modernity.

As it appears on the map of liberal modernity, civil society, Marx ([1843] 1978) wrote, "exists only in order to guarantee for each of its members the presentation of his person, his rights, and his property. . . . [A]s a member of civil society, [man] is an individual separated from the community, withdrawn into himself, wholly preoccupied with his private interest" (p. 43). In the market, private individuals treat one another as means, degrade themselves and each other, and become the "playthings of alien powers" (p. 34). In publics, citizenship is reduced to a means for preserving the rights of man "as an isolated monad, withdrawn into himself [and] the citizen is declared to be the servant of egoistic 'man' [as publics themselves] are degraded to a level below the sphere where he functions as a partial being" (pp. 42–43). In the real world of liberal modernity, according to Marx, civil society is driven by the market and the capitalist relations of production on which it rests. Publics occupy a subservient position. Conflict, poverty, inequality, and alienation, not individual freedom, grow from the ground of this civil society.

Capitalism, Marx and many others noted in the mid-nineteenth century, is not hospitable to close, enduring social relations. The bourgeoisie, he wrote, "has pitilessly torn asunder the motley feudal ties that bound man to his 'natural superiors', and has left remaining no other nexus between man and man than naked self-interest, than callous 'cash payment'" (Marx and Engels [1848] 1978:475). While Marx saw some good in the ever-disruptive character of capitalist development—"barbarians are brought into civilization," "rural idiocy is ended," the productive forces are continuously improved—he knew that capitalism's central dynamics, commodification and proletarianization especially, deteriorated the deeper sources of solidarity which fed the civil society defended by Durkheim and Mead. Commodification, transforming goods and services for which people once relied on the goodwill of others into commodities bought and sold on the market, and proletarianization, stripping people of their means of production and other resources that enable them to be self- and mutually reliant, force people to become increasingly dependent on the market economy which supplies the commodities and on the capitalists and their organizations which have appropriated the means of production and the resources of ordinary competence. Commodification and proletarianization combine, Marx argued, to close off the opportunities for interpersonal cooperation and to shut down the social contexts in which people develop the skills and carry on the practices of mutuality.

For Weber, rationalization is the driving force of modernity, and it underlies commodification and proletarianization. The inescapable fate of the modern world, rationalization expands by diminishing personal ties and sentimental attachments and by increasing people's reliance on the administrative experts who rationally design and impersonally manage the large-scale, purposively constructed organizations that dominate the lives of modern people. In the middle of the cold, calculated iron cage liberal modernity has nearly become, there exists a spiritual crisis, the result of the disenchantment of the world, the loss of cultural ideals and consensual values capable of providing meaning, direction, purpose, and a context congenial to the building of character. In bureaucratically structured workplaces and the bureaucratic welfare state where rationally calculated rules are followed "without regard for persons," Weber ([1921] 1946b) discovered that "the casing for a new serfdom is ready" (p. 215). Hostile to the claims of sociability which take people from rationally planned, formally specified courses of action, the rationalized structures of modernity produce rational actors whose ability to select the most efficient means for the pursuit of a given end comes at the expense of their capacity to sustain the cultural values that give meaning to that end.

Bureaucratic rationalization is an unavoidable accompaniment to modernity. The key question, Weber argued, concerns, "what we oppose to this machinery, in order to keep a portion of humanity free from this parceling out of the soul, from this total dominance of the bureaucratic ideal of life" (quoted in Bellamy 1992:188). Weber's response to this question included a repudiation of the socialist solution offered by Marx, which, in his view, would simply extend and complete the process of rationalization ushered in by modern capitalism. Only within liberal modernity, that is, within the context established by the capitalist market economy and liberal democracy, is it possible to launch an effective opposition to the machinery of bureaucratic rationalization. The task, for Weber, involves the revitalization of the spirit of calling, the devotion to vocation, that gave discipline, vigor, initiative, moral guidance, and a sense of responsibility to the strong and creative individuals who were the entrepreneurs, businessmen, and skilled workers of early modern capitalism. The extensive bureaucratic organization of work and life has destroyed this possibility for most. Nevertheless, there remain within the iron cage a few with sufficient strength of character, and, Weber argued, democracy should be structured to provide them with the opportunity to assume leadership roles. The plebicitarian leadership democracy Weber advocated would permit "an elite gifted with exceptional powers of self-overcoming and discipline [and devoted to] a high mission . . . to bear the burdens of ruling and to cope with the disappearance of a commonly shared and available meaning in a world disenchanted by rationalization" (Goldman 1988:165–66). Not bound by the requirement to be accountable and responsive to the democratically expressed will of the people—something, in any event, rarely produced by modernity's rational actors whose passive mass politics fill the vacuum left by the rationalization of public life—the new aristocracy, firmly committed to politics as a vocation, would have the opportunity to exercise the kind of inspiring leadership that could counter the spiritual crisis of the age (Weber [1919] 1946a).

Marx and Weber agreed that liberal modernity advanced in ways that irrevocably damaged the foundations of the civil society endorsed by Durkheim and Mead. For Marx, the capitalist market economy fuels the devitalization of the interpersonal, solidaristic spheres of society and publics. For Weber, rationalization, particularly in its noneconomic forms and most especially through the bureaucratic state, is the primary force responsible for the loss of sentimental ties and moralizing contexts and the transformation of the public into the mass. Liberal modernity thus forecloses the option favored by Durkheim and Mead. The choice is not between the interpersonal realm of civil society and the impersonal sphere of market and state. It is, rather, a choice between the private market economy and the public state. Marx, of course, chose the state, the socialist state, the dictatorship of the proletariat, which through rational planning and expert administration would eliminate the irrationalities of the capitalist market and harness the immense productive power generated by capitalism to the satisfaction of human purposes. Weber sided with the capitalist market economy, convinced that even a social democratic welfare state far more modest in scope than Marx's socialist state would constitute an unassailable solidification of the iron cage. In time, the premise underlying this choice, namely that the market and the state are the only two viable games in the town of liberal modernity, came to be widely accepted as modernity's individuals looked less to themselves as members of societal groups and participants in publics and more to the market and the state for solutions to their problems, sometimes favoring the free market over the intrusive, heavy-handed state, other times preferring the guidance of the caring welfare state over the anarchic, uncompassionate market. To the detriment of modern people, the sociological view of civil society outlined by Durkheim and Mead receded into the background, its language of solidarity hardly ever spoken at all.

Contemporary Sociology. The two best known and most powerfully rendered contemporary sociological critiques of liberal modernity are the ones developed by Jurgen Habermas and Alan Wolfe. It is no accident that each draws heavily from the classical sociological critique elaborated in the works of Marx, Durkheim, Weber, and Mead to trace out the processes by which the capitalist market economy and the liberal democratic welfare state have invaded and seriously weakened the interpersonal spheres of society and public life.

In Habermas's account, liberal modernity's development is characterized as the colonization and consequent deformation of the lifeworld by the system. The lifeworld comprises the private sphere of society, most especially the family and those associations centered around it, and democratic publics. Therein, coordination is sought and social relations are formed on the basis of communicative action, a cooperative process of mutual interpretation through which people struggle to achieve understanding and consensus. The lifeworld sustains meaning by transmitting or critically reappropriating cultural tradition; it fosters group solidarity; and it promotes the development of socially competent and responsible adults in possession of strong identities (Habermas 1989a:138–41). The system consists of the capitalist market economy and the bureaucratic welfare state. Here, coordination is carried out and social relations are defined in terms of impersonal steering mechanisms, money in the case of the market, power in the case of the state. Money and power "encode a purposive-rational attitude toward calculable amounts of value and make it possible to exert generalized, strategic influence on the decisions of other participants while *bypassing* processes of consensus-oriented communication" (p. 183).

This purposive-rational attitude, an obstacle to the mutual understanding that underlies solidarity, has been brought to the lifeworld, Habermas argues, as the capitalist market has commodified and the welfare state has extended the reach of bureaucratic administration to more and more areas of social life. "To the degree that the economic system subjects the lifeforms of private households and the life of consumers and employees to its imperatives, consumerism and possessive individualism," Habermas writes,

> motives of performance and competition gain the force to shape behavior. . . . As the private sphere is undermined and eroded by the economic system, so too is the public sphere by the administrative system. The bureaucratic disempowering and desecration of spontaneous process of

opinion- and will-formation expand the scope for engineering mass loyalty and make it easier to uncouple political decision-making from concrete, identity-forming contexts of life. (1989a:325)

The monetarization and bureaucratization of the lifeworld imposes market and administrative principles of organization on the activities of civil society. As a result, group and public solidarities become weaker, skills and practices of mutual assistance diminish, adult identities become more tenuous, and individuals as consumers dependent on the market and clients dependent on the state go about their lives with a reduced sense of personal and collective agency.

Wolfe's analysis of the contemporary forms taken by liberal modernity parallels Habermas's. In some liberal modern countries, the United States in particular, Wolfe finds, civil society—families, communities, public life—is primarily organized by the self-interested logic of the market; in others, the Scandinavian countries especially, civil society is structured more by the administrative logic and coercive authority of the welfare state. In both contexts, people's sense of personal responsibility for the well-being of others suffers. "The position of present generations is strengthened at the expense of those before and after," Wolfe writes (1989),

> either because of the market's emphasis on rational choice or because of the state's receptivity to interest-group politics. Ties between anonymous others expressed through volunteerism and charity can weaken, either because they are sacrificed to the market's emphasis on egoism or because of the state's assumption of impersonal responsibility. Finally, culture . . . tends to thin out, vulnerable to both the origination of cultural production by the market and the replacement of cultural ties by political ones that emphasize rights. (p. 188)

Increasingly guided by the calculated self-interest appropriate to market transactions and the sense of entitlement promoted by the welfare state, the relations of civil society lose their capacity to sustain mutuality, to teach social obligation, to nourish solidarity, and to develop moral competence. The paradox of liberal modernity, according to Wolfe, is that it makes people "need one another more but trust one another less. . . . Modern people need to care about the fates of strangers, yet do not know how to treat their loved ones" (p. 5).

Habermas and Wolfe agree that the societal and public spheres of interpersonal solidarity encompassed by civil society have been shrunk and deformed by the intrusion of the capitalist market economy and the bureaucratic welfare state. They also agree on the need to revitalize Durkheim's and Mead's sociological project for the reconstruction of civil society. However, when it comes to defining the content of the project, the two take divergent paths. Where Habermas focuses on the construction of democratic public life, Wolfe emphasizes the strengthening of the intimate, small-scale settings of society.

Habermas proposes a "radical reformism" committed to the view that "the socially integrating force of solidarity should be in a position to stake its claim against the other social forces, money and administrative power" (1990:19). The solidarity Habermas defends is not that engendered by particularistic societal groups and communities, for it is too limiting, often antidemocratic, and, in any event, dependent on increasingly obsolete traditional structures of everyday life. It is, rather, the solidarity created by the rational public discourse carried on by autonomous actors in publics. Its achievement requires that the conditions of mutuality found in the particularistic settings of society "be transferred to the sphere of legally and administratively mediated social relations through the preconditions of nonexclusive processes for the formation of public opinion and democratic political will" (Habermas 1990:19). In the modern world, Habermas claims, mutually supportive coexistence only can exist as "an *abstract* idea . . . a legitimate, intersubjectively shared expectation" (1990:15) institutionalized in the form of proceduralized popular sovereignty.

> The point of conceiving mutually supportive relations abstractly is to separate the symmetries of mutual recognition, presupposed by communicative action . . . from the concrete ethical practice of naturalized forms of behavior, and generalize them into the reflexive forms of agreement and compromise whilst simultaneously safeguarding them through legal institutionalization [of] forms of communication that regulate the flow of the discursive formation of public opinion and political will. (p. 16)

The task, in short, is to reconstruct democratic public life by legally establishing the procedures for reflexive and open processes of public discourse. The aim is to create a post-conventional civil society, a civil society beyond the established particularistic conventions of societal groups and communities, one wherein solidarity rests on a consensus forged and upheld by individuals interacting in accord with the abstract ethical principles of proceduralized popular sovereignty. The "democratization of the values, norms, institutions, and social identities rooted ultimately in a political culture" (Arato and Cohen 1992:212) that subjects each to public scrutiny and discursive adjudication would signal the presence of a modernized civil society strong enough to hold its own against the capitalist market economy and the bureaucratic welfare state.

For Wolfe, the effective reconstruction of civil society requires not the revitalization of democratic public life and the ensuing democratization of the intimate sphere of society, but just the reverse—the strengthening of the intimate sphere and the extension of its moral codes to the more distant public realm we share with strangers. Mutually supportive coexistence is capable of sustaining a solidarity strong enough to withstand the encroachments of liberal modernity—not as an abstract idea, as Habermas claims, but as a lived reality in "families, communities, friendship networks, voluntary organizations, and social movements . . . because it can only be within the intimate realm, surrounded by those we know and for whom we care, that we learn the art of understanding the moral position of others" (Wolfe 1989:233). Wolfe reverses Habermas's emphasis on public solidarity achieved by reason, logic, and open discourse guided by abstract procedures over particularistic solidarities rooted in sentiment, intuition, emotion, and common sense, to favor a solidarity of the heart over a solidarity of the head. For Wolfe, the intimate realm should serve as a model for public life. Doing it the other way, applying the principles and procedures of democracy to the intimate realm, might enhance people's sense of abstract justice but at a cost to their capacity to care about and take personal responsibility for particular others. It is better, according to this view, to move from the intimate sphere to the sphere of public life, treating strangers the way we treat friends, rather than the other way around, treating friends in accordance with procedures established to guide civil intercourse among strangers.

Like Durkheim and Mead, Habermas and Wolfe recognize the importance of revitalizing civil society in liberal modernity. Like Marx and like Weber, they understand the enormous difficulties of the task, beset as it is on the one side by the powerful commodifying tendencies of the capitalist market economy and on the other by the equally strong rationalizing tendencies of the bureaucratic welfare state. Faced with these difficulties, Habermas proposes a reconstructed civil society with an active, legally institutionalized democratic public life at its center, while Wolfe directs us to a civil society founded on a thriving intimate realm of small-scale social settings. Habermas's approach, Wolfe charges, subordinates the capacity to care cultivated in such settings to procedures of justice whose effectiveness ultimately depends on the development of that capacity. Wolfe's approach, Habermas argues, makes difficult the creation of general public standards to which particularistic moral codes must be held accountable if individual autonomy and democracy are to prevail. A better approach, it seems, would call for the strengthening of both the intimate and the public spheres of civil society, recognizing with Wolfe that people who know how to meet their obligations to loved ones are more likely to meet their obligations to distant others, and agreeing with Habermas that a vital public life serves to help assure that loved ones are treated with respect and dignity. Aware of the ongoing tensions between society and public life, this approach, the one originally suggested by Durkheim and

Mead, emphasizes that the integrity of each is most threatened by the market economy and the bureaucratic state and is most safely secured by the strong presence of the other.

In a series of essays on the moral crisis of contemporary social life, the political theorist Michael Walzer comes closest to this approach. Advanced liberal countries, whether market-oriented, like the United States, or state-oriented, like Sweden, Walzer (1991) argues, have put the associational life of civil society at serious risk. The result is

> the steady attenuation of everyday cooperation and civic friendship . . . cities . . . noisier and nastier than they once were. Familial solidarity, mutual assistance, political like-mindedness—all these are less certain and less substantial than they once were. Other people, strangers on the street, seem less trustworthy than they once did. The Hobbesian account of society is more persuasive than it once was. (p. 293)

Under the onslaught of the market and the state, the social settings that produce and reproduce trust, solidarity, and civility have withered.

The solution for Walzer (1989), as it was for Durkheim and Mead, is the revitalization of the associational networks of civil society where people engage one another for "the sake of sociability itself" and "become part of a world of family, friends, comrades, and colleagues . . . connected to one another and responsible for one another" (p. 29). The connections and responsibilities sustained in civil society give a nourishing context to individual freedom, providing both a place for individuals to stand together against the injustices of the market and the state and a constraint on the selfishness that transforms individual freedom into an instrument of social disorganization, abandonment, distrust, and irresponsibility. Like Durkheim and Mead, Walzer argues that the task is not simply to "recapture the density of associational life" (p. 30) by trying to re-create older forms of civil society. Instead that density has to be reconstructed to satisfy the conditions of freedom and equality. Walzer, too, rejects the claim that we must choose between the morally informed, deep social attachments of civil society on the one hand, and the achievements of modernity on the other. He knows that the latter are dependent ultimately on the former, that the honesty, trust, and civility necessary for effective markets and legitimate democratic welfare states are learned only in the rich associational life of civil society. He also knows that the market and the state are necessary to check the unequal power relations and the tendencies toward exclusivity and intolerance that often arise in civil society (Walzer 1986:94–95). The promise of modernity, according to Durkheim, Mead, and Walzer, cannot be realized by the market and the state alone. It requires in addition the vigorous social attachments, the dense social engagements, and the powerful sense of social obligation that liberal modernity opposes and the liberal market and the liberal state diminish.

In envisioning a solidaristic civil society, Durkheim, Mead, and Walzer suggest a language of solidarity capable of holding its own against the dominant languages of economic self-interest and state-enforced individual rights. In contrast to the market's and the state's language of individualism, civil society's language of solidarity allows individuals to name and express their needs for belonging, benevolence, and community and thus to begin to undertake the practices necessary to the satisfaction of these needs. The language of solidarity does not celebrate solidarity over the individual and his or her freedom. Rather, it celebrates the solidarities of civil society as an indispensable basis of the individual and that freedom. It gives the individual and freedom the context and substance taken away by liberalism's languages of the market and rights. It has us recognize the enabling and ennobling qualities of society as it demands constant vigilance against those societal forces that stifle, exclude, fuel prejudice, and thus preclude the possibilities for freedom and equality opened up by liberal modernity's market and state. And it alerts us to the dangers of liberal modernity's most influential assumption—that in the absence of society we become free individuals. At the end of the century, as social cartographers throughout the world rediscover the idea of civil society, it is important to approach it as Durkheim and Mead did at the beginning of the century, in terms of the language of solidarity.

CONCLUSION

"If the moral force of liberalism is still stimulating," C. Wright Mills observed in 1952, "its sociological content is weak; it has no theory of society adequate to its moral aims" ([1952] 1963:191). Nearly a half-century later, liberalism's moral force has been nearly extinguished and its moral aims largely subverted by the economic and political arrangements designed and developed in its name. Consider the response of George Will, the leading American right-wing commentator, to the news that the rate of growth of inequality in wealth and income and the gap between rich and poor is higher in the United States than in other Western countries. "A society that values individualism, enterprise, and the market economy," Will (1995) writes, "is neither surprised nor scandalized when the unequal distribution of marketable skills produces large disparities in the distribution of wealth. . . . Certainly there is today no prima facie case against the moral acceptability of increasingly larger disparities of wealth" (p. 51). The absence of surprise and scandal recorded by Will testifies not to the robustness of individualism in the United States today, but to its collapse, and, as well, to the collapse of a society capable of nurturing an enduring and responsible individualism. Sociology provides the theory of society that liberalism lacks. In it, society—social institutions and communitarian interdependencies—is regarded as indispensable to the cultivation of morally competent, attentive individuals, a place where people acquire some of the virtues that make them active citizens in the ongoing public life that combines with society to constitute civil society. Sociology's theory of society endorses the individual, and it values the market economy and the democratic state, acknowledging both the contributions each makes to the possibility of moral individualism and the important role each plays in checking the dark side of civil society as expressed in patriarchal institutions, bigoted communities, and uninformed and intolerant public opinion.

The individual unable to make a case against the large and still increasing inequalities in wealth and income is the individual outside society, the individual unencumbered by institutional identity and the obligations of associational life. For a time, this individual sought and found security in a growing market economy which supplied stable jobs, rising wages, and the comforts of consumerism, and in a welfare state that provided a wide range of benefits and protections. In the current era of downsizing and flexibility, market and government become increasingly unreliable for most, and the result is a sense of insecurity deep and pervasive enough to deserve the name 'anomie.' Standing alone, without the resources generated in society and in publics, liberalism's individual is confused and anxious.

As the twenty-first century dawns, Ralf Dahrendorf argues, modern societies appear to be faced with two options: "economic growth and political freedom without social cohesion, and . . . economic growth and social cohesion without political freedom" (1995:30). The first option, the American model, links economic growth to a growing inequality that turns political freedom into an avenue across which conflicts between classes, races, generations, sexes, and regions are played out. The second option, the Asian model, is an authoritarian capitalism that favors social cohesion by using economic growth to reduce inequality and, more directly, by using government to squash dissident views and movements. "The onset of anomie," Dahrendorf (1995) warns, "gives rise to the temptation of authoritarianism, which is more tempting to some based on the perceived success of the Asian model" (p. 33).

There is, of course, a third option, one in which people turn not to an inequality-generating market economy, nor to the authoritarian state, but to one another. This is the sociological option, and it may become more prominent as more people recognize the futility of finding security in the market economy and the welfare state. Recently, in response to shrinking government services and programs, neighborhood associations and civic groups have arisen to assume a variety of responsibilities. In Queens, New York, a neighborhood association took charge of after-school tutoring and art classes; in Brooklyn, housing project residents formed a nightly street patrol; in Austin, Texas, voluntary associations were created to help sustain a threatened health and nutrition program at area parks; in St. Paul, Minnesota, neighborhood groups were established to provide home health care services and companionship to live-at-home elderly (Belluck 1996; Rosen 1996). Each of these efforts receives financial support and technical assistance from city, state, or the federal government, and most are carried out in close collaboration with government agencies. These examples are small in number, and their combined impact on the problems besetting the United States is no doubt negligible. Nevertheless, they hint at the direction suggested by the sociological option.

The sociological option favors economic growth, social cohesion, and political freedom, and is particularly concerned to assure that economic growth occurs in ways congenial to a civil society that is the ground of social cohesion and political freedom. The primary task is the revitalization of civil society—the strengthening of social institutions, the rebuilding of communitarian interdependencies, and the reinvigoration of publics—as a sphere whose autonomy is respected and supported by the market economy and the state. Freedom exists in effective participation in communities that possess the autonomy and resources that enable them to influence significantly their own destinies. In public life, such freedom is called self-government; in social life, it takes the form of informal social control. To argue that the market economy and the state must be made congenial to civil society is to say that each must accommodate the conditions that promote the qualities of character and the practices of solidarity on which depend self-government and informal social control. Minimally, this requires that some responsibility for welfare provision be separated from the state and that some income and goods be separated from the market economy.

The Welfare State.   The key to overcoming social breakdown in America's inner-city underclass, argues Paul Starr, is "the reconstruction of civil society in minority communities [and] the strengthening of 'intermediate' institutions . . . which provide the organizational foundation for collective development and effective public representation" (1992:4). In Starr's proposal, the substantial capital support required to initiate community self-development is provided by government. Given the aim of such support, namely, the revitalization of the neighborhood groups, service clubs, churches, voluntary associations, credit unions and other community development financial institutions, and local businesses, and the sense of family responsibility that underlay an autonomous civil society, the extension of welfare expenditure would not entail the expansion of the state. One way of breathing new life into the conditions that promote a vigorous and autonomous civil society is to delegate some welfare responsibilities and supply the public funds adequate to the discharge of these responsibilities to existing or newly emerging local groups and associations. Assisted by broad federal race-neutral programs that would secure affordable education and health care for lower- and middle-income Americans, community self-development programs, in Starr's view, stand a good chance of success.

Starr's point—more welfare but a smaller welfare state—is extended in Paul Hirst's defense of what he calls "associationalism," the goal of which is to significantly narrow the scope of state administration so that the provision of welfare becomes more social or associational in form and less bureaucratic and centralized. Hirst's associationalism rests on two central principles:

> First, that the state should cede functions to [voluntary self-governing] associations, and create the mechanisms of public finance whereby they can undertake them. Second, that the means to the creation of an associative order in civil society are built up, such as alternative sources of mutual finance for associative economic enterprises, agencies that aid voluntary bodies and their personnel to conduct their affairs effectively, and so on. (1994:21)

With associationalism, government's role as service provider is delimited. Its primary tasks in the area of welfare come to include raising the public funds that pay for welfare services; assuring that such funds are used properly by the voluntary self-governing associations that are the service providers, ensuring, that is, that their provision of services to their members clearly meets the standards set by government; and protecting the provider associations and their members from forces that threaten to overwhelm them (Hirst 1994:24, 167–171). Like Starr, Hirst is convinced that the devolution of welfare provision from far-away bureaucratic state agencies to nearby groups and associations will give people good reason and good opportunities to assemble for the purpose of mutual benefit.

The "devolution of welfare provision" is the most prominent mantra of the political Right as it leads the effort to dismantle the welfare state by replacing federal entitlements with far less well funded and reliable block grants. Hirst's associationalism differs from the agenda put forth by the political Right in both substance and intent. First, it does not reduce public expenditure on welfare services. Rejecting the extremely dubious proposition advanced by the political Right that churches and charities, suddenly bloated by massive increases in individual donations, will fill the gap left by reduced government spending, associationalism targets public funds as the primary source of welfare services. Second, it does not call for a weaker governmental presence in the market economy, in part because the public funds supportive of welfare depend on some redistribution of income and wealth from the rich to the poor and the vitality of associational service providers requires the regulation of some kinds of business activity. Third, the private agencies central to associationalism—the service clubs, labor unions, and neighborhood and church groups that organize to provide for welfare services—are expected to be accountable to their members and to the larger public authority vested in the state (where the private agencies most valued by the Right—business enterprises—are held accountable only to their owners). Finally, where the policies of the Right diminish the public sphere, associationalism anticipates a revitalized public sphere rising from the more active involvement of people in the provision of welfare services to those with whom they share associational life (Hirst 1994:22).

So far, Hirst's associationalism is consistent with the sociological option. Yet, this consistency is lost when Hirst insists that associationalism, like the strategies proposed by the political Right and the political Left, justify itself in terms of liberal individualism's highest ideal, the free individual as uninhibited chooser of his or her own ends and obligations. The "core ethical claim of associationalism, that individuals ought to associate and should be free to do so," Hirst writes, "is justified on essentially individualistic terms, that it enhances both the freedom and the individuation of the individual" (p. 50). The product of free and intelligent choices made by rational and self-interested individuals, voluntary self-governing associations claim no priority over individuals and their right to choose. "From the right to be a voluntary member of an association we derive the most basic right in an associative society, that is, the . . . right of exit. The unquestioned right of exit ensures that associations are communities of choice" (Hirst 1994:52–53). Unlike communities of choice, which "fit in with the dominant trend of modern human aspirations," communities of fate comprising social obligations, communal expectations, and institutional demands not freely chosen "are inconsistent with individuation and are difficult to defend as necessary in a world peopled by literate, at least minimally informed individuals who have the desire to shape their lives by choice" (p. 54, 55).

Committed to the right of the individual to choose freely his or her own ends and to the understanding of the individual as a rational calculator of self-interest, Hirst's associationalism falls victim to rhetoric of liberal individualism. A richer associational life, he asserts, requires neither deeper reservoirs of altruism nor higher levels of civic engagement but only the motivations given by "the self-interest of members of the public who choose to support an association and the self-interest of its officials, whose livelihood is connected with building it up" (1994:52). We know better than this. We know, to cite the words of Hirst himself, that "the market requires . . . moral and self-denying individuals if it is to be equitable. Honesty, fair-dealing, and a respect for law are essential to an impersonal and efficient market, but they cannot be supplied by it. . . . They are a gift from society and its moral order" (1994:64). Society as a gift-giving moral order is home to moral individuals who value loyalty and voice before exit, and who seek involvement in cooperative processes that allow them to participate in the creation of common ends and a shared way of life. An associationalism imbued with rights and market rhetoric does fit in with "the dominant trend of modern human aspirations," as Hirst says, but it also fits in with the primary consequence of this trend, namely, the further erosion of that gift-giving moral order which even Hirst regards as essential to a tolerable existence in the contemporary world.

The associationalism favored by the sociological option is justified by its contributions to solidarity. Like Hirst's associationalism, it promotes the devolution of substantial welfare responsibilities to local groups and associations but does so in ways that enliven civil society. Sociological associationalism, like Hirst's, demands neither the reduction of public welfare funds nor the weakening of the government's role in economic governance, though it does insist on the accountability of groups and associations to public authority, and anticipates their contribution to an active and effective public life. A good illustration of sociological associationalism is found in Raffaella Nanetti's (1988) account of governmental decentralization in Italy.

In an effort to combat an increasingly unresponsive, ineffective, and corrupt national state bureaucracy, Italy, in 1970, initiated a process of decentralizing a broad range of state responsibilities to twenty regional governments. Often linked through multipurpose communal associations, regions acquired considerable policy-making power. In northern and central Italy, many regional governments themselves decentralized, delegating responsibility for the delivery of a wide range of social services to area-wide districts and neighborhood groups, some newly established, others long in existence. From the 1970s on, a sustained effort has been made to shift the provision of social services away from the state and, as well, from the dominant Catholic Church, to regional and municipal governments, and from there to local districts, voluntary associations, and neighborhood groups. Where it has worked, decentralization has been accompanied by heightened levels of civic participation. More individuals volunteer their services to management committees and governing boards, and more voluntary groups arise to assist neighborhood councils in maintaining and supervising the use of recreational facilities, gardens, day care centers, libraries, and art, theater, and film clubs, and in meeting the special needs of the elderly, children, and the handicapped (Nanetti 1988:148–49). Today, Nanetti notes, "there is a strong positive correlation between the level and quality of public services and the demand from citizens to participate in their management" (p. 184).

Not only has decentralization sparked an increase in both the participation of citizens in the management of public services and the number of voluntary associations and neighborhood groups involved in their delivery, it also has encouraged the growth of service cooperatives and mutual aid societies. Service cooperatives are nonprofit enterprises staffed by professionals, not volunteers, and are responsible for supplementing public services and providing lower-cost alternatives to services offered in the market. Self-financed and self-managed mutual aid societies are composed of groups of families or other users who "pay a small fee to cover the operating costs of the services which the society offers free of charge to members . . . for example, the care of the family when the mother is temporarily hospitalized, the provision of sitters for children and companionship for the elderly at home" (Nanetti 1988:156). In northern and central Italy (where Putnam discovered the social capital–generating civic regions), the decentralization of welfare and other social services improved their accessibility and quality. It also made interaction more engaged and committed, and thus advanced the solidarity that enables people to exercise greater control over their collective destiny. Indeed, as Nanetti discovers, it is the reward of such solidarity, and not the promise of greater individual freedom to fashion ends in accord with personal preferences, that motivated the remarkable upsurge in the level of participation in associational life (1988:155–57).

A welfare state appropriate to civil society has much to learn from the Italian experience and from the proposals of Starr and Hirst. It would be a state whose unshakeable commitment to the basic welfare of all its citizens and their children requires it to use its taxation power in a progressive way to acquire the public funds that will pay for welfare services; to establish national policies seriously dedicated to the improvement of education and health care; to set national standards that define acceptable welfare services and to monitor service providers in light of these standards; and to facilitate the decentralization of service delivery by delegating responsibilities to regional and local groups, associations, and clubs with the expectation that they attract the involvement of their members at a level sufficient to the resuscitation of the area's civil society. A civil welfare state would honor the individual rights of its citizens. However, it would justify itself to the moral individuals who are its citizens not as a bureaucratic device to satisfy entitlements but as part of the collective answer to the question, "What do we owe to one another?" Drawing its sustenance from a solidarity that has at its center respect for the worth and dignity of others as individuals, a civil welfare state demands of its citizens a personal stake in the welfare of others, asking them to give not only tax dollars but also of themselves. A civil welfare state, then, depends on compassionate people adept at the practices of mutual aid. Accordingly, it must assure the vitality of the civil society from which such people come.

The Market Economy. In the United States, the market economy, always considerably more powerful than the welfare state, has contributed most to the social breakdown which defines the underclass. "Inner cities have always featured high levels of poverty," writes William Julius Wilson (1996:27–28), "but the current levels of joblessness in some neighborhoods are unprecedented. . . . Many of today's problems—crime, family dissolution, and welfare—are fundamentally a consequence of the disappearance of work." The market that helps produce an underclass by taking jobs away from the inner city while intensifying the hold the consumerist ethos has on its residents, is the very same market that gives us an overclass whose vastly enlarged share of the nation's wealth and income does little to disguise the weakened institutional and communal life that they, like most other Americans, share with the underclass poor. The demoralization of social life has been furthered immeasurably by the deregulation of economic life. Indeed, the effort to advance market deregulation over the past two decades has effectively disembbeded the market economy from social context.

A civil market economy—a market economy friendly to civil society— is socially embedded. A socially embedded market economy is attentive to the purposes given by institutional ideals and deliberative public opinion and congenial to the formation of the social and civic virtues that enable people to realize those purposes. Throughout most of American history, Michael Sandel (1996) writes, "debates about economic policy have not [as they have over the past forty years] focused solely on the size and distribution of the national product. [Rather] they also addressed a different question, namely, what economic arrangements are most hospitable to self-government?" (p. 124). A civil market economy operates in ways consistent with freedom as self-government and as social control. Indeed, it is limited by the expectation that the pursuit of economic growth be undertaken with respect for the autonomy of public life (self-government), the autonomy of social life (social control), and the solidarity that underlies each.

Quickly and continually providing accurate information and economic incentive, the market economy is an enormously efficient device for producing and allocating goods and services. In addition, it affords the ground for the important freedom of choice in personal expression, work, and consumption. A civil market economy sacrifices neither market efficiency nor basic market freedoms in its accommodation to social and political freedoms. Yet, in defense of these freedoms, it supports those forces that work to modify the market's inherent tendency to distribute ever more unequally the conditions of welfare that sustain civil society. Some of these forces take governmental form, for instance, a progressive tax code. Others are the consequence of the moralizing energies generated within revitalized civil society. "The point to stress," David Miller (1989:32) notes, "is that, for markets to operate effectively, individuals and enterprises must receive primary profits, but the proportion of those profits that they need to keep as private income depends on how far they require material (as opposed to moral) incentives. The market is flexible in this respect." Thus, for people in whom the moral disposition has been developed, the market incentive of private material gain may be reduced with no loss in efficiency and with a gain in the amount of resources available for redistribution. A civil market economy is not socialized in Marx's sense of greater state control and ownership. Rather, it is moralized, in Durkheim's sense of being a place where profit-seeking, preference-satisfying individuals are moved not only by self-interest but as well by a moral sense rooted in developed social sentiments.

The redistribution of the income and wealth generated by a civil market economy runs counter to the growing inequality produced by the political Right's deregulated market. It also differs from the redistributive schemes associated with the political Left's welfare state in that it is justified in terms of solidarity, and not in terms of the individual's right to a package of benefits that permits one to select a self-preferred way of life. Solidaristic redistribution aims at establishing that minimal level of equality required for inclusion. It seeks not the end of inequality, but the end of those severe inequalities that exclude groups of people—the desperately poor of the underclass and the exorbitantly rich of the overclass, among them—from the solidaristic life of civil society. Its task is simple: "To assure that every citizen is at least on board" (Dahrendorf 1996:196–97). The responsibility for the fates of others which resides at the center of solidarity often is expressed as mutual self-interest, in the context of which acts of cooperation and mutual aid are valued for their contributions to the individual's pursuit of personal ends. Here, Paul Spicker (1992:73) observes, "people support others who are supporting them— and those who have not been able to contribute . . . will either not be included or be included only on inferior terms to others who do contribute," a logic played out in the difference between relatively generous insurance-based welfare programs and the always meagerly funded and stigmatized means-tested welfare programs. The solidarity in which a civil market economy is embedded goes beyond mutual self-interest. It is the more inclusive solidarity of moral individualism which honors redistribution as a practice of social responsibility which brings all on board and at a level where each is capable of developing the virtues that allow effective participation in autonomy-enhancing self-government and social control. It is, in short, the solidarity of the gift community whereby the gift of redistribution raises the recipients to the point where they are able to pass the gift along, a process, as we saw in the last chapter, that broadens the scope and deepens the roots of inclusion and integration.

A civil market economy differs from the uncivil market economy currently existing in the United States in its treatment of large corporations, in its response to the joblessness created by new technologies and globalization, and in its appreciation for what observers variously call the "voluntary," "third," or "social service" sector of the economy. In the embedded civil market economy, corporations are tied to social purposes once again. Initially, in return for the privileges and immunities of limited liability granted them by government, corporations were expected to take some responsibility for the public welfare. As this expectation lost force, corporations became mere money-making machines with little concern for the health, education, and well-being of their employees, residents of the localities in which they existed, and the citizens of the larger society. In a civil market economy, federally chartered corporations are expected to formulate employment and investment policies respectful of the natural and social habitats (no longer regarded as mere externalities) and of the conditions of civil society. High levels of corporate public accountability and social responsibility are achieved, first, by assuring that all who have a stake in the success of the corporation—not only shareholders, but employees, the community, and region that houses the corporation's operations—have their interests represented at the level of corporate policy making and decision making; and second, by linking corporate access to tax advantages and other forms of governmental assistance to socially responsible performances. Alternatives to large corporations—small- and medium-sized firms and worker- and community-owned enterprises—are actively encouraged in a civil market economy, perhaps by government-supported lending and investment banks committed to local and regional economic development (see Rowe 1996; Block 1993; Rifkin 1996b; Hirst 1994:chaps. 4, 5).

Seeking economic growth, a civil market economy embraces new technology and participates competitively in the global economy. Thus, it links itself to two developments greatly responsible for the rising levels of joblessness, working poor, and falling wages that plague the contemporary uncivil market economy. In a civil market economy, however, productivity gains are not confined to boosting executive salaries, the incomes of highly educated knowledge workers, and stockholder dividends; they are shared. A reduced work week, job sharing, and longer periods set aside for vacation, family and related leaves, and job retraining increase the number of available jobs but ultimately are insufficient to reverse the paradox created by the new technologies: Productivity increases are tied to decreases in the number of necessary work hours. To avoid the problems this creates in the uncivil market economy, its civil counterpart accommodates a citizen's income, an income independent of the market economy.

A citizen's income is a guaranteed annual income given to each citizen regardless of his or her wealth, employment status, or other income. It expresses each citizen's claim "to a share in the value of common resources," James Robertson (1996) writes, and is offered to provide people some measure of security amidst the volatile unpredictability promoted by new technology and globalization, and to do so in ways that "enable them to become less dependent on employers and officials of the state" (pp. 50–58). Complementing the minimum wage, social insurance programs, and the localized and regionalized system of welfare provision, the citizen's income sharply reduces poverty while it makes job-sharing more feasible and attractive. While most current proponents advocate a citizen's income as an unconditional right of each individual man, woman, and child in society, the citizen's income supported by a civil market society is different. First, its allocation takes into account the social context in which each man, woman, or child finds him- or herself, recognizing each not simply as an isolated individual but as a participant in social life. Care is taken to assure that as it enlarges independence from the market economy and the welfare state, the citizen's income does nothing to undermine the social and economic interdependencies that sustain close, especially familial, social attachments. Second, this citizen's income expressly links right to responsibility, and thus is conditional on participation. The participation criterion may be met through the labor market, with the usual exemptions granted to those prevented from work by illness, disability, or old age, or it may be satisfied, in A. B. Atkinson's words, by "people engaged in approved forms of education or training, caring for young, elderly, or disabled dependents or undertaking approved forms of voluntary work. . . . The condition involves neither *payment* nor *work*; it is a wider definition of social contribution" (1996:68–69). The citizen's income makes it possible for more people to contribute to the life of society by participating in socially important projects outside the market economy.

The primary beneficiary of the citizen's income conditional on participation is what Jeremy Rifkin (1995) calls the "third" or "voluntary" sector. "With the employed having more free time at their disposal and the unemployed having idle time on their hands," Rifkin writes,

> the opportunity exists to harness the unused labor of millions of people toward constructive tasks outside the private and public sectors. The talents and energy of both the employed and the unemployed—those with leisure hours and those with idle time—could be effectively directed toward rebuilding thousands of local communities and creating a third force that flourishes independent of the marketplace and the public sector. (p. 239)

Alongside the civil market economy, nonprofit organizations, many of them involved in the local and regional distribution of welfare services, prosper, and large numbers of people participate in community service programs which offer mentors to disadvantaged youth, home care to the elderly and the handicapped, or renovated apartments and low-cost housing to the poor. Others serve in public hospitals and shelters, as literacy teachers, volunteer firefighters, and disaster relief workers, and in environmental protection programs and crisis centers (Rifkin 1995:240). While workers in the current market economy "are motivated by material gain and view security in terms of increased consumption," Rifkin notes, participants in the third sector "are motivated by service to others and view security in the sense of grounding in the larger community" (1996a:24).

While the citizen's income is an important foundation of the expanded sector of goods and services production and distribution not driven by the imperative to enlarge stockholder value, it also has the potential to threaten Rifkin's vision of the third sector as home to a vibrant associational life nurtured by the motivation to be of service to others. If the citizen's income comes to be regarded as a wage for activities that are now strictly voluntary, then, like the givers of blood studied by Richard Titmuss, people currently disposed to make gifts of their time and energy to public shelters, literacy campaigns, and home care programs for the elderly may withdraw, making the third sector more heavily dependent on those whose participation is motivated only by the citizen's income as economic incentive. In these circumstances, the third sector could easily enough be transformed into a form of workfare that offers low-level, stigmatized employment and reduces the work of caring and mutual assistance to the paid labor of those displaced by the new technologies and globalization.

The strongest force standing against this possibility is the felt authority of the collective ideal of moral individualism identified by Durkheim. If firmly anchored in civil society—in viable institutions, in revitalized neighborhoods and communities, in a lively associational life, and in practices of civic engagement—the ideal of moral individualism places the achievement of solidarity, the kind of solidarity that feeds the freedoms of self-government and social control, high on the list of purposes for which the state and the market economy are responsible. Toward this end, limits are set on the juridifying reach of the state and the commodifying tendencies of the market; and the state, as it carries out the protection of individual rights, and the market, as it goes about the business of satisfying individual preferences, are expected to respect the conditions that nourish civil society as a sphere of solidarity. Where civil society is valued as much as the state and the market economy, the work required to sustain it—in part, the work provided by Rifkin's third sector—becomes immune to stigmatization. Add to this the giftlike character of both the citizen's income and the possibility for the honorable, socially important work it affords. Offered not in the language of individual rights and entitlements, but in the interests of solidarity, the citizen's income is a gift we make one another in recognition of the respect we owe each other as worthy and dignified individuals. As a gift, the citizen's income not only evokes gratitude, it also brings its recipients to the level at which they are able to keep the gift in motion, in this case, by passing along in their work generosity, goodwill, and graciousness.

A civil welfare state and a civil market economy, then, respect the space where civil society as a sphere of solidarity grows. In the past, when such space was more readily available, people threatened by the anomically destructive forces of liberal modernity quickly and ably used this space to construct social institutions, community associations, local cooperative structures, and networks of civic engagement, both to protect themselves against the perils of excessive individualism and to sustain the satisfactions of mutuality and belonging. For instance, as noted earlier, in the nineteenth century workers in Western Europe and later in the United States established friendly societies and other mutual aid associations to combat the deterioration of traditional social responsibility which accompanied the first wave of liberal modernization (Hird 1996). In the last half of the nineteenth century, the English middle class, resisting the spread of egoism and the cash nexus, helped create the ideals, statuses, and rituals that defined the institution of the modern nuclear family (Regan 1993; Gillis 1996). In the aftermath of the social decay and economic insecurity produced by the Great Depression, Americans, Alan Wolfe (1989) notes, "took refuge from the economy in civil society. Long marriages, whether satisfying or not, were combined with relatively stable communities and a commitment to the expansion of the public sector, all to create a system in which people could to some degree rely on one another for support" (p. 76).

But that was then, and this is now, as the realists remind us; and now, even if the space for civil society were reconstructed, does it make sense to assume that liberal individualist speakers of market and rights rhetoric, long habituated to the ways of the market economy and the welfare state, possess the resources, the know-how, and dispositions to create the social institutions, communitarian interdependencies, and networks of civic engagement that constitute an autonomous civil society? There are reasons to be skeptical, if not seriously pessimistic, and many of them have been presented here. If, as I have argued, Americans as liberal individuals lack developed social sentiments, experience with ongoing and reliable practices of mutual assistance, and a language capable of expressing the need for belonging and solidarity, they may respond to current insecurities and discontents by taking the ethos of individual survivalism to even greater extremes, by trying to recapture the past in closed, hate-filled, self-righteous groups hostile to outsiders, or, if the money is there, by escaping to well-guarded private enclaves sufficiently distanced from the miseries and the dangers of social collapse. Is sociology able to do anything about this?

In his important Presidential Address to the American Sociological Association, the late James Coleman argues that sociology can do something constructive once it abandons its "critical mistake," namely, continuing the search, initiated by the classical sociological tradition, for ways to revitalize the bases of morally dense solidarity. Strong families and kinship groups, vibrant neighborhoods, and moralizing communities cannot be regenerated in the modern world, Coleman insists, and probably all to the good given the intolerance and oppressiveness that accompany the primordial contexts that nurture such social settings. Their demise provides an opportunity for sociologists to become involved centrally in the rational reconstruction of society. As designers of institutions and architects of a purposively constructed social order, sociologists will be able to enhance their value to society by building systems of social control that rely not on constraint and negative sanction but "primarily on positive incentives and rewards for performance" (Coleman 1993:14). The classical sociological tradition, especially as it is represented by the commitment to civil society as a sphere of the solidarity-grounded individualism found in Durkheim's and Mead's work, has been rendered obsolete by developments that have placed rationally designed, impersonal organizations at the center of social life. Let it go, Coleman advises sociologists, and commence the real work of designing institutions that will "optimize relevant outcomes" (1993:14).

In contrast to Coleman, I have argued that the classical sociological tradition, especially Durkheim's contribution to it, continues to offer both a powerful critique of liberal modernity and a clear, though general, set of directions for advancing the moral reconstruction of society. Rather than follow Coleman's lead and seek a solution to the problems of weakened social order and diminished social obligation in the very forces that produced the problems, it would be better to guide our search by Durkheim's vision of vigorous, morally dense associations regulating themselves in accordance with moral principles supportive of individualism and authoritative enough to counter the self-interest actively encouraged by Coleman's rational system. Sociology's task is not simply to keep this vision alive but to enlarge its presence and deepen its appeal. To accomplish this, sociology must revitalize and popularize its language of solidarity, making available a rhetoric that enables people to express their needs for belonging and mutuality, to make sense of their developing social sentiments, and to respect those social settings that make possible the moral competencies that fortify and enrich the individual freedom advanced by liberal modernity.

In its effort to invigorate its language of solidarity, sociology could learn from the approach successfully taken by the ecology movement and environmental science in their attempt to alert people, children as well as adults, to the damage done to the natural ecology, to promote an abiding respect for the natural environment, and to encourage the alteration of behaviors destructive of the natural habitat. By raising awareness of and appreciation for the social habitat to the same level, sociology would improve the prospects for civil society. If it is to succeed in this endeavor, it first must rescue the words of solidarity—family values, responsibility, virtue, character, village, and civil society—from the distortions imposed on them in the current politics of social breakdown. Mandatory school uniforms, television V-chips, "three strikes and you're out" laws that add to the prison population, Personnel Responsibility Acts that make more precarious the lives of poor children, and Defense of Marriage Acts that deny homosexuals access to the institution of marriage—all are offered as ways of shoring up the cracked and bowed beams of social obligation. Yet, what modern solidarity most requires—knowledge of, the inclination to, and the resources for securing social institutions, communitarian interdependencies, and networks of civic engagement—is rarely acknowledged.

Sociology's job is to acknowledge this and to assure that its language of solidarity is readily available for that time when most Americans, having learned that the demands they make through liberal individualism's market and rights rhetorics go unheard, are compelled to figure out different ways of organizing their lives. With sociology's language of solidarity at hand, they may decide to call on one another for assistance in the gift-giving, trust-creating ways that make people good parents, good neighbors, and good citizens.

References

Agulhon, Maurice. 1982. *The Republic in the Village.* New York: Cambridge University Press.

Anderson, Elijah. 1990. *Streetwise.* Chicago: University of Chicago Press.

———. 1992. "The Story of John Turner." *Public Interest* 108(Summer):3–34.

———. 1994. "The Code of the Streets." *Atlantic Monthly* May:81–94.

Anderson, Elizabeth. 1990. "Is Women's Labor a Commodity?" *Philosophy and Public Affairs* 19:71–92.

Arato, Andrew, and Jean Cohen. 1992. "Civil Society and Social Theory." Pp. 199–219 in *Between Totalitarianism and Postmodernity,* edited by P. Beilharz, G. Robinson, and J. Rundell. Cambridge, MA: MIT Press.

Arblaster, Anthony. 1984. *The Rise and Decline of Western Liberalism.* Oxford: Blackwell.

Atkinson, A. B. 1996. "The Case for Participation Income." *Political Quarterly* 67:67–70.

Attali, Jacques. 1991. "The Ideology of Reversibility." *New Perspective Quarterly* Spring:20–21.

Atwood, Margaret. 1985. *The Handmaid's Tale.* New York: Fawcett.

Auletta, Ken. 1982. *The Underclass.* New York: Random House.

Banfield, Edward. 1958. *The Moral Basis of a Backward Society.* New York: Free Press.

Barber, Benjamin. 1984. *Strong Democracy.* Berkeley and Los Angeles: University of California Press.

———. 1989. "Liberal Democracy and the Costs of Consent." Pp. 54–68 in *Liberalism and the Moral Life,* edited by N. Rosenblum. Cambridge, MA: Harvard University Press.

Barrett, Katherine. 1988. "Re-Expressing Parenthood." *Yale Law Review* 98(December):293–340.

Baumeister, Roy, and Mark Leary. 1996. "The Need to Belong: Desire for Interpersonal Attachments as a Fundamental Human Motivation." *Psychological Bulletin* 117:497–529.

Bell, Daniel. 1995. "Residential Community Associations: Community or Disunity?" *The Responsive Community* 5(4):25–36.

Bellah, Robert, Richard Madsen, William Sullivan, Ann Swidler, and Stephen Tipton. 1985. *Habits of the Heart.* Berkeley and Los Angeles: University of California Press.

————. 1991. *The Good Society.* New York: Knopf.

Bellamy, Richard. 1992. *Liberalism and Modern Society.* University Park: Pennsylvania State University Press.

Belluck, Pam. 1996. "In an Era of Shrinking Budgets, Community Groups Blossom." *New York Times* February 26:A1, 36.

Berger, Peter, and Thomas Luckmann. 1966. *The Social Construction of Reality.* New York: Anchor.

Berkowitz, Peter. 1996. "The Art of Association." *New Republic* June 24:44–49.

Berry, Kathleen. 1991. "A Multibillion Dollar Business in a Non-profit World." *New York Times* July 7:C8.

Best, Michael, and William Connolly. 1976. *The Politicized Economy.* Lexington, MA: Heath.

Blau, Peter. 1964. *Exchange and Power in Social Life.* New York: Wiley.

Block, Fred. 1993. "Remaking Our Economy." *Dissent* Spring:166–71.

Blum, Lawrence. 1990. "Vocation, Friendship, and Community." Pp. 175–97 in *Identity, Character and Morality,* edited by O. Flanagan and A. Rorty. Cambridge, MA: MIT Press.

Boisjoly, Johanne, Greg Duncan, and Sandra Hofferth. 1995. "Access to Social Capital." *Journal of Family Issues* 16:609–31.

Bowles, Samuel. 1991. "What Markets Can—and Cannot—Do." *Challenge* July–August:11–16.

Bowles, Samuel, and Herbert Gintis. 1986. *Democracy and Capitalism.* New York: Basic.

Braithwaite, John. 1989. *Crime, Shame, and Reintegration.* New York: Cambridge University Press.

Callahan, Daniel. 1987. *Setting Limits.* New York: Simon & Schuster.

Carrier, James. 1991. "Gifts, Commodities, and Social Relations." *Sociological Forum* 6:119–36.

Carton, Paul. 1991. "Mass Media Culture and the Breakdown of Values Among Inner-City Youth." *Future Choices* 2(Winter):11–14.

Chira, Susan. 1994. "Study Confirms Worst Fears on U.S. Children." *New York Times* April 12:A1.

Cladis, Mark. 1992a. *A Communitarian Defense of Liberalism.* Stanford, CA: Stanford University Press.

————. 1992b. "Durkheim's Individual in Society." *Journal of the History of Ideas* 53:71–90.

Clinton, Hillary. 1996. *It Takes a Village and Other Lessons Children Teach Us.* New York: Simon & Schuster.

Cobb, Clifford, Ted Halstead, and Jonathan Rowe. 1995. "If the GDP Is Up, Why Is America Down?" *Atlantic Monthly* October:59–78.

Coleman, James. 1988. "Social Capital in the Creation of Human Capital." *American Journal of Sociology* 94(Supplement):95–120.

————. 1990a. *Foundations of Social Theory.* Cambridge, MA: Harvard University Press.

————. 1990b. *Equity and Achievement in Education.* Boulder, CO: Westview.

————. 1990c. "How Worksite Schools and Other School Reforms Can Generate Social Capital." *American Education* Summer:35–46.

———. 1991. "Prologue: Constructed Social Organization." Pp. 1–14 in *Social Theory for a Changing Society,* edited by P. Bourdieu and J. Coleman. Boulder, CO: Westview.

———. 1993. "The Rational Reconstruction of Society." *American Sociological Review* 58:1–15.

Coleman, James, and Thomas Hoffer. 1987. *Public and Private High Schools.* New York: Basic.

Collins, Randall. 1988. *Theoretical Sociology.* San Diego, CA: Harcourt Brace Jovanovich.

Csikszentmihayli, Mihaly. 1993. "Contexts of Optimal Growth in Childhood." *Daedalus* 122:31–56.

Csikszentmihayli, Mihaly, and Eugene Rochberg-Halton. 1981. *The Meaning of Things.* Cambridge: Cambridge University Press.

Currie, Elliot. 1991. "Crime in the Market Society." *Dissent* Spring:254–60.

———. 1993. *Reckoning.* New York: Hill & Wang.

Cushman, Philip. 1990. "Why the Self Is Empty." *American Psychologist* 45:599–611.

Dahrendorf, Ralf. 1985. *Law and Order.* Boulder, CO: Westview.

———. 1995. "A Precarious Balance: Economic Opportunity, Civil Society, and Political Liberty." *The Responsive Community* 5(3):13–39.

———. 1996. "On the Dahrendorf Report." *Political Quarterly* 67:194–97.

Day, Kathleen. 1993. *S. and L. Hell.* New York: Norton.

Dewey, John. 1988. "Creative Democracy—The Task Before Us." Pp. 224–29 in *John Dewey: The Later Works,* vol. 14, edited by J. Boydson. Carbondale: Southern Illinois Press.

Didion, Joan. 1993. "Trouble in Lakewood." *New Yorker* July 26:46–65.

Diller, Lawrence. 1996. "The Run on Ritalin." *Hastings Center Report* March–April:12–18.

Durkheim, Émile. [1893] 1947. *The Division of Labor in Society.* New York: Free Press.

———. [1897] 1951. *Suicide.* J. Spaulding, translator. New York: Free Press.

———. [1950] 1958. *Professional Ethics and Civic Morals.* Glencoe, IL: Free Press.

———. [1925] 1961. *Moral Education.* New York: Free Press.

———. [1912] 1965. *Elementary Forms of the Religious Life.* New York: Free Press.

———. [1890] 1973. "The Principles of 1789 and Sociology." Pp. 34–42 in *Émile Durkheim on Morality and Society,* edited by R. Bellah. Chicago: University of Chicago Press.

———. 1974. *Sociology and Philosophy.* New York: Free Press.

Earls, Felton, and Mary Carlson. 1993. "Towards Sustainable Development for American Families." *Daedalus* 122:93–121.

Eberstadt, Nicholas. 1994. "Why Babies Die in D.C." *Public Interest* 115(Spring):3–16.

Edsall, Thomas. 1996. "Public Grows More Receptive to Anti-Government Message." *Washington Post* January 31:A1, 5.

Egan, Timothy. 1995. "Many Seek Security in Private Communities." *New York Times* September 3:A1, 22.

Elkind, David. 1995. "School and Family in the Post-Modern World." *Phi Delta Kappan* September:8–14.

Emerson, Ralph Waldo. 1876. *Essays*. Boston: Houghton, Mifflin, and Company.

Erikson, Erik. 1968. *Identity: Youth and Crisis*. New York: Norton.

Erikson, Kai. 1976. *Everything in Its Path*. New York: Simon & Schuster.

———. 1991. "Notes on Trauma and Community." *American Imago* 48:455–71.

Freeman, Richard. 1996. "Toward an Apartheid Economy?" *Harvard Business Review* September–October:114–21.

Fukuyama, Francis. 1992. *The End of History and the Last Man*. New York: Free Press.

———. 1995. *Trust*. New York: Free Press.

Furstenberg, Frank, and Mary Elizabeth Hughes. 1995. "Social Capital and Successful Development Among At-Risk Youth." *Journal of Marriage and the Family* 57:580–92.

Gehlen, Arnold. 1980. *Man in the Age of Technology*. New York: Columbia University Press.

Gergen, Kenneth. 1991. *The Saturated Self*. New York: Basic.

Gilder, George. 1981. *Wealth and Poverty*. New York: Basic.

Gilligan, Carol. 1982. *In a Different Voice*. Cambridge, MA: Harvard University Press.

Gillis, John. 1996. *A World of Their Own*. New York: Basic.

Glass, James. 1980. "Hobbes and Narcissism." *Political Theory* 8:335–63.

Glassman, James. 1990. "The Great Banks Robbery." *New Republic* October 8:16–21.

Glendon, Mary Ann. 1991. *Rights Talk*. New York: Free Press.

Goldberger, Paul. 1995. "The Gospel of Church Architecture, Revised." *New York Times* April 20:C1, 6.

Goldman, Harvey. 1988. *Max Weber and Thomas Mann: Calling and the Shaping of the Self*. Berkeley and Los Angeles: University of California Press.

Gonzalez, David. 1993. "Seeking Security, Many Retreat Behind Bars and Razor Wire." *New York Times* July 17:A1.

Goodin, Robert. 1985. "Vulnerabilities and Responsibilities." *American Political Science Review* 79:775–87.

Gouldner, Alvin. 1980. *Two Marxisms*. New York: Seabury.

Habermas, Jurgen. 1974. "The Public Sphere." *New German Critique* 3:49–55.

———. 1989a. *The Theory of Communicative Rationality*, vol. 2. Boston: Beacon.

———. 1989b. *The Structural Transformation of the Public Sphere*. Cambridge, MA: MIT Press.

———. 1990. "What Does Socialism Mean Today?" *New Left Review* 183 (September–October):3–21.

Hacker, Andrew. 1992. "The Myths of Racial Division." *New Republic* March 21:21–25.

Hagan, John, Hans Merkins, and Klaus Boehnke. 1995. "Delinquincy and Disdain: Social Capital and the Control of Right-Wing Extremism Among East and West Berlin Youth." *American Journal of Sociology* 100:1028–52.

Hall, Robert. 1987. *Émile Durkheim: Ethics and the Sociology of Morals*. New York: Greenwood.

———. 1991. "Communitarian Ethics and the Sociology of Morals." *Sociological Focus* 24:93–104.

Hallowell, Edward, and John Ratey. 1994. *Driven to Distraction.* New York: Pantheon.

Hamburg, David. 1992. *Today's Children.* New York: Times Books.

Hampden-Turner, Charles. 1971. *Radical Man.* Garden City, NY: Doubleday.

———. 1975. *From Poverty to Dignity.* Garden City, NY: Doubleday.

Handler, Joel. 1990. *Law and the Search for Community.* Philadelphia: University of Pennsylvania Press.

Hardimon, Michael. 1994. "Role Obligations." *Journal of Philosophy* 91:333–63.

Heath, Douglas. 1994. *Schools of Hope.* San Francisco: Jossey-Bass.

Held, Virginia. 1990. "Mothering Versus Contract." Pp. 287–304 in *Beyond Self-Interest,* edited by J. Mansbridge. Chicago: University of Chicago Press.

Hilbert, Richard. 1986. "Anomie and the Moral Regulation of Society." *Sociological Theory* 4(Spring):1–19.

Hird, Christopher. 1996. "Building Societies: Stakeholding in Practice and Under Threat." *New Left Review* 218(July–August):40–52.

Hirschman, Albert. 1970. *Exit, Voice, and Loyalty.* Cambridge, MA: Harvard University Press.

———. 1986. *Rival Views of Market Society.* New York: Viking.

Hirschmann, Nancy. 1992. "Political Obligation, Freedom, and Feminism." *American Political Science Review* 86:179–88.

Hirst, Paul. 1994. *Associative Democracy.* Amherst: University of Massachusetts Press.

Hobbes, Thomas. [1651] 1963. *Leviathan.* New York: Meridian.

Hochschild, Jennifer. 1991. "The Politics of the Estranged Poor." *Ethics* 101:560–78.

Honneth, Axel. 1992. "Pluralization and Recognition: On the Self-Misunderstanding of Postmodern Social Theorists." Pp. 163–72 in *Between Totalitarianism and Postmodernity,* edited by P. Beilharz, G. Robinson, and J. Rundell. Cambridge, MA: MIT Press.

Horvitz, Allan. 1990. *The Logic of Social Control.* New York: Plenum Press.

Hyde, Lewis. 1979. *The Gift.* New York: Vintage.

Ingrassia, Michele, and John McCormick. 1994. "Why Leave Children with Bad Parents?" *Newsweek* April 25:52–54.

Jacobs, Lesley. 1993. "The Enabling Model of Rights." *Political Studies* 41:381–93.

Janowitz, Morris. 1978. *The Last Half-Century.* Chicago: University of Chicago Press.

Jencks, Christopher. 1988. "Deadly Neighborhoods." *New Republic* June 13:23–32.

———. 1990. "Varieties of Altruism." Pp. 53–67 in *Beyond Self-Interest,* edited by J. Mansbridge. Chicago: University of Chicago Press.

Kant, Immanuel. [1785] 1950. *The Moral Law.* New York: Barnes & Noble.

Kass, Leon. 1992. "Organs for Sale? Propriety, Prosperity, and the Price of Progress." *Public Interest* 107(Spring):65–86.

Katz, Michael. 1989. *The Underserving Poor.* New York: Pantheon.

Kempton, Arthur. 1991. "Native Sons." *New York Review of Books* April 11:55–61.

Kennedy, David. 1995. "Residential Associations as State Actors." *Yale Law Review* 105:761–93.

Kernberg, Otto. 1975. *Borderline Conditions and Pathological Narcissism.* New York: Aronson.

Kirp, David. 1989. *Learning by Heart*. New Brunswick, NJ: Rutgers University Press.

Kohlberg, Lawrence. 1981. *The Philosophy of Moral Development*. San Francisco: Harper & Row.

———. 1984. *Essays on Moral Development*. San Francisco: Harper & Row.

Kramer, Michael. 1994. "Clinton's House Rules." *Time* May 9:55.

Kroker, Arthur, Marilouise Kroker, and David Cook. 1990. "Panic USA: Hyper-modernism as America's Postmodernism." *Social Problems* 37:443–59.

Kymlicka, Will. 1990. *Contemporary Political Philosophy*. New York: Oxford University Press.

Lane, Robert. 1981. "Market and Politics: The Human Product." *British Journal of Political Science* 11:1–16.

———. 1991. *The Market Experience*. New York: Cambridge University Press.

Lasch, Christopher. 1978. *The Culture of Narcissism*. New York: Norton.

———. 1984. *The Minimal Self*. New York: Norton.

———. 1992. "Hillary Clinton, Child Saver." *Harper's* October:74–82.

———. 1995. *The Revolt of the Elites*. New York: Norton.

Leach, Penelope. 1994. *Children First*. New York: Knopf.

Lemann, Nicholas. 1991. *The Promised Land*. New York: Knopf.

Levi, Margaret. 1996. "Social and Unsocial Capital." *Politics and Society* 24:45–55.

Levin, David. 1987. "Clinical Stories: A Modern Self in the Fury of Being." Pp. 479–538 in *Pathologies of the Modern Self*, edited by D. Levin. New York: New York University Press.

Lewis, David, and Andrew Weigert. 1985. "Trust as Social Reality." *Social Forces* 63:967–85.

Lind, Michael. 1995. *The Next American Nation*. New York: Free Press.

Lipson, Michael, and Abigail Lipson. 1996. "Psychotherapy and the Ethics of Attention." *Hastings Center Report* January–Febraury:17–22.

Logan, John, and Harvey Molotch. 1987. *Urban Fortunes*. Berkeley and Los Angeles: University of California Press.

Luke, Tim. 1989–1990. "Xmas Ideology: Unwrapping the New Deal and the Cold War Under the Christmas Tree." *Telos* 82(Winter):157–73.

Macpherson, C. B. 1962. *The Political Theory of Possessive Individualism*. Oxford: Oxford University Press.

———. 1977. *The Life and Times of Liberal Democracy*. Oxford: Oxford University Press.

Maland, Charles. 1980. *Frank Capra*. Boston: Twayne.

Marx, Karl. [1843] 1978. "On the Jewish Question." Pp. 26–52 in *The Marx–Engels Reader*, edited by R. Tucker. New York: Norton.

Marx, Karl, and Friedrich Engels. [1848] 1978. "The Manifesto of the Communist Party." Pp. 469–500 in *The Marx–Engels Reader*, edited by R. Tucker. New York: Norton.

Mauss, Marcel. 1967. *The Gift*. New York: Norton.

McClelland, Peter. 1990. *The American Search for Economic Justice*. Cambridge, MA: Blackwell.

McCloskey, Herbert, and John Schaar. 1965. "Psychological Dimensions of Anomy." *American Sociological Review* 30:14–40.

Mead, George Herbert. 1962. *Mind, Self, and Society*. C. Morris, editor. Chicago: University of Chicago Press.

——. 1964. *On Social Psychology*. A. Strauss, editor. Chicago: University of Chicago Press.

Mestrovic, Stjepan, and Helene Brown. 1985. "Durkheim's Concept of Anomie as Dérèglement." *Social Problems* 33:81–99.

Mill, John Stuart. [1859] 1975. *On Liberty*. Indianapolis, IN: Hackett.

Miller, David. 1989. "Why Markets?" Pp. 25–49 in *Market Socialism*, edited by J. LeGrand and S. Estrin. Oxford: Clarendon Press.

Mills, C. Wright. [1952] 1963. "Liberal Values in the Modern World." Pp. 187–95 in *Power, Politics, and People*, edited by I. G. Horowitz. New York: Oxford University Press.

Mincy, Ronald, Isabel Sawhill, and Douglas Wolf. 1990. "The Underclass: Definition and Measurement." *Science* 248(April 27):450–52.

Moon, J. Donald. 1993. *Constructing Community*. Princeton, NJ: Princeton University Press.

Moore, Thomas. 1992. *Care of the Soul*. New York: HarperCollins.

——. 1996. *The Re-enchantment of Everyday Life*. New York: HarperCollins.

Morin, Richard. 1996. "Who's in Control? Many Don't Know or Care." *Washington Post* January 29:A1, 6.

Moynihan, Daniel. 1993. "Defining Deviancy Down." *American Scholar* 62:17–30.

Murray, Charles. 1984. *Losing Ground*. New York: Basic.

——. 1992. "Discussing Welfare Dependency Is Irrelevant." *Public Welfare* Spring:24–25.

——. 1993. "The Coming White Underclass." *Wall Street Journal* October 29:8.

——. 1994a. "Does Welfare Bring More Babies?" *Public Interest* Spring:18–30.

——. 1994b. "What to Do About Welfare." *Commentary* December:26–34.

Murray, Thomas. 1987. "Gifts of the Body and the Needs of Strangers." *Hastings Center Report* April:30–38.

Myrdal, Gunnar. 1962. *The Challenge to Affluence*. New York: Pantheon.

Nanetti, Raffaella. 1988. *Growth and Territorial Politics: The Italian Model of Social Capitalism*. London: Pinter.

Niebuhr, Gustav. 1995a. "Where Shopping-Mall Culture Gets a Big Dose of Religion." *New York Times* April 16:A1, 14.

——. 1995b. "The Minister as Marketer." *New York Times* April 18:A1, 20.

Nightingale, Charles. 1993. *On the Edge*. New York: Basic.

Nisbet, Robert. 1966. *The Sociological Tradition*. New York: Basic.

——. 1988. *The Present Age*. New York: Harper & Row.

Orru, Marco. 1987. *Anomie*. Boston: Allen & Unwin.

Pateman, Carol. 1989. *The Disorder of Women*. Stanford, CA: Stanford University Press.

Pearce, Frank. 1989. *The Radical Durkheim*. London: Allen & Unwin.

Pettit, Philip. 1995. "The Cunning of Trust." *Philosophy and Public Affairs* 23:202–25.

Piaget, Jean. 1965. *The Moral Judgement of the Child*. New York: Free Press.

Piliavin, Jane, and Hong-Wen Chang. 1990. "Altruism: A Review of Recent Theory and Research." *Annual Review of Sociology* 16:27–65.

Pizzo, Stephen, Mary Fricker, and Bob Muolo. 1989. *Inside Job*. New York: McGraw-Hill.

Poole, Ross. 1991. *Morality and Modernity*. New York: Routledge.

Poponoe, David. 1988. *Disturbing the Nest*. Hawthorne, NY: Aldine de Gruyter.

———. 1991. "Family Decline in the Swedish Welfare State." *Public Interest* 102(Winter):65–77.

Putnam, Robert. 1993a. *Making Democracy Work: Civic Traditions in Modern Italy*. Princeton, NJ: Princeton University Press.

———. 1993b. "The Prosperous Community." *American Prospect* Spring:35–42.

———. 1995a. "Tuning In, Tuning Out: The Strange Disappearance of Social Capital in America." *PS: Political Science and Politics* 28:664–83.

———. 1995b. "Bowling Alone, Revisited." *The Responsive Community* 5:18–33.

———. 1995c. "Bowling Alone: America's Declining Social Capital." *Journal of Democracy* 6:65–78.

Radin, Margaret J. 1987. "Market Inalienability." *Harvard Law Review* 100:1849–1937.

Regan, Milton. 1993. *Family Law and the Pursuit of Intimacy*. New York: New York University Press.

Reich, Robert. 1991. *The Work of Nations*. New York: Vintage.

Rifkin, Jeremy. 1995. *The End of Work*. New York: Putnam.

———. 1996a. "A New Social Contract." *Annals of American Political and Social Science* 544(March):16–26.

———. 1996b. "Civil Society in the Information Age." *Nation* February 26:11–16.

Robertson, James. 1996. "Towards a New Social Compact: Citizen's Income and Radical Tax Reform." *Political Quarterly* 67:50–58.

Roche, Maurice. 1992. *Rethinking Citizenship*. Cambridge: Polity Press.

Rosen, Marty. 1996. "Keeping the Elderly in the Neighborhood." *The Responsive Community* 6:81–83.

Rowe, Jonathan. 1996. "Reinventing the Corporation." *Washington Monthly* April:16–23.

Ruston, J. P. 1980. *Altruism, Socialization, and Society*. Englewood Cliffs, NJ: Prentice-Hall.

Sampson, Robert. 1995. "The Community." Pp. 193–216 in *Crime*, edited by J. Q. Wilson and J. Petersilia. San Francisco: ICS Press.

Sandel, Michael. 1984. "Morality and the Liberal Ideal." *New Republic* May 7:15–17.

———. 1988. "The Crisis of Authority." *New Perspectives Quarterly* Fall:8–16.

———. 1989. "Moral Argument and Liberal Toleration: Abortion and Homosexuality." *California Law Review* 77:521–38.

———. 1992. "The Procedural Republic." Pp. 12–28 in *Communitarianism and Individualism*, edited by S. Avineri and A. DeShalit. New York: Oxford University Press.

———. 1996. *Democracy's Discontent*. Cambridge, MA: Harvard University Press.

Selznick, Philip. 1987. "The Idea of a Communitarian Morality." *California Law Review* 75:445–63.

———. 1992. *The Moral Commonwealth*. Berkeley and Los Angeles: University of California Press.

Shalin, Dmitri. 1988. "G. H. Mead, Socialism, and the Progressive Agenda." *American Journal of Sociology* 93:913–51.

————. 1992. "Critical Theory and the Pragmatist Challenge." *American Journal of Sociology* 98:237–79.

Sherrill, Robert. 1990. "S. and L.s, Big Banks and Other Triumphs of Capitalism." *The Nation* November 19:589–624.

Shils, Edward. 1991. "The Virtues of Civil Society." *Government and Opposition* 26:3–20.

Siegel, Fred. 1988. "Dependent Individualism." *Dissent* Fall:437–40.

Silver, Alan. 1985. "'Trust' in Social and Political Theory." Pp. 52–67 in *The Challenge of Social Control*, edited by G. Suttles and M. Zald. Norwood, NJ: Ablex.

Simmel, Georg. [1908] 1950. *The Sociology of Georg Simmel*, edited by K. Wolff. New York: Free Press.

Simmons, Roberta. 1991. "Altruism and Sociology." *Sociological Quarterly* 32:1–22.

Singer, Peter. 1973. "Altruism and Commerce." *Philosophy and Public Affairs* 2:312–320.

————. 1977. "Freedoms and Utilities in the Distribution of Health Care." Pp. 149–73 in *Markets and Morals*, edited by G. Dworkin. Washington, DC: Hemisphere.

Skogan, Wesley. 1990. *Disorder and Decline*. New York: Free Press.

Smith, Adam. [1776] 1910. *An Inquiry into the Wealth of Nations*. New York: Dutton.

Smothers, Ronald. 1995. "Tell It to Mom and Dad and the Authorities." *New York Times* November 14:E4.

Solomon, Marion. 1988. *Narcissism and Intimacy*. New York: Norton.

Solow, Robert. 1995. "But Verify." *New Republic* September 11:36–39.

Spicker, Paul. 1992. "Equality Versus Solidarity." *Government and Opposition* 27:66–77.

Spiegler, Marc. 1996. "Scouting for Souls." *American Demographics* March:42–49.

Starr, Paul. 1992. "Building Minority Institutions." *Current* February:4–9.

Swidler, Ann. 1992. "Inequality and American Culture." *American Behavioral Scientist* 35:606–29.

Taylor, Charles. 1989. *Sources of the Self*. Cambridge, MA: Harvard University Press.

Thorne, Emanuel. 1990. "Tissue Transplants." *Public Interest* 98(Winter):37–48.

Titmuss, Richard. 1970. *The Gift Relationship*. London: Allen & Unwin.

Tonnies, Ferdinand. [1888] 1957. *Community and Society*. East Lansing: Michigan State University Press.

Turnbull, Colin. 1972. *The Mountain People*. New York: Simon & Schuster.

————. 1978. "Rethinking the Ik: A Functional Non-Social System." Pp. 49–75 in *Extinction and Survival in Human Populations*, edited by C. Vaughlin and J. Brody. New York: Columbia University Press.

Van Biema, David. 1996. "Emperor of the Soul." *Time* June 24:64–68.

Veroff, Joseph, Elizabeth Douvan, and Richard Kulka. 1981. *The Inner American*. New York: Basic.

Wallis, Claudia. 1994. "Life in Overdrive." *Time* July 18:43–50.

Wallwork, Ernest. 1985. "Sentiment and Structure: A Durkheimian Critique of Kohlberg's Moral Theory." *Journal of Moral Education* 14:87–101.

Walzer, Michael. 1982. "Socialism and the Gift Relationship." *Dissent* Fall:431–41.

———. 1986. "Toward a Theory of Social Assignments." Pp. 79–96 in *American Society,* edited by W. Knowlton and R. Zeckhauser. Cambridge, MA: Ballinger.

———. 1989. "The Good Life." *New Statesmen and Society* October 6:28–30.

———. 1991. "The Idea of Civil Society." *Dissent* Spring:293–304.

Weber, Max. [1919] 1946a. "Politics as a Vocation." Pp. 77–128 in *From Max Weber,* edited by H. Gerth and C. W. Mills. New York: Oxford University Press.

———. [1921] 1946b. "Bureaucracy." Pp. 196–244 in *From Max Weber,* edited by H. Gerth and C. W. Mills. New York: Oxford University Press.

Westman, Jack. 1994. *Licensing Parents.* New York: Plenum Press.

Whitehead, Barbara Dafoe. 1993. "Dan Quayle Was Right." *Atlantic Monthly* April:47–84.

Will, George. 1995. "What's Behind Income Disparity." *Cortland Standard* April 24:5.

Willis, Donald. 1974. *The Films of Frank Capra.* Metuchen, NJ: Scarecrow.

Wilson, James Q. 1993. *The Moral Sense.* New York: Free Press.

Wilson, William Julius. 1987. *The Truly Disadvantaged.* Chicago: University of Chicago Press.

———. 1991a. "Studying Inner-City Social Dislocations." *American Sociological Review* 56:1–14.

———. 1991b. "The Poor Image of Black Men." *New Perspectives Quarterly* Summer:26–29.

———. 1996. "Work." *New York Times Magazine* August 28:27–31, 40, 48, 52–54.

Wolfe, Alan. 1989. *Whose Keeper?* Berkeley and Los Angeles: University of California Press.

Wuthnow, Robert. 1991. *Acts of Compassion.* Princeton, NJ: Princeton University Press.

Yarosh, Steven. 1994. "A Place for Safe Housing in the Fourth Amendment." *The Responsive Community* 4:29–41.

Zakaria, Faveed. 1995. "Bigger Than the Family: Smaller Than the State." *New York Times Book Review* August 13:1, 25.

Zuriff, G. E. 1996. "Medicalizing Character." *Public Interest* Spring:94–99.

Zwiebach, Burton. 1988. *The Common Life: Ambiguity, Agreement, and the Structure of Morals.* Philadelphia: Temple University Press.

Author Index

Agulhon, Maurice, 160
Anderson, Elijah, 37–38
Anderson, Elizabeth, 13–14, 126–127
Arato, Andrew, 169
Arblaster, Anthony, 56–57
Arrow, Kenneth, 102–103
Atkinson, A.B., 182–183
Attali, Jacques, 126
Atwood, Margaret, 14
Auletta, Ken, 23

Barber, Benjamin, 56–57
Barrett, Katherine, 18, 20
Baumeister, Roy, 86
Bell, Daniel, 43–44
Bellah, Robert, 8, 9, 16, 17, 47, 48, 54, 56, 85, 141, 143
Belluck, Pam, 174
Berger, Peter, 17
Berkowitz, Peter, 140–141
Berry, Kathleen, 116–117
Best, Michael, 59
Blau, Peter, 119
Block, Fred, 181
Blum, Lawrence, 16
Boehnke, Klaus, 99
Boisjoly, Johanne, 98, 102–103
Bowles, Samuel, 60–61, 157
Braithwaite, John, 34
Brown, Helene, 67

Callahan, Daniel, 15
Carrier, James, 111–112
Carlson, Mary, 12
Chang, Hong-Wen, 113–114
Cladis, Mark, 82
Clinton, Hillary, 2–7, 9, 11–12

Cobb, Clifford, 104–105
Cohen, Jean, 169
Coleman, James, 2–5, 7–9, 11–12, 35–37, 39, 102–103, 128–129, 151–152, 185
Collins, Randall, 81, 122
Connolly, William, 59
Cook, David, 70–71
Csikszentmihalyi, Mikaly, 1, 12, 140–141
Currie, Elliot, 30–33, 39
Cushman, Philip, 53

Dahrendorf, Ralf, 67–68, 173, 180–181
Day, Kathleen, 108–109
Dewey, John, 163–164
Diller, Lawrence, 137–138, 141–142
Douvan, Elizabeth, 60–61
Duncan, Greg, 98, 102–103
Durkheim, Emile, 67–69, 71–72, 77–84, 121–123, 158–164, 166–167, 180

Earls, Felton, 12
Eberstadt, Nicholas, 41–42
Egan, Timothy, 43
Elkind, David, 142–143
Emerson, Ralph Waldo, 110–111
Erikson, Erik, 35, 119
Erikson, Kai, 51–53, 55

Fricker, Mary, 108–109
Fukuyama, Francis, 97–103, 130, 155
Furstenberg, Frank, 98–99, 102–103

Gehlen, Arnold, 16–17
Gergen, Kenneth, 54–55

197

Gilder, George, 28
Gilligan, Carol, 76–77
Gillis, John, 184
Gintis, Herbert, 157
Glass, James, 53–54
Glassman, James, 109–110
Glendon, Mary Ann, 9
Goldberger, Paul, 139–140
Goldman, Harvey, 166
Goodin, Robert, 62
Gonzalez, David, 21
Gouldner, Alvin, 66

Habermas, Jurgen, 153–156, 166–171
Hacker, Andrew, 41–42
Hagan, John, 99
Hall, Richard, 80
Hallowell, Edward, 138
Halstead, Ted, 104–105
Hamburg, David, 1
Hampden-Turner, Charles, 68–69
Handler, Joel, 11
Hardimon, Michael, 17–18
Heath, Douglas, 138–139
Held, Virginia, 119–120
Hilbert, Richard, 67–69
Hird, Christopher, 184
Hirschman, Albert, 61–62
Hirschmann, Nancy, 157–158
Hirst, Paul, 174–177, 181
Hobbes, Thomas, 48–50
Hochschild, Jennifer, 39–41
Hoffer, Thomas, 35
Hofferth, Sandra, 98, 102–103
Honneth, Axel, 71
Horvitz, Allan, 33
Hughes, Mary Elizabeth, 98–99, 102–103
Hyde, Lewis, 112, 117–118

Jacobs, Lesley, 62
Janowitz, Morris, 33
Jencks, Christopher, 40, 114

Kant, Immanuel, 74–75
Kass, Leon, 117
Katz, Michael, 23

Kirp, David, 92–94
Kempton, Arthur, 41
Kennedy, David, 43–44
Kernberg, Otto, 53–54
Kohlberg, Lawrence, 75–76
Kramer, Michael, 38–39
Kroker, Arthur, 70–71
Kroker, Marilouise, 70–71
Kulka, Richard, 60–61
Kymlicka, Will, 73–74

Lane, Robert, 60–61
Lasch, Christopher, 5–6, 11, 42–44, 53–55, 137
Leach, Penelope, 4–5, 7, 9, 11–12
Leary, Mark, 86
Lemann, Nicholas, 24–25, 28
Levi, Margaret, 134
Levin, David, 54
Lewis, David, 34–35
Lind, Michael, 42–43
Lipson, Abigail, 140
Lipson, Michael, 140
Logan, John, 21–22
Luckmann, Thomas, 17
Luke, Tim, 105

Macpherson, C.B., 56–58
Madsen, Richard, 8–9, 16–17, 47–48, 56, 85, 141, 153–154
Maland, Charles, 105, 107–108
Marx, Karl, 158–159, 163–166
Mauss, Marcel, 119–120
McClelland, Peter, 28–30
McCloskey, Herbert, 68–70
Mead, George Herbert, 158–167
Merkins, Hans, 99
Mestrovic, Stjerpan, 67
Mill, John Stuart, 47, 57–58, 157
Miller, David, 180
Mills, C. Wright, 172
Mincy, Ronald, 23–27
Molotoch, Harvey, 21–22
Moon, J. Donald, 85–86
Moore, Thomas, 124–125
Moynihan, Daniel Patrick, 67–68
Muolo, Bob, 108–109

Murray, Charles, 28–30, 39, 144
Murray, Thomas, 110–111
Myrdal, Gunnar, 23

Nanetti, Raffaella, 177–178
Niebuhr, Gustav, 139
Nightingale, Carl, 24–25, 40, 69–70
Nisbet, Robert, 8–9, 54, 121–122

Orru, Marco, 67

Pateman, Carol, 157
Pearce, Frank, 84
Pettit, Philip, 118
Piaget, Jean, 161–162
Piliavin, Jane, 113–114
Pizzo, Stephen, 108–109
Poole, Ross, 82–83
Poponoe, David, 63–65
Putnam, Robert, 36–37, 97–101, 108–
    109, 129–131, 134

Ratey, John, 138
Radin, Margaret Jane, 8, 127
Regan, Milton, 132–134, 184
Reich, Robert, 41–42
Rifkin, Jeremy, 181–184
Robertson, James, 181–182
Rochberg-Halton, Eugene, 140–141
Roche, Maurice, 28
Rowe, Jonathan, 104–105, 181
Rosen, Marty, 174
Ruston, J.P., 113

Sampson, Robert, 99
Sandel, Michael, 9–10, 63, 133–134,
    179–180
Sawhill, Isabel, 23–27
Schaar, John, 68–70
Selznick, Philip, 18, 89–90, 151, 161–
    162
Shalin, Dimitri, 89–90
Sherrill, Robert, 109
Shils, Edward, 155–156
Siegel, Fred, 11
Silver, Alan, 34–35, 65
Simmel, Georg, 119

Simmons, Roberta, 113–114
Singer, Peter, 115–117
Skogan, Wesley, 22–23
Smith, Adam, 58–59
Solomon, Marion, 53
Solow, Robert, 103–104
Spicker, Paul, 180–181
Spiegler, Marc, 139
Starr, Paul, 174
Sullivan, William, 8–9, 16–17, 47–48,
    56, 85, 141, 153–154
Swidler, Ann, 8–9, 16–17, 47–48, 56,
    85, 141, 153–154

Taylor, Charles, 70
Tipton, Steven, 8–9, 16–17, 47–48, 56,
    85, 141, 153–154
Titmuss, Richard, 114–116, 127, 183–
    184
Tonnies, Ferdinand, 150–151
Turnbull, Colin, 49–51

Veroff, Joseph, 60–61

Wallis, Claudia, 137–138
Wallwork, Ernest, 79–80
Walzer, Michael, 117–118, 170–172
Weber, Max, 158–159, 164–166
Weigert, Andrew, 34–35
Westman, Jack, 7
Whitehead, Barbara Dafoe, 1–2, 19–
    20, 146–147
Will, George, 172
Willis, Donald, 105
Wilson, James Q., 86–87
Wilson, William Julius, 23–27, 179
Wolfe, Alan, 7–8, 11–12, 19, 62–65, 67,
    90–91, 159, 167–171, 184
Wolfe, Douglas, 23–27
Wuthnow, Robert, 94–95

Yarosh, Steven, 38–39

Zakaria, Fareed, 148
Zuriff, G.E., 143
Zwiebach, Burton, 89–90

Subject Index

Altruism, 113–114
Anomie
  and authoritarianism, 173
  Durkheim on, 67–69
  expression of, 67–70
  and liberal individualism, 67–68,
    71–72
  and postmodernism, 70–72
  as a psychological condition, 68–70
  in the underclass, 69–70
Associationalism
  liberal, 175–177
  sociological, 177–179
Attention-deficit disorder, 137–139,
  142–143
Attentiveness
  and communitarian interdependen-
    cies, 140–141
  definition, 140
  and moral responsiveness, 140
  and social institutions, 140–141

Bounty system, 3–4
Buffalo Creek, 51–53
Building and loan societies, 105–106,
  108–110

Children's rights, 4–8
Citizen's income, 181–184
Civil society
  and associationalism, 175–177
  and citizen's income, 181–184
  and civility, 156
  Durkheim on, 158–164, 166–167
  feminist critique of, 157–158
  Habermas on, 166–171
  liberal conception of, 149–159

  as lifeworld, 167–168
  and market economy, 154–155, 167–
    169, 178–184
  as market relations and publics,
    155–158
  Marx on, 158–159, 163–166
  Mead on, 158–167
  in the politics of social breakdown,
    148–149
  and primordial attachments, 156–157
  and publics, 153–154, 163–164
  revitalization of, 172–186
  sociological view of, 66, 158–186
  and solidarity, 149, 171–181
  and the third sector, 181–184
  Walzer on, 170–172
  Weber on, 158–159
  and the welfare state, 156, 167–169,
    174–179
  Wolfe on, 167–171
Commodification
  definition, 8
  of gifts, 114–115
  of lifeworld, 167
  and loss of competence, 164–165
  of motherhood, 13–14
  of parental obligations, 4, 7
  of the sacred, 124–128
Communitarian interdependencies
  and attentiveness, 140–141
  definition, xi, 34
  and morality, 86–89
  and neighborhood, 23–27
  and right-wing policy, 146–148
  and social capital, 36–37, 99
  and social control, 34
  and trust, 34–36

Constitutional law, 133–134
Contractual relations
   features, 110–112
   in gesellschaft, 150–151
   and right-wing politics, 146–148
   and social obligation, 111–112
   in surrogate mothering, 13–14, 126–127
Corporate responsibility, 181
Culture
   of decency, 38
   of inattentiveness, 142–143
   of narcissism, 52–53, 137
   of personal freedom, 39–42

Democracy
   liberal, 58–59
   and social capital, 99–101
Deregulation
   market, 39–41, 146–147
   social, 39–41

Exit, 59, 61–62, 176

Family
   and attentiveness, 141–143
   deinstitutionalization of, 18–20, 40,
      63–65, 145, 146
   instability and the underclass, 24–26
   juridification of, 10–11
   and market economy, 31–32, 41
   parent-child relations in, 1–8
   and primordial social organization,
      151–152, 154, 156–157, 160–161
   and privatization, 133–134
   and social capital, 36, 98–99, 131
   as a social institution, 16–18, 184
   and trust, 34–36
   and welfare state, 28–30, 63–65
Feminism
   critique of civil society, 157–158
   morality, 76–77
Freedom
   and gifts, 116–117
   and liberalism, 39–42, 57–58
   and the market, 58–59, 116

   as self-government, 58–59, 174,
      179–180
   as social control, 162–163, 174, 179–180
Friendly societies, 107, 160

Gemeinschaft, 150–153
Gesellschaft, 150–153
Gifts
   and altruism, 113–114
   of blood, 114–118
   and charity, 117–118
   and civil society, 183–184
   commodification of, 114–115
   and community, 107, 112–113, 120
   and compassion, 95–96
   and contractual relations, 110–113
   and equality, 117–118
   and gratitude, 110–111
   and markets, 114–118
   and mothering, 119–120
   movement of, 112–113
   and noncommodification, 127–128
   and sacredness, 120, 126–128
   and social capital, 135
   and social obligation, 110–113, 119
   and trust, 118–120
Government decentralization, 177–178
Gratitude
   and gifts, 110–111, 119
   and trust, 118–120
Gross Domestic Product, 104

IK, 49–51
Inattentiveness
   as attention-deficit disorder, 137–139
   culture of, 142–143
   and decrease in social support, 141–143
   as deficit of character, 138–139
   and market-orientation, 143
   and megachurches, 139–140
   and the political right, 143–144
   and self-esteem, 142–143
Incivility, 22–23

Individualism
  conservative opposition to, 77–78
  liberal, 47–48, 56–57, 73, 83–84, 89–96
  moral, 81–84, 88–96
Intersubjectivity, 83
It's a Wonderful Life, 105–110

Juridification
  definition, 10
  and gifts, 117–118
  of parental obligation, 11–12

Kantianism, 73–76, 78–80, 91

Left-wing politics
  analysis of the underclass, 30–33
  as an expression of liberalism, 2, 10–12, 47–48
  and rights rhetoric, 9, 19, 39–40
  solution to bad parenting, 4–8
  solution to underclass, 32–33
Liberalism
  and anomie, 67–68
  and associationalism, 176–177
  and civil society, 149–159
  and compassion, 94–95
  and disaster, 54–55
  and freedom, 57–58
  hostility toward society, 47–48
  and individualism, 2, 47–48, 56–57, 73
  and the Left, 2, 10–12, 47–48
  and the market, 57–58, 65
  as modernity, 150–159
  contrasted to moral individualism, 83–84, 91–96
  and morality, 73–76, 159, 172–173
  and the private sphere, 153–155
  and privatization, 132–133
  and publics, 153–154
  and the Right, 2, 10–12, 47–48
  and the sacred, 126, 134
  and the state, 58, 61–62, 65, 153

Market
  approach to bad parenting, 2–5
  and civil society, 167–168, 178–184
  colonization of lifeworld, 167–168
  and commodification, 8–9, 13–14, 114–115, 124–128
  and communitarian interdependencies, 146–148
  and exit, 61–62
  and gifts, 114–118
  principles, 58–59
  as psychological environment, 59–61
  and social institutions, 146–147
  and the underclass, 30–33
Market rhetoric, 4, 7–8, 39–41, 102–103, 146–148
Megachurches, 139–140
Moral individualism
  and ambiguity, 89–90
  as antidote to anomie, 78
  and autonomy, 81–82
  as collective ideal, 82–84
  and external constraint, 82
  and gifts, 128
  and intersubjectivity, 82–83
  contrasted to liberal individualism, 83–84, 89–96
  and prudence, 89–90
  and sacredness, 125–126
  and solidarity, 183–186
  as standard for evaluating social institutions and communitarian interdependencies, 88–89
Moral passages, 90–95
Morality
  and communitarian interdependencies, 86–88
  of constraint, 161–162
  of cooperation, 161–162
  Durkheim on, 73, 77–84
  and feminism, 75–76
  Kantian view, 73–75, 78–80, 91
  Kohlberg's developmental model, 75–76
  and moral passages, 90, 92–96
  and natural sociability, 86–87
  preference-based approach, 92–93
  rights-based approach, 92–93
  and social institutions, 85–86

and social sentiments, 87
utilitarian view, 73–74, 78–79, 91
Moral reconstruction of society, 162–
164, 185–186
Mothering
and commercial surrogacy, 13–14,
126–127
and gifts, 119–120
and trust, 119–120

Narcissism, 52–55, 137
Neighborhood
bad, 23–24, 26–27, 44–45
and communitarian interdependencies, 23–27
decline of, 22–23
use-values, 21

Overclass
and bad neighborhoods, 44–45
definition, 42–43
parallels to the underclass, 42–45
withdrawal to fortified communities, 44–45

Parenthood
bad, 1–2
deinstitutionalization of, 18–20
good, 12–13, 16
licensing of, 7
obligations of, 1, 4, 145–148
as a social institution, 16–19
Pre-modern–Modern distinction, 150–
153
Primordial social organization, 151–
152, 161–162
Privatization
as individualization, 132–133
as sacralization, 133–135
Publics
and civil society, 149, 153–154, 168–
169
and solidarity, 149, 153–154, 163–
164
Public–private distinction, 153–155,
157–158

Purposively constructed social organization, 151–152

Rational reconstruction of society,
185–186
Rationalization, 164–166
Rights rhetoric, 9, 13, 39–40
Right-wing politics
analysis of the underclass, 28–30
and bad parenting, 2–5, 145–148
and inattentiveness, 143–144
as expression of liberalism, 2, 10–
12, 47–48
and market rhetoric, 4, 7–9, 39–41,
102–103, 146–148
and social capital, 129–131
and the weakening of social obligation, 145–148

Sacred
commodification of, 124–126
Durkheim on, 120–123
and gifts, 120
and modernity, 125–129
and moral individualism, 125–
126
and privatization, 132–134
and the profane, 120–121
as the social, 121–122
and social obligation, 122–123
and soul, 122–125
weakening of, 123–124
Savings and loans, 109–110
Self
anomic, 68–71
loose, 8–9, 11, 54
dependent, 11, 54–55
inattentive, 138–139
narcissistic, 52–55
empty, 54
postmodern, 54–55
and market, 59–61
moral, 73–77, 82–82, 89–96
Social breakdown
as deinstitutionalization, xi, 18–
20
and gross domestic product, 104

as the loss of social control, xi, 39, 37–39
the politics of, 148–149
Social capital
in civic regions, 99–100
and communitarian interdependencies, 36–37, 99
definition, 35–36
democracy, 99–101
and economic prosperity, 101–102
and gifts, 105–121, 135
and good neighborhoods, 36–37
as an imprecise concept, 103–104
and the market, 129–130
and market rhetoric, 102–103
and networks of engagement, 98–100, 129–130
and privatization, 132–134
and reciprocity, 97, 100
and social control, 99
sociological criticism of, 105
and spontaneous sociability, 98, 101–102
and trust, 35–36, 97, 102
in uncivic regions, 100–101
weakening of, 39–40, 128–132
and the welfare state, 130
Social control
and autonomy, 162–163
and civil society, 174
and communitarian interdependencies, 34
definition, 33
loss of, 34, 37–39
and morality of cooperation, 162–163
and public opinion, 163–164
and social capital, 36–37, 99
and trust, 34–36
Social institutions
and attentiveness, 140–141
features, 12–20, 85
language of, 85–86
and market rhetoric, 146
and morality, 85–86, 89
and rights rhetoric, 145–146
and right-wing policy, 145–147
and self-respect, 85–86

Social obligation
bases of, 145
commodification of, 8–9
and communitarian interdependencies, 20
and gifts, 110–113, 119
impact of right-wing policies on, 145–148
juridification of, 10–11
sacredness of, 122–123
and social institutions, 16–18
and trust, 35–36
and vulnerability, 15, 18
Sociology
and civil society, 149–150, 158–172
and compassion, 95–96
and the language of solidarity, 117–118, 170–172, 186
and liberalism, 66–67
and social capital, 105
Solidarity
and government decentralization, 177–179
and income redistribution, 180–181
language of, 172, 186
in the liberal conception of civil society, 149
particularistic, 119, 153–154, 170
in the sociological conception of civil society, 160–161, 171–172
universalistic, 149, 153, 163–164, 169
Soul
loss of, 128–132
and sacredness, 122–125
State of nature, 48–50
Survivalist ethos
in Buffalo Creek survivors, 52–53
in the IK, 50–51
and inattentiveness, 143
in liberal modernity, 55–56
and narcissism, 53–54
and right-wing politics, 147–148
and sacredness, the loss of, 128–130
and social capital, the weakening of, 101
in the state of nature, 49–50
Swedish welfare state, 63–65

Television
 and the loss of social capital, 131–32
 and the underclass, 40–41
Third sector, 181–184
Trust
 and communitarian interdependencies, 34–36
 definition, 34
 generalized, 102
 and gifts, 117–121
 and mothering, 118–120
 and social capital, 35–36, 97–98, 102–103
 and social obligation, 35–36

Underclass
 and anomie, 69–70
 definition, 23–24
 development, 24–27
 and family instability, 25–26
 and joblessness, 25–27

left-wing explanation of, 30–33
 measures of, 24–25
 as mirror of larger society, 39–42
 right-wing explanation of, 28–30
 Wilson on, 23–26
Utilitarianism, 73–74, 78–79, 91

Vocation, 16, 165–166
Vulnerability, 15–16, 145–146

Welfare state
 approach to bad parenting, 4–11
 and civil society, 168–169, 174–179
 colonization of lifeworld, 167–168
 features, 61–63
 and juridification, 10–11
 and liberalism, 62
 neutrality of, 9–10
 and social capital, 130–131
 in Sweden, 63–65
 and the underclass, 28–33